ANNO DOMINI
A short history of the
first millennium AD

Laurent Guyénot

ISBN : 9798388857941

For Kaoru,
to whom I owe the best of mystelf,
and who endures the worst.

CONTENT

revised February 2024

INTRODUCTION
Don't know much about chronology...

When I first heard of *recentism* — the theory that some periods of ancient history are more "recent" than admitted by conventional history —, it was a notion that resonated with a number of observations that had intrigued me during my doctoral research in medieval culture.[1]

One puzzling problem concerned the history of European "folk-lore". Ethnographers of the nineteenth century, encouraged by German and French tenants of "comparative mythology," were struck by a certain familiarity of medieval popular tales with ancient pagan myths. Alfred Nutt (1856-1910), for example, wrote about the mythical Tuatha Dé Danann of Ireland: "the oldest manuscripts present them in a guise so clearly mythological that we can see them as the dispossessed inmates of an Irish pantheon."[2] Since Ireland was supposedly Christianized in the fifth century, for Irish monks to record the stories of the Tuatha Dé Danann (in the *Lebor Gabála*) in the eleventh century means that these stories had run underground for six centuries. This has never been convincingly explained.

I stumbled on a few other odd chronological shortcuts. What a surprise, for example, to discover that in the middle of the eleventh century, among the Bretons of Wales and Cornwall, supposedly Christianized eight centuries earlier, the cult of King Arthur, associated with several shrines and relics, was very popular. It was reported that anyone telling the Bretons that their Arthur was dead for real would have difficulty escaping with his life.[3] How can this be, if Arthur had lived in the sixth century?

The literary genre of the Grail novels, to which I devoted my book *La Lance qui saigne*,[4] is another mystery, and Richard Barber, in *The Holy Grail: Imagination and Belief,* can find no convincing answer to the question: "Why, when the medieval Church never officially recognized the Grail stories, did the Grail become a powerful religious icon, but only to non-clerics?"[5] It is quite certain that the Fisher King of Chrétien de Troyes's *Conte du Graal* is not only a figure of Christ, but also an avatar of Osiris, while Perceval represents Horus, and the Red Knight refers to Seth the Red, Osiris' brother and murderer. Chretien de Troyes's cryptic use of the Egyptian myth suggests that it was easily recognizable by his target audience.[6] Pagan survival of this type pose the problem of their transmission over centuries.

I didn't pay too much attention to these questions, until I came to notice that the men of the Middle Ages seemed to live in a different time frame. For them, the Roman Empire belonged to a recent past. In fact, they thought of themselves as still living in a Roman world, and they were longing for the rebirth of the Empire. Their architecture, which we call "Romanesque" was simply "Roman" to them. Knights thought of themselves as members of the equestrian order founded under Augustus.[7]

In short, there is a sense that, within the worldview that can be construed from our records of lay culture in the tenth and eleventh centuries, the collapse of the Roman Empire was not 600 years away, but just around the corner. Could it be that our long chronology of the first millennium is an artefact of clerical scholarship, an illusion created in the scriptoriums of the papal states? But why?

The fact is that, for historians, the tenth century is a barrier beyond which it is difficult to see anything clearly. Firstly, manuscripts from that century and earlier ones are extremely rare and are never dated in any absolute manner.

Don't we have primary sources from Antiquity, Late Antiquity and the early Middles Ages? Yes we do, but a clear distinction should be made between two kinds of primary sources: those for which we possess manuscripts dating back to their period of composition (let's call them first-hand primary sources), and those for which we have only copies made centuries after their dates of composition (second-hand primary sources). In the latter case, the actual date of authorship is only hypothetical, and so is the accuracy of the copy. Historians rarely make that distinction, although it is a crucial one: we don't have first-hand primary sources from before the tenth century, let alone, of course, Antiquity. History is, by definition, the interpretation of written material. But doing ancient history based on books allegedly written during Greek or Roman Antiquity but known only from medieval or late-medieval manuscripts, should require a very different approach from doing medieval history on the basis of medieval manuscripts. But, as we shall see in the first chapter, that distinction is neglected by historians of Antiquity.

Secondly, the tenth century had been catastrophic, literally, to the point of creating some form of traumatic amnesia. It was, writes Guy Blois in *The Transformation of the Year One Thousand,* "a period which is among the most mysterious in our history," and "has left few traces in our collective memory." In some regions, "twenty to twenty-five years sufficed to transform the social landscape from top to bottom."

> "There was no gentle progress by imperceptible transitions from one situation to another. There was drastic upheaval, affecting all aspects of social life: a new distribution of power, a new relation of exploitation (the *seigneurie*), new economic mechanisms (the irruption of the market), and a new social and political ideology. If the word revolution means anything, it could hardly find a better application."[8]

Sources of information from the tenth century are almost non-existent, and the sources from the eleventh century are not very explicit about the ills of the tenth century. The people of the early eleventh century lived with a sense of a radical rupture between the last century — a time of destruction, disintegration, and confusion — and their present — a time full of promises which would soon give birth to what historians call the "Renaissance of the Twelfth Century".

The monk Rodulfus Glaber, writing between 1026 and 1040, says that in December of 997, "there appeared in the air an admirable wonder: the form, or perhaps the body itself, of a huge dragon, coming from the north and heading south, with dazzling lightning bolts. This prodigy terrified almost all those who saw it in the Gauls." Rodulfus also mentions that, between 993 and 997,

> "Mount Vesuvius (which is also called Vulcan's Caldron) gaped far more often than his wont and belched forth a multitude of vast stones mingled with sulphurous flames which fell even to a distance of three miles around. ... It befell meanwhile that almost all the cities of Italy and Gaul were ravaged by flames of fire, and that the greater part even of the city of Rome was devoured by a conflagration. ... At this same time a horrible plague raged among men, namely a hidden fire which, upon whatsoever limb it toned, consumed it and severed it from the body. ... Moreover, about the same time [997], a most mighty famine raged for five years in the whole Roman world [*in universo Romano orbe*], so that no region could be heard of which was not hunger stricken for lack of bread, and many of the people were starved to death. In those days also, in many regions, the terrible famine compelled men to make their food not only of unclean beasts and creeping things, but even of men's, women's, and children's flesh, without regard even of kindred; for so fierce waxed this hunger that grown-up sons devoured their mothers, and mothers, forgetting their maternal love, ate their babes."[9]

Patrick Geary has studied the phenomenon of collective memory loss in the tenth century. He writes on *Phantoms of Remembrance: Memory and Oblivion at the End of the First Millennium*:

> "Those living on the other side of this caesura felt themselves separated by a great gulf from this earlier age. Already in the eleventh century those people who

undertook to preserve the past in written form, for their contemporaries or their posterity, seemed to know little and understand less of their familial, institutional, cultural, and regional past. ... And yet they were deeply concerned with this past, possessed by it almost, and their invented past became the goal and justification of their programs in the present."[10]

From the "Ground Zero" of the Tenth Century Collapse, people recreated this past from bits and pieces—as a form of "recovered memory". It is this recreation that they transmitted to future generations:

"Much of what we think we know about the early Middle Ages was determined by the changing problems and concerns of eleventh-century men and women, not by those of the more distant past. Unless we understand the mental and social structures that acted as filters, suppressing or transforming the received past in the eleventh century in terms of presentist needs, we are doomed to misunderstand those earlier centuries."[11]

On what basis, then, can we reconstruct the history of the first millennium, if it ended with a break in collective memory that makes it inscrutable to us? This is where the proponents of chronological revisionism part from academic historians: the latter use pre-established chronological boxes, which they only have to fill in: they know that between Antiquity and the Classical Middle Ages, there is Late Antiquity and then the High Middle Ages, two fairly obscure periods that need to be filled in with whatever scarce information can fit there. If the man of the eleventh century knew little of these periods, it was because he was ignorant, goes the common wisdom. The alternative, which I explore here, is that the man of the eleventh century, however confused he was, nevertheless deserves to be heard, when he tells us that he has just left the Roman Empire.

Is it conceivable that our chronology of the centuries before the classical Middle Ages is so faulty? Hadn't an accurate count of years been kept since at least the fourth century? In the comment section of my one of my *Unz*

Review articles, medieval philologist Eric Knibbs objected to the theory that our chronology in *Anno Domini* (AD) was elaborated and imposed by the Gregorian reformers of the eleventh century or their immediate predecessors.[12] He has signaled a few cases where AD dates were already in use in ninth-century manuscripts. For instance, on codex Sankt-Gallen, Stiftsbibliothek 272, we read "*anno DCCC.VI. ab incarnatione domini*" ("In the year 806 from the incarnation of the Lord").[13] In Ms. lat. 2341, Paris, Bibl. nat., future dates for the celebration of Easter are given in the form "*ANNO INCARNATIONIS DOMINI NOSTRI IESU CHRISTI DCCCXLIII*" ("the year of the incarnation of our lord Jesus Christ 843").[14] Another case is Clm 14429 at the Bayerische Staatsbibliothek, which indicates on the first folio the date when it was copied: "*anno domini DCCCXXI*" ("the year of the Lord 821").[15] However, the objection is inconclusive, because the standardization of AD dates was still a work in progress, and there is no way of knowing if scribes were using them consistently.

The problem is illustrated by the above-mentioned Rodulfus Glaber, writing between 1026 and 1040. In Book II, §8 of his autograph manuscript, Rodulfus gives the date "888 of the Word incarnate" instead of 988 (according to the editor's footnote in my Latin-French edition). In Book 1, §23, he mentions an event during the pontificate of Benedict VIII (1012-1024) and dates it from "the year 710 of the Lord's incarnation." The modern editor corrects him in footnote: "In fact in 1014, but the manuscript corrected by Rodulfus carries indisputably the date 710; nothing explains such a mistake."[16] One thing that can explain such mistakes is the floating state of the chronology. Most probably, Rodulfus borrowed these "erroneous" dates from others without realizing they were tuned to a different dating scale. Even a manuscript carrying a date like 806 AD could be misdated, that is, written by someone counting years with a shorter chronology. What is illustrated by Rodulfus is that the AD dating system did not become settled overnight, and that different people could ascribe different AD dates to very recent times. A case by case examination of supposedly ninth-century manuscripts with AD dates should determine if the dating is consistent with these manuscripts surviving the Tenth Century Collapse.

Starting from the premise that AD dates were well established long before the Gregorian Reform, historians have assumed that, when medieval men saw the year 1000 approach, they must have feared the worst. This assumption is now considered false: our sources are mute about the supposed "fears of the year 1000." Historians who nevertheless insist that they were real, like Richard Landes, resort to funny arguments like "a consensus of silence that masks a great deal of concern. ... medieval writers avoided the subject of the millennium whenever and wherever possible."[17] More convincingly, the missing "fears of the year 1000" make a strong argument that the AD computation came in common use after the year 1000.

When, then, did our standard first-millennium chronology become the dominant consensus? What is the *terminus ad quem,* the latest possible date, for that cultural artifact? The earliest partial chronicles with dates given in "year of the Incarnation" appear in the tenth century, with for instance the Chronicle of Moissac (*Chronicon Moissiacense*). But there was no attempt at a systematic chronology encompassing the first millennium before the late eleventh century, with the Chronicle of Sigebert of Gembloux, which became a reference for future historians.

The author presents himself as a continuator and imitator of Eusebius. He therefore begins his chronicle in 381, the date on which the chronicle of Eusebius, continued by Jerome, ends. Sigebert's chronicle had a considerable influence. According to Mireille Chazan, "we must even consider that it was the arrival of Sigebert's chronicle that led, from the last third of the 12th century, to the flourishing of the genre of the universal chronicle in France." "From 1190 to 1328, eight universal chronicles are thus based on that of Sigebert. [...] the chronicle of Sigebert, by its extent, by the precision of its dating system, by its coherence represented for [later chroniclers] a fundamental contribution and deeply marked their work." In the thirteeth century, Sigebert's chronicle "became the direct or indirect basis of most universal chronicles."[18]

How reliable is Sigebert's chronology? Are the sources he used correct, and is his use of them justified? Sigebert's method does not seem to have been the subject of in-depth critical examination. We are therefore, for the last six centuries of the first millennium, in a situation almost identical to that concerning the first four centuries, for which we are totally dependent on Eusebius and Jerome. Not quite, it is true, because we know at least part of Sigebert's sources. The doubts that can be cast on the chronology of the first four centuries, as we will see, are much stronger than those raised by the following six centuries.

But my point here is that we must firmly exclude from consideration theories claiming that our standard first-millennium European chronology was invented after the eleventh century. Such theories exist, which is why I prefer to state that point clearly.[19]

If, however, we are looking for the first worldwide chronology synchronizing the histories of all known civilizations, that is another matter. The universal timeline which we rely on today, allowing us to place with relative precision all major events in world history, is a sophisticated cultural construct that was not completed before the late sixteenth century. Portuguese and Spanish explorers and conquerors played a big part in this conquest of time. As wrote Serge Gruzinski in *La Machine à remonter le temps* ("Time Machine"):

> "Little by little, across the entire planet, the relationship with the past is becoming more homogenous. ... Over the centuries, while Europeans physically invade planetary spaces and relate them to their vision of the world, they conquer the memories of the societies they invade or

contaminate. In these countries, confronted with a past, a present and a future formatted in the European way or simply seduced by the modernity that this way of thinking projects, receive (or adopt) a history which they internalize as the westernization of the world progresses and European globalization reshapes minds and imaginations. From the moment any point on the globe is within reach of any initiative coming from Western Europe, nothing prevents any society from being historicized, that is to say endowed with a past linked to a history of the world conceived and written from ours."[20]

Jesuits played a prominent role in that computation, but the main architect of the chronology we are now familiar with was a French Huguenot named Joseph Scaliger (1540-1609), who set out to harmonize all available chronicles and calendars (Hebrew, Greek, Roman, Persian, Babylonian, Egyptian). His main works on chronology, written in Latin, are *De emendatione temporum* (1583) and *Thesaurus temporum* (1606). The Jesuit Denys Pétau (or Dionysius Petavius, 1583-1652) built on Scaliger's foundation to publish his *Tabulae chronologicae*, from 1628 to 1657.

Also influential was Irish Calvinist scholar James Ussher (1581-1656), whose *Annales veteris testamenti, a prima mundi origine deducti* ("Annals of the Old Testament,

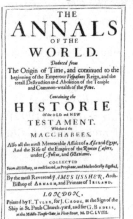

deduced from the first origins of the world"), published in 1650 and augmented in 1654, determined that Creation happened in 4004 BC. (His contemporary John Lightfoot set the beginning at precisely 9 am on 23 October.) Usher's chronology is still considered accurate on dates such as the death of Alexander in 323 BC or that of Julius Caesar in 44 BC.

So our global chronology, the backbone of textbook history, is a scientific construct of modern Europe. Like other European norms, it was accepted by the rest of the world during the period of European cultural domination. The Chinese, for example, had already compiled, during the Song dynasty (960-1279), a long historical narrative, but it was Jesuit missionaries who reshaped it to fit in their BC-AD calendar, resulting in the thirteen volumes of the *Histoire Générale de la Chine* by Joseph-Anne-Marie de Moyriac de Mailla, published between 1777 and 1785.[21] Once Chinese history was securely riveted to Scaligerian chronology, the rest followed. But some nations had to wait until the nineteenth century to find their place in that framework. India, for example, had very ancient records, but no consistent chronology until the British gave her one. In 1965 the renowned Indian historian and Sanskrit scholar Damodar D. Kosambi wrote:

> "India has virtually no historical records worth the name ... In India there is only vague popular tradition, with very little documentation above the level of myth and legend. We cannot reconstruct a complete list of kings. . . . What little is left is so nebulous that virtually no dates can be determined for any Indian personality till the Muslim period. This has led scholars to state that India has no history."[22]

Truth be told, the chronology of ancient, pre-Roman, empires was never completely settled. In *The Chronology of Ancient Kingdoms Amended*, Isaac Newton (1642-1727) had suggested to reduce drastically the by-then-accepted antiquity of Greece, Egypt, Assyria, Babylon and Persia. Today, ancient chronology is still open to debate in the academic community, as illustrated for example by Peter James's *Centuries of Darkness: a challenge to the conventional chronology of Old World archaeology* (1993), foreworded by Cambridge professor of archaeology Colin Renfrew (more in the Appendix).

But as we approach the Common Era, the chronology is considered untouchable, except for minor adjustments, because of the abundance of written sources. I have never read, in any recent book by a professional historian on Roman or medieval times, any question about the accepted date of this or that event, give or take a few years. Historians simply don't deal with chronology. They leave it to chronologists. But chronologists are an extinct species. The last ones were spotted in 1770, working on "the art of verifying the dates of historical facts from the charts, chronicles and other ancient monuments since the birth of Our Lord by the means of a chronological table etc."

Today, this art is lost, because it is not needed anymore. Chronology is like going to the Moon: we did it, but we are not sure how we did it.[23] The difference is that there are no official plans to do it again. Why do it again? Dates are all secure now! Wikipedia tells you exactly what day every single European king was crowned and died.

Are we so sure? As I said, until the ninth century AD, no primary source provides reliable absolute dates. Events are dated relatively to some other event of local importance, such as the foundation of a town or the accession of a ruler. Dating recent events in *Anno Domini* (AD) only became common in the eleventh century. So the general timeline of the first millennium still rests on a great deal of uncertain assumptions. Yet it was carved into stone long before the beginning of scientific excavations (nineteenth, mainly twentieth century), and, as we shall see, its authority is such that archaeologists surrender to it even when their stratigraphic data contradicts it.

Modern methods of dating are of little help, as we shall see. Dendrochronology (tree-ring dating) is relative and calibrated on the standard timeline one way or another, and radiocarbon is so imprecise that it is rarely used independently for the Common Era. These methods are not worthless, but they cannot date stone buildings anyway. For this, the only scientific criterion is stratigraphy, that is, the relative depth of archaeological strata. The chronological revisionism of Professor Gunnar Heinsohn, presented in chapter 4, is so convincing because it is based on the hard evidence of stratigraphy-based archaeology.

Apart from that, we are left with the classic material of historians, literature. But, if the history of the first millennium was written in the second millennium, what confidence should we put in it? For Roman Antiquity, there are serious doubts about the authenticity of the writings of some ancient Roman historians "discovered" in the late Middle Ages or the Renaissance. The suspicion that Roman Antiquity was, to some extent, a fabulation of later ages, finds support in considerations such as the following one, made by French medievalist Robert Folz:

> "In 1143, the Capitol became the residence of the Council of the Commune of Rome. ... in an environment where the past was the object of such a passion as in Rome, any attempt at new creation had necessarily to take the aspect of a restoration of the past: the Council of the Commune was called Senate, the senatorial era was used in the dating of acts, while the sign SPQR also reappeared. It all happened as if we were returning to the tradition of republican Rome."[24]

The founders of the medieval Roman Republic opposed the pope's rule over the city, and supported the Hohenstaufen emperors' plan to make Rome the capital of their newly called "Holy Roman Empire". So it is not surprising to discover, as we shall in the first chapter, that the Roman patriots of the fourteenth century were the very "humanists" who "saved from oblivion" the glory of ancient Republican and Imperial Rome, and launched what came to be called the "Renaissance".

Historiography is political, and so is chronology, in an age when prestige and hierarchy depends on ancientness. We will find many illustrations of that principle. Let me here give only one, mentioned by Heinrich Fichtenau in *Living in the Tenth Century: Mentalities and Social Orders*. When the cities of Reims and Trier were competing for the honor of crowning emperor Otto the Great, Reims came up with the claim of having been founded by Remus after he was expelled by his brother Romulus; Trier responded by claiming to have been founded by Trebeta, the son of Ninus and a contemporary of Abraham. Both produced texts to back their claim.[25]

There is no question that the greatest forgers of history were churchmen. Eric Knibbs will   not dispute that statement, having written in *Ansgar, Rimbert and the Forged Foundations of Hamburg-Bremen*:

> "In the middle of the twelfth century, Archbishop Hartwig I falsified a wide range of privileges relating to his diocese, with the aim of re-extending his province northwards to include new Christian communities along the Baltic shore, and in Iceland and Greenland as well. ... Hartwig's forgery program was not the only attempt to recast the early history of Hamburg-Bremen. As the quarrel between Pope Gregory VII and Emperor Henry IV unfolded, the eleventh-century archbishop Liemar appears to have falsified a series of ninth-century privileges to emphasize that his predecessors had enjoyed the status of papal legates since the time of Ansgar. And still earlier, at the beginning of the eleventh century, Archbishop Liäwizo forged two further documents in order to secure possession of a monastery at Ramelsloh, against the contrary claims of the bishop of Verden."[26]

As we shall see, forgeries are the rule rather than the exception for clerical diplomas, and they were nowhere more abundant than in papal chancelleries. The Donation of Constantine was the centerpiece of this industry of historical and legal forgery developed in episcopal and papal scriptoriums. It shows Constantine the Great giving to "Sylvester the universal pontiff and to all his successors until the end of the world" all the imperial insignia: diadem, tiara, shoulder band, purple mantle, crimson tunic, scepters, spears, standards, banners, "and all the advantage of our [Constantine's] high imperial position, and the glory of our power." On the basis of this forgery, the popes would later claim to have been given, by the first Christian emperor himself, the full extent of imperial authority, and the right to confer it to the emperor of their choice, or to take it away from him — and even, in the case of vacancy, to rule as emperors themselves. But why stop there, thought the forger. He has Constantine also cede to the pope "our imperial Lateran palace", as well as "the city of Rome and all the provinces, districts and cities of Italy or of the western regions."

It is no exaggeration that European history was, to a large extent, shaped by this single papal forgery. The Italian priest Arnold of Brescia (1090-1155), co-founder of the Commune of Rome, saw in it the hand of the Antichrist (he paid for the blasphemy with his life). One of his supporters, by the name of Wetzel, wrote to Emperor Frederick Barbarossa that it is known to everyone in Rome that the Donation is "a lie and a heretical legend."[27] Yet from the eighth till the fifteenth century, the papacy's imperial policy rested entirely on this gigantic lie.

On the geopolitical level, the Donation was the keystone of a great historical hoax by which Rome claimed universal supremacy and treated the Byzantine Orthodox as schismatic. Significantly it was not until the mid-fifteenth century, when Constantinople fell to the Ottomans, that the Donation was recognized as a forgery.

The deception, I came to suspect, has been so thorough and systematic that it has tampered with the chronology —

the ADN of history, so to speak —, resulting in a historical sequence of events from Rome to Constantinople which has never ceased to puzzle historians. Consider for example these remarks on Constantine the Great by French medievalist Ferdinand Lot:

> "New Rome, in his mind, was to be all Roman. He transported part of the Senate there and had palaces built for the old families he attracted there. The laws were all Roman. The language of the Court, of the offices was Latin. ... And here is what happened: Constantinople became a Greek city again. Two centuries after its foundation, the descendants of the Romans transplanted into the *pars Orientis* had forgotten the language of their fathers, no longer knew anything of Latin literature, and considered Italy and the West as a half-barbaric region. By changing their language they had changed their soul. Constantine thought he was regenerating the Roman Empire. Without suspecting it, he founded the Empire so aptly called 'Byzantine'."[28]

The unlikeliness of this scenario is so cognitively dissonant with the unanimous faith in its certainty that it is simply repressed. But when one starts to investigate with a critical mind, one bumps, again and again, on contradictions. Consider, for example, the enigma about the so-called Arch of Constantine in Rome. The sequence of construction is so inconsistent with the standard chronology that scholars assume that the three top stages were fitted with reliefs and statues looted from earlier but unknown imperial buildings, as mentioned in the Wikipedia page and illustrated by the drawing below. This incomprehensible "fact", we are told, "has generated a vast amount of discussion," and explanations range from "lack of time" to "a breakdown of the transmission in artistic skills."

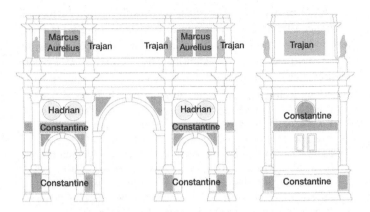

Professor Gunnar Heinsohn, whom I will introduce in the fourth chapter, has a better explanation: the correct chronology is here engraved in stone, literally, but historians are unable to see it.[29] Among other chronological inconsistencies, Heinsohn notes that, although Constantinople was founded in the early fourth century, Hadrian had already built an aqueduct there two centuries earlier.[30] In reality, Heinsohn argues, "Hadrian's aqueduct carries water to a flourishing city 100 years after Constantine, and not to a supposed wasteland centuries earlier. The mystery disappears. When Justinian renovates the great Basilica Cistern, which gathers water from Hadrian's aqueduct, he does so not 400 years, but less than 100 years after it was built."[31]

My suspicion of a major distortion in our Western-centered history, and the possibility that this distortion has affected the chronology, has kept growing as I learned, among many other facts that will be presented in this book, that Constantine was a native of the Balkans who had never set foot in Rome before he conquered it from Maxentius, or that the Romans of Italy saw themselves as descendants of Eastern immigrants — a belief illustrated by Virgil's *Aeneid* and by the very name of Rome (*Romos,* Latinized in *Romus,* is a Greek word meaning "strong") —, or that the

Byzantines had always called themselves "Romans", and their Greek language "Romaic", and never regarded the "Latins" as their ancestors. Such facts do not fit well with the generally accepted picture of the relationship between Rome and Constantinople.

The conventional narrative has been shaped by Latin propaganda at the expense of Constantinople. A distorted historiography has resulted in the West, based on the occultation of Byzantium. Few medievalists are aware of it. Not much has changed since Cambridge professor Paul Stephenson wrote in 1972: "The excision of Byzantine history from medieval European studies does indeed seem to me an unforgivable offense against the very spirit of history."[32]

When the Byzantine Empire is mentioned, it is almost as a ghost or a pale copy of the Western Roman Empire. But that image is singularly lacking in historical perspective. Not only was the Byzantine civilization the center of the known world during the whole Middle Ages, but Constantinople had inherited more from Athens than from Rome. Its philosophical, scientific, poetic, mythological and artistic traditions came directly from classical Greece, with hardly any Italian contribution. It was Constantinople that passed the cultural wealth of Greece to Rome. Without the conservation work of the Imperial Library of Constantinople, we would not know Plato, Aristotle, Thucydides, Herodotus, Aeschylus, Sophocles, Euripides, or Euclid. In Constantinople, the light of classical Greece has never suffered an eclipse,[33] and it was Photios, Patriarch of Constantinople from 858 to 867, who became the best advocate of the Macedonian Renaissance by his work of conservation of ancient Greek books.

Greek culture radiated from Constantinople to the confines of the known world, from Persia to Egypt and from Ireland to Spain. The eleventh and twelfth centuries saw a vast movement of translation from Greek into Latin of philosophical and scientific works (medicine, mathematics, geography, astronomy, etc.). In *Aristote au mont Saint-Michel. Les racines grecques de l'Europe chrétienne* (translated in German and Greek, but not in English), historian Sylvain Gouguenheim debunks the common opinion that the spread of Greek philosophy and science in the Middle Ages is to be credited mostly to Muslims. In most cases, the Greek heritage was transmitted to Italian cities directly from Constantinople.[34] Between the fifth and thirteenth centuries, Europe gravitated towards Constantinople.

If this reality escapes us today, it is because of our incurable eurocentrism, which Oswald Spengler denounced, but in vain:

> "The ground of West Europe is treated as a steady pole, a unique patch chosen on the surface of the sphere for no better reason, it seems, than because we live on it—and great histories of millennial duration and mighty far-away Cultures are made to revolve around this pole in all modesty. It is a quaintly conceived system of sun and planets. We select a single bit of ground as the natural centre of the historical system, and make it the central sun. From it all the events of history receive their real light, from it their importance is judged in perspective. But it is in our own West-European conceit alone that this phantom 'world-history,' which a breath of scepticism would dissipate, is acted out."[35]

This book challenges the conventional historical framework of the Mediterranean world from the Roman Empire to the Crusades. It is a contribution to a debate that has gained new momentum in recent decades in the fringe of the academic world, mostly in Germany, Russia, and France.

In the first two chapters, I will show that our standard narrative of the first millennium AD is based on more fragile sources and conjectures than is usually believed, and that it has serious structural inconsistencies. At this stage, I will not address directly questions of chronology, but confine myself to highlighting the most serious weaknesses of the traditional scheme. On the way, I will formulate a few working hypotheses to explain the unreliability of certain sources, but the reader must keep in mind that some of these hypotheses will be rejected in the third to fifth chapters in favor of another hypothesis based on a paradigm shift in chronology.

This essay reflects my personal approach to the case, influenced by my training as a medievalist, even if, for the most part, the arguments are inspired by the work of other scholars. My purpose is to show that questioning the basic timeline of history is not a preconceived goal, but is a response to an accumulation — even a saturation — of contradictions in the very structure of our standard narrative.

I insist on the provisional nature of all the hypotheses put forward in this essay. It is an *experiment*—and not a final statement—in chronological revisionism, as indicated in the subtitle. To be perfectly honest, I finished this book with a sense of failure: at this stage, none of the hypotheses seem perfectly satisfying to me. The final proof for any of them escapes us. The conventional paradigm is recognized as faulty, but the search for a new paradigm is still unfinished business. There is no certainty about the extent of the distortion of our first-millennium chronology, and no certainty about the time when the greatest and final distortion happened. The reader is entitled to judge some theories presented in this book (particularly in chapter 4) exaggerated or even extravagant, but testing the limits is part of the experiment. Chronological revisionism remains a work in progress. Nevertheless, as frustrating as the final result is, the quest itself is a transforming experience. If no final destination has been reached, many rewarding discoveries have been made on the way. Readers, I hope, will learn as much as they unlearn. Chronology, anyway, is not the only subject of this book, as it is only brought into the discussion in the third chapter.

Four chapters of this book were published as articles on the webzine *The Unz Review*, under the anonymous signature of "The First Millennium Revisionist." They are reproduced here with some improvements, many of them owing to the contributions of commenters. I warmly express my gratitude to them, and to Ron Unz for providing such an inspiring forum for unconventional viewpoints. The final chapter is simply an "Appendix" because it deals with the chronology of eras before the first millennium AD.

CHAPTER 1
How fake is Roman Antiquity?

Tacitus and Bracciolini

One of our most detailed historical sources on imperial Rome is Cornelius Tacitus (56-120 AD), whose major works, the *Annals* and the *Histories,* span the history of the Roman Empire from the death of Augustus in 14 AD, to the death of Domitian in 96.

Here is how the French scholar Polydor Hochart introduced in 1890 the result of his investigation on "the authenticity of the *Annals* and the *Histories* of Tacitus":

"At the beginning of the fifteenth century scholars had at their disposal no part of the works of Tacitus; they were supposed to be lost. It was around 1429 that Poggio Bracciolini and Niccoli of Florence brought to light a manuscript that contained the last six books of the Annals and the first five books of the Histories. It is this archetypal manuscript that served to make the copies that were in circulation until the use of printing. Now, when one wants to know where and how it came into their possession, one is surprised to find that they have given unacceptable explanations on this subject, that they either did not want or could not say the truth. About eighty years later, Pope Leo X was given a volume containing the first five books of the Annals. Its origin is also surrounded by darkness.

Why these mysteries? What confidence do those who exhibited these documents deserve? What guarantees do we have of their authenticity?

In considering these questions we shall first see that Poggio and Niccoli were not distinguished by honesty and loyalty, and that the search for ancient manuscripts was for them an industry, a means of acquiring money.

> We will also notice that Poggio was one of the most
> learned men of his time, that he was also a clever
> calligrapher, and that he even had in his pay scribes trained
> by him to write on parchment in a remarkable way in
> Lombard and Carolin characters. Volumes coming out of
> his hands could thus imitate perfectly the ancient
> manuscripts, as he says himself.
>
> We will also be able to see with what elements the
> Annals and the *Histories* were composed. Finally, in
> seeking who may have been the author of this literary
> fraud, we shall be led to think that, in all probability, the
> pseudo-Tacitus is none other than Poggio Bracciolini
> himself."[36]

Hochart was not the first author to question the authenticity of Tacitus' work. According to Clarence Mendell, since 1775 there had been already five attempts to discredit the works of Tacitus as either forgeries or fiction.[37] Hochart was building up on the work of John Wilson Ross published twelve years earlier, *Tacitus and Bracciolini: The Annals forged in the XVth century* (1878).

Hochart's demonstration proceeds in two stages. First, he traces the origin of the manuscript discovered by Poggio and Niccoli, using Poggio's correspondence as evidence of deception.[38] Then Hochart deals with the emergence of the second manuscript, two years after Pope Leo X (a Medici) had promised great reward in gold to anyone who could provide him with unknown manuscripts of the ancient Greeks or Romans. Leo rewarded his unknown provider with 500 golden crowns, a fortune at that time, and immediately ordered the printing of the precious manuscript. Hochart concludes that the manuscript must have been supplied indirectly to Leo X by Jean-François Bracciolini, the son and sole inheritor of Poggio's private library and papers, who happened to be secretary of Leo X at that time, and who used an anonymous intermediary in order to elude suspicion.

Both manuscripts are now preserved in Florence, so their age can be scientifically established, can't it? That is questionable, but the truth, anyway, is that their age is simply assumed. For other works of Tacitus, such as *Germania* and *De Agricola,* we don't even have any medieval manuscripts. David Schaps tells us that *Germania* was ignored throughout the Middle Ages but survived in a single manuscript that was found in Hersfeld Abbey in 1425, was brought to Italy and examined by Enea Silvio Piccolomini, later Pope Pius II, as well as by Bracciolini, then vanished from sight.[39] No wonder historians today think that Tacitus did not know what he was talking about, and certainly never met a German Barbarian.[40] No wonder, also, Machiavelli's depiction of the Germans of his own time differed so little from Tacitus' that Gaetano Mosca thought he "evidently wrote under the influence of Tacitus."[41] Russian born American historian and linguist Leo Wiener, wrote in *Tacitus' Germania and other Forgeries* (1920):

> "The utter worthlessness of the Germania is patent, beyond any possibility of defence. Only the mentally blind will defend it … It is sad to contemplate that Germanic history and allied subjects are based on the *Germania* and the *Getica*, two monuments of conscious fraud and unconscious stupidity."[42]

Poggio Bracciolini (1380-1459) was a libertine and cynical character, who in his *Liber facetiarum* made fun of both the duplicity of the clergy and the credulity of the people. In one his "facetious" stories, a bishop eats partridges on a Friday, and declares to his disapproving valet: "Do you not know that I am a priest? Which is more difficult, to turn bread into the body of Christ, or partridges into fish?" After which the priest "made the sign of the cross, commanded the partridges to turn into fish, and ate them as such."[43]

The same Poggio is credited for "rediscovering and recovering a great number of classical Latin manuscripts, mostly decaying and forgotten in German, Swiss, and French monastic libraries" (Wikipedia). Hochart believes that Tacitus' books are not his only forgeries. Under suspicion come other works by Cicero, Lucretius, Vitruvius, Quintilian, and Ammianus Marcellinus to name just a few.

Lucretius' only known work, *De rerum natura* "virtually disappeared during the Middle Ages, but was rediscovered in 1417 in a monastery in Germany by Poggio Bracciolini" (Wikipedia). So was Quintilian's only extant work, a twelve-volume textbook on rhetoric entitled *Institutio Oratoria*, whose discovery Poggio recounts in a letter:

> "Amid a tremendous quantity of books, we found Quintilian safe and sound, though filthy with mould and dust. For these books were in a foul and gloomy dungeon at the bottom of one of the towers, where not even men convicted of a capital offence would have been confined."
> (Letter to Guarino da Verona, 1416)[44]

Ammianus Marcellinus is a historian of crucial importance for our knowledge of Late Antiquity. Although living in the Greek-speaking East, he wrote in Latin in the 390s, taking his model from Tacitus. He comes out as a kind of monotheistic pagan believing in the goddess Fortuna, but benevolent toward Christianity. Of his *Res Gestae*, covering the period from 96 to 378, only the part corresponding to the years 353 to 378 is known. One single medieval manuscript has been preserved, dated to the ninth or tenth century (Vaticanus Latinus 1873). Poggio Bracciolini claimed to have discovered it in 1417, in Fulda, Germany. Most scholars agree that this manuscript is a transcript from an earlier manuscript, the Codex Hersfeldensis, of which the scholar Sigismund Gelenius published an edition in 1533, before the manuscript disappeared, although six pages were found in 1875, and three more in 1986.[45]

To get a sense of the prose of such Classical authors as Ammianus, whose work covers a whole bookshelf in university libraries, here is the standeard translation of the very beginning of what has been preserved:

> "After the events of an expedition full of almost insuperable difficulties, while the spirits of all parties in the

state, broken by the variety of their dangers and toils, were still enfeebled; while the clang of trumpets was ringing in men's ears, and the troops were still distributed in their winter quarters, the storms of angry fortune surrounded the commonwealth with fresh dangers through the manifold and terrible atrocities of Caesar Gallus: who, when just entering into the prime of life, having been raised with unexpected honour from the lowest depth of misery to the highest rank, exceeded all the legitimate bounds of the power conferred on him, and with preposterous violence threw everything into confusion."[46]

How did people write like that, when punctuation was not even invented? More importantly, how did they write, *physically*? Let's listen to the expert, classicist and philologist Edwin P. Menes:

"There's a lot of dispute about ancient book production, but the author most likely wrote on wax tablets (which allowed easy correction). The finished work on wax would then have been copied onto a papyrus roll by a secretary, for final correction by the author. From there it would go to friends for further comment or it might enter the book trade immediately, either via a commercial seller or via a private publisher."[47]

This is just Menes' best guess. The truth is that the acts of writing, publishing, and even reading in Antiquity remain quite mysterious.

Assuming Hochart is right to suspect Poggio of massive fraud, was Poggio the exception that confirms the rule of honesty among the humanists to whom humankind is indebted for "rediscovering" the great classics? Hardly, as we shall see. Even the great Erasmus (1465-1536) succumbed to the temptation of forging a treatise under the name of saint Cyprian (*De duplici martyrio ad Fortunatum*), which he pretended to have found by chance in an ancient library. Erasmus used this stratagem to voice his criticism of the Catholic confusion between virtue and suffering. In this case, heterodoxy gave the forger away. But how many forgeries went undetected for lack of originality? Giles

Constable writes in "Forgery and Plagiarism in the Middle Ages": "The secret of successful forgers and plagiarists is to attune the deceit so closely to the desires and standards of their age that it is not detected, or even suspected, at the time of creation." In other words: "Forgeries and plagiarisms … follow rather than create fashion and can without paradox be considered among the most authentic products of their time."[48]

We are here focusing on literary forgeries, but there were other kinds. Michelangelo himself launched his own career by faking antique statues, including one known as the *Sleeping Cupid* (now lost), while under the employment of the Medici family in Florence. He used acidic earth to make the statue look antique. It was sold through a dealer to Cardinal Riario of San Giorgio, who eventually found out the hoax and demanded his money back, but didn't press any charges against the artist. Apart from this recognized forgery, Lynn Catterson has made a strong case that the sculptural group of "Laocoön and his Sons," dated from around 40 BC and supposedly discovered in 1506 in a vineyard in Rome and immediately acquired by Pope Julius II, is another of Michelangelo's forgery[49].

When one comes to think about it seriously, one can find several reasons to doubt that such masterworks were possible any time before the Renaissance, one of them having to do with progress in human anatomy.

And what about those impressively realistic Roman busts? Why was nothing comparable made throughout Late Antiquity and the Middle Ages? The historian Henri Pirenne has informed us that the Barbarians who settled on the territory of the Empire in the fifth century, far from hating the Empire, "admired it. All they wanted was to settle there and enjoy it. And their kings aspired to Roman dignities."[50] They adopted the Roman language, Roman law, Roman customs. They imitated the Romans in everything, Pirenne tells us. Why not in sculpture? Did Clovis, who "boasted of receiving the title of consul,"[51] find no Roman sculptor to cut his portrait?

So many antique works raise so many questions. For instance, comparing Marcus Aurelius' bronze equestrian statue (formely thought to be Constantine's), with, say, Louis XIV's, makes you wonder: how come nothing remotely approaching this level of achievement can be found between the fifth and the fifteenth century?[52]

And by the way, Marcus Aurelius may be a historical figure, but his real place in history is far from clear. "The major sources depicting the life and rule of Marcus are patchy and frequently unreliable" (Wikipedia), the most important one being the highly dubious *Historia Augusta*

(more later). Besides, the standard explanation for why he wrote his *Meditations* in Greek (Romans "walked away from using Latin" in literary works after the early 100s AD) is far from satisfactory.

The anachronism in our representation of Antiquity is overwhelming, no matter how much we repress it or rationalize it under the stress of cognitive dissonance. It is not just about art, but also about mentality. Gaetano Mosca, wrote about this sense of temporal disruption in *The Ruling Class* (1939):

> "One has only to read a medieval writer—a writer, preferably, who is somewhat posterior to the fall of the western Empire and not too close to the Renaissance—to perceive at once how much more profoundly, how much more basically theological, medieval thinking was than the thinking of antiquity. Medieval writers and the people about them are immensely more remote, immensely more different, from us, than the contemporaries of Aristotle or Cicero ever were."[53]

Consider for example the "modernity" of Cicero's definition of the *Res Publica* as "an assemblage of people in large numbers associated in an agreement (*consensus*) with respect to justice and a partnership for the common good" (*On the Republic* I.39).

The lucrative market of literary forgeries

"Literary Forgery in Early Modern Europe, 1450-1800" was the subject of a 2012 conference, whose proceedings were published in 2018 by the John Hopkins University Press (who also published a 440-page catalog, *Bibliotheca Fictiva: A Collection of Books & Manuscripts Relating to Literary Forgery, 400 BC-AD 2000*). One of the forgers discussed in that book is Annius of Viterbo (1432-1502), who produced a collection of eleven texts, attributed to a Chaldean, an Egyptian, a Persian, and several ancient Greeks and Romans, purporting to show that his native town of Viterbo had been an important center of culture during the Etruscan period. Annius attributed his texts to recognizable ancient authors whose genuine works had conveniently perished, and he went on producing voluminous commentaries on his own forgeries.

This case illustrates the combination of political and mercantile motives in many literary forgeries. History-writing is a political act, and in the fifteenth century, it played a crucial role in the competition for prestige between Italian cities. Tacitus' history of Rome was brought forward by Bracciolini thirty years after a Florentine chancellor by the name of Leonardo Bruni (1369-1444) wrote his *History of the Florentine people* (*Historiae Florentini populi*) in twelve volumes (by plagiarizing Byzantine chronicles). Political value translated into economic value, as the market for ancient works reached astronomical prices: it is said that with the sale of just one copy of a manuscript of Titus Livy, Bracciolini bought himself a villa in Florence. During the Renaissance, "the acquisition of classical artifacts had simply become the new fad, the new way of displaying power and status. Instead of collecting the bones and body parts of saints, towns and wealthy rulers now collected fragments of the ancient world. And just as with the relic trade, demand far outstripped supply" (from the website of San Diego's "Museum of Hoaxes").[54]

In the mainstream of Classical Studies, ancient texts are assumed to be authentic unless they are proven forged. Cicero's *De Consolatione* is now universally considered the work of Carolus Sigonius (1520-1584), an Italian humanist born in Modena, only because we have a letter by Sigonius himself admitting the forgery. But short of such a confession, or of some blatant anachronism, historians and classical scholars will simply ignore the possibility of fraud. They would never, for example, suspect Francesco Petrarca, known as Petrarch (1304-1374), of faking his discovery of Cicero's letters, even though he went on publishing his own letters in perfect Ciceronian style. Jerry Brotton is not being ironic when he writes in *The Renaissance Bazaar*: "Cicero was crucial to Petrarch and the subsequent development of humanism because he offered a new way of thinking about how the cultured individual united the philosophical and contemplative side of life with its more active and public dimension. ... This was the blueprint for Petrarch's humanism."[55]

The medieval manuscripts found by Petrarch are long lost, so what evidence do we have of their authenticity, besides Petrarch's reputation? Imagine if historians seriously questioned the authenticity of some of our most cherished classical treasures. How many of them would pass the test? If Hochart is right and Tacitus is removed from the list of reliable sources, the whole historical edifice of the Roman Empire suffers from a major structural failure, but what if other pillars of ancient historiography crumble under similar scrutiny? What about Titus Livy, author a century earlier than Tacitus of a monumental history of Rome in 142 verbose volumes, starting with the foundation of Rome in 753 BC through the reign of Augustus. It is admitted, since Louis de Beaufort's critical analysis (1738), that the first five centuries of Livy's history are a web of fiction.[56] But can we trust the rest of it? It was also Petrarch, Brotton informs us, who "began piecing together texts like Livy's *History of Rome,* collating different manuscript fragments, correcting corruptions in the language, and imitating its style in writing a more linguistically fluent and rhetorically persuasive form of Latin."[57] None of the manuscripts used by Petrarch are available anymore. Petrarch was part of a circle of Italian propagandists who celebrated Rome's past glory. "His intentions," writes French medievalist Jacques Heers, "were deliberately political." He was "one of the most virulent writers of his time, involved in a great quarrel against the papacy of Avignon, and this relentlessness in fighting determined his cultural as well as political options."[58]

What about the *Augustan History* (*Historia Augusta*), a Roman chronicle that Edward Gibbon trusted entirely for writing his *Decline and Fall of the Roman Empire*? It has since been exposed as the work of an impostor who has masked his fraud by inventing sources from scratch. It contains about 150 alleged documents, including 68 letters, 60 speeches and proposals to the people or the senate, and 20 senatorial decrees and acclamations, almost all of them now considered fraudulent. However, for some vague reason, it is assumed that the forger lived in the fifth century, which is supposed to make his forgery worthwhile anyway. In reality, some of its stories sound like cryptic satire of Renaissance mores, others like Christian calumny of pre-Christian religion. How likely is it, for example, that the hero Antinous (literally "like a spirit"), worshipped throughout the Mediterranean Basin as an avatar of Osiris, was the gay lover (*eromenos*) of Hadrian, as told in *Augustan History?* Such questions of plausibility are simply ignored by professional historians.[59] But they jump to the face of any lay reader unimpressed by scholarly consensus. For instance, just reading the summary of Suetonius' *Lives of the Twelve Cesars* on the Wikipedia page should suffice to raise very strong suspicions, not only of fraud, but of mockery, for we are obviously dealing here with biographies of great imagination, but of no historical value whatsoever.

Works of fiction also come under suspicion. We owe the complete version of the *Satyricon,* supposedly written under Nero, to a manuscript discovered by Poggio Bracciolini in Cologne.[60] Apuleius' novel *The Golden Ass* was also found by Poggio in the same manuscript as the fragments of Tacitus' *Annales* and *Histories.* It was unknown before the thirteenth century, and its central piece, the tale of Cupid and Psyche, seems derived from the more archaic version found in the twelfth-century *Roman de Partonopeu de Blois.*[61]

The question can be raised of why Romans would bother writing and copying such works on papyrus *volume.* And who bought and read them? But the more important question is: Why would medieval monks copy and preserve them on expensive parchments? This question applies to all pagan authors, for none of them reached the Renaissance in manuscripts older than the ninth century (by the most optimistic estimate). "Did the monks, out of pure scientific interest, have a duty to preserve for posterity, for the greater glory of paganism, the masterpieces of antiquity?" asks Hochart.

And not only masterpieces, but bundles of letters! In the early years of the sixteenth century, the Veronian Fra Giovanni Giocondo discovered a volume of 121 letters exchanged between Pliny the Younger (friend of Tacitus) and Emperor Trajan around the year 112. This "book", writes Latinist scholar Jacques Heurgon, "had disappeared during the whole Middle Ages, and one could believe it definitively lost, when it suddenly emerged, in the very first years of the sixteenth century, in a single manuscript which, having been copied, partially, then completely, was lost again."[62] Such unsuspecting presentation is illustrative of the blind confidence of classical scholars in their Latin sources, unknown in the Middle Ages and magically appearing from nowhere in the Renaissance.

The strangest thing, Hochart remarks, is that Christian monks are supposed to have copied thousands of pagan volumes on expensive parchment, only to treat them as worthless rubbish:

> "To explain how many works of Latin authors had remained unknown to scholars of previous centuries and were uncovered by Renaissance scholars, it was said that monks had generally relegated to the attics or cellars of their convents most of the pagan writings that had been in their libraries. It was therefore among the discarded objects, sometimes among the rubbish, when they were allowed to search there, that the finders of manuscripts found, they claimed, the masterpieces of antiquity."

In medieval convents, manuscript copying was focused on religious books such as psalters, gospels, missals, catechisms, and saints' legends. They were mostly copied on papyrus. Parchment and vellum were reserved for luxury books, and since it was a very expensive material, it was common practice to scrape old scrolls in order to reuse them. Pagan works were the first to disappear. In fact, their destruction, rather than their preservation, was considered a holy deed, as hagiographers abundantly illustrate in their saints' lives.

How real is Julius Caesar?

Independently of Hochart, and on the basis of philological considerations, Robert Baldauf, professor at the university of Basle, argued that many of the most famous ancient Latin and Greek works are of late medieval origin (*Historie und Kritik*, 1902). "Our Romans and Greeks have been Italian humanists," he says. They have given us a whole fantasy world of Antiquity that "has rooted itself in our perception to such an extent that no positivist criticisms can make humanity doubt its veracity."

Baldauf points out, for example, German and Italian influences in Horace's Latin. On similar grounds, he concludes that Julius Cesar's books, so appreciated for their exquisite Latin, are late medieval forgeries. Recent historians of Gaul, now informed by archaeology, are actually puzzled by Cesar's *Commentarii de Bello Gallico* — our only source on the elusive Vercingetorix. Everything in there that doesn't come from book XXIII of Poseidonios' *Histories* appears either wrong or unreliable in terms of geography, demography, anthropology, and religion.[63]

A great mystery hangs over the supposed author himself. We are taught that "Caesar" was a cognomen (nickname) of uncertain meaning and origin, and that it was adopted after Julius Caesar's death as imperial title; we are asked to believe, in other words, that the emperors all called themselves Caesar in memory of that general and dictator who was not even emperor, and that the term gained such prestige that it went on to be adopted by Russian "Czars" and German "Kaisers". But that etymology has long been challenged by those (including Voltaire) who claim that "Caesar" comes from an Indo-European root word meaning "king", which also gave the Persian *Khosro* (Xerxes). These two origins cannot both be true, and the second seems well grounded. What is indisputable is that the German *Kaiser* derives not from the Latin *Caesar* but from the Greek *Καῖσαρ*: this fact alone is a serious challenge to our Rome-centered Western historiography, and a clue that medieval German emperors were emulating the flourishing Eastern (Byzantine) Roman Empire, not the long-dead and elusive Western Roman Empire (more in the next chapter).

Cesar's gentilice (surname) Iulius does not ease our perplexity. We are told by Virgil that it goes back to Cesar's supposed ancestor Iulus or Iule. But it happens to be an Indo-European root word designating the sunlight or the day sky, identical to the Scandinavian name for the solar god, *Yule* (*Helios* for the Greeks, *Haul* for the Gauls, *Hel* for the Germans, from which derives the French Noël, *Novo Hel*). From *Iule* is derived Jupiter (*Jul Pater*). So is "Julius Caesar" the "Sun King"?

Consider, in addition, that: 1. Roman emperors were traditionally declared adoptive sons of the sun-god Jupiter or of the "Undefeated Sun" (*Sol Invictus*). 2. The first emperor, Octavian Augustus, was allegedly the adoptive son of Julius Caesar, whom he divinized under the name Iulius Caesar Divus (celebrated on the 1st of January), while renaming in his honor the first month of summer, July. If Augustus is both the adoptive son of the divine Sun and the adoptive son of the divine Julius, and if in addition Julius or Julus is the divine name of the Sun, it means that the divine Julius is none other than the divine Sun (and the so-called "Julian" calendar simply meant the "solar" calendar). Has Julius Caesar been brought down from heaven to earth, transposed from mythology to history? That is a common process in Roman history, according to Georges Dumézil, who explains the notorious poverty of Roman mythology by the fact that it "was radically destroyed at the level of theology

[but] flourished in the form of history," which is to say that Roman history is a literary fiction built on mythical structures.[64]

The Romans' lack of mythology is a point that deserves careful consideration. "not even the most important and most vital gods have any mythology," Dumézil notes. He suggests that the Romans simply discarded their own mythology because of "the invasion of Greek mythology, which was much richer and much more prestigious." This is mere speculation. The fact remains:

> "This kind of almost completely demythologized religion, surviving only in rites whose mythological and even theological justifications have been forgotten, is seldom found in other parts of the Indo- European world."[65]

The mystery surrounding Julius Caesar is of course of great consequence, since on him rests the historiography of Imperial Rome. If Julius Caesar is a fiction, then so is much of Imperial Rome.

At this point, most readers will have lost patience. With those whose curiosity surpasses their skepticism, we shall now argue that Imperial Rome is actually, for a large part, a fictitious mirror image of Constantinople, a fantasy that started emerging in the eleventh century in the context of the cultural war waged by the papacy against the Byzantine empire, and solidified in the fifteenth century, in the context of the plunder of Byzantine culture that is known as the Renaissance. This, of course, will raise many objections, some of which will be addressed here, others in further chapters.

First objection: Wasn't Constantinople founded by a Roman emperor, namely Constantine the Great? So it is said. But then, how real is this legendary Constantine? And what is his real place in history? Is he an Eastern or a Western Emperor?

How real is Constantine the Great?

If Julius Caesar is the alpha of the Western Roman Empire, Constantine is the omega. One major difference between them is the nature of our sources. For Constantine's biography, we are totally dependent on Christian authors, beginning with Eusebius of Caesarea, whose *Life of Constantine,* which includes the story of the emperor's conversion to Christianity, is a mixture of eulogy and hagiography. Its modern editors tell us:

> "it has proved extremely controversial. Some scholars are disposed to accept its evidence at face value while others have been and are highly skeptical. Indeed, the integrity of Eusebius as a writer has often been attacked and his authorship of the VC [*Vita Constantini*] denied by scholars eager to discredit the value of the evidence it provides, with discussion focusing particularly on the numerous imperial documents which are cited verbatim in the work."[66]

The common notion derived from Eusebius is that Constantine moved the capital of his Empire from Rome to Byzantium, which he renamed in his own honor. But that scenario lacks credibility. The very notion of Constantine's *translatio imperii* is replete with inner contradictions. First, Constantine didn't really move his capital to the East, because he was himself from the East. He was born in the Balkans, in Naissus (today Nis in Serbia), in the region then called Moesia. In broad terms, Constantine may be called a Dacian, or a Scythian. According to standard history, Constantine had never set foot in Rome before he marched on the city and conquered it from Maxentius.

Constantine wasn't just a Roman who happened to be born in Moesia. His father Constantius Chlorus also came from Moesia. So did his colleague and rival Licinius. And so did his predecessor Diocletian, who was born there, built his palace there (Split, today in Croatia), and died there. In Byzantine chronicles, Diocletian is given as *Dux Moesiae,*[67] which can mean "king of Moesia", for well into the Early Middle Ages, *dux* was more or less synonymous with *rex.*[68]

It is said that Diocletian gave an Oriental style to his emperorship, and even to his army, equipping them with Persian bows.[69] Textbook history tells us that, on becoming emperor, Diocletian decided to share his power with Maximian as co-emperor. That is already odd enough. But instead of keeping for himself the historical heart of the empire, he left it to his subordinate and settled in the East. Seven years later, he divided the Empire further into a tetrarchy; instead of one Augustus Caesar, there was now two Augustus and two Caesars. Diocletian retired to the far eastern part of Asia Minor, bordering on Persia. Like Constantine after him, Diocletian never reigned in Rome; he visited it once in his lifetime. He resided most of his life in Nicomedia, on the eastern shore of the Bosphorus, where Licinius also settled.

This leads us to the second inner contradiction of the *translatio imperii* paradigm: Constantine didn't really move the imperial capital from Rome to Byzantium, because Rome had ceased to be the imperial capital in 286, being replaced by Milan. By the time of Diocletian and Constantine, the whole of Italy had actually fallen into anarchy during the Crisis of the Third Century (AD 235–284). When in 402 AD, the Eastern emperor Honorius restored order in the Peninsula, he transferred its capital to Ravenna on the Adriatic coast. So from 286 on, we are supposed to have a Roman Empire with a deserted Rome.

The conundrum only thickens when we compare Roman and Byzantine cultures. According to the *translatio imperii* paradigm, the Eastern Roman Empire is the continuation of the Western Roman Empire. But Byzantium scholars insist on the great differences between the Greek-speaking Byzantine civilization and the earlier civilization of the Latium. For example, the Byzantines "were not a warlike people" as were the Romans, notes Byzantinist Anthony Kaldellis:

> "They preferred to pay their enemies either to go away or to fight among themselves. Likewise, the court at the heart

of their empire sought to buy allegiance with honors, fancy
titles, bales of silk, and streams of gold. Politics was the
cunning art of providing just the right incentives to win
over supporters and keep them loyal. Money, silk, and
titles were the empire's preferred instruments of
governance and foreign policy, over swords and armies."[70]

The Byzantine civilization owed nothing to Rome, and
everything from Greece. Culturally, it was closer to Persia
and Egypt than to Italy, which it treated as a colony. At the
dawn of the second millenium AD, it had almost no
recollection of its supposed Latin past, to the point that the
most famous byzantine philosopher of the eleventh century,
Michael Psellos, confused Cicero with Caesar.

How does the textbook story of Constantine's *translatio
imperii* fit in this perspective? It doesn't. In fact, the notion
is highly problematic. Unwilling, for good reasons, to accept
at face value the Christian tale that Constantine moved to
Byzantium in order to leave Rome to the Pope alone,
historians struggle to find a reasonable explanation for the
transfer, and they generally settle for this one: after the old
capital had fallen into irreversible decadence (soon to be
sacked by the Gauls), Constantine decided to move the heart
of the Empire closer to its most endangered borders. Does
that make any sense? Even if it did, how plausible is the
transfer of an imperial capital over a thousand miles, with
senators, bureaucrats and armies, resulting in the
metamorphosis of a Roman empire into another Roman
empire with a totally different political structure, language,
culture, and religion?

One of the major sources of this preposterous concept is
the false Donation of Constantine. While it is admitted that
this document was forged by medieval popes in order to
back their ambition to rule Rome, its basic premise, the
translation of the imperial capital to the East, has not been
questioned. I suggest that Constantine's *translatio imperii*
was actually a mythological cover for the very real opposite
movement of *translatio studii,* the transfer of Byzantine

culture to the West that started before the crusades and evolved into systematic plunder after. Late medieval Roman culture rationalized and disguised its less than honorable Byzantine origin by the opposite myth of the Roman origin of Constantinople.

This will become clearer in the next chapter, but here is already one example of an insurmountable contradiction to the accepted filiation from the Western Roman Empire to the Eastern Roman Empire. One of the most fundamental and precious legacy of the Romans to our Western civilization is their tradition of civil law. Roman law is still the foundation of our legal system. How come, then, Roman law was imported to Italy from Byzantium at the end of the eleventh century? Specialists like Harold Berman or Aldo Schiavone are adamant that knowledge of Roman laws had totally disappeared for 700 years in Western Europe, until a Byzantine copy of their compilation by Justinian (the *Digesta*) was discovered around 1080 by Bolognese scholars. This "700-year long eclipse" of Roman law in the West, is an undisputed yet almost incomprehensible phenomenon.[71]

Who were the first "Romans"?

One obvious objection to the idea that the relationship between Rome and Constantinople has been inverted is that the Byzantines called themselves Romans (*Romaioi*), and believed they were living in *Romania*. Persians, Arabs and Turks called them *Rumis*. Even the Greeks of the Hellenic Peninsula called themselves *Romaioi* in Late Antiquity, despite their detestation of the Latins. This is taken as proof that the Byzantines considered themselves the heirs of the Roman Empire of the West, founded in Rome, Italy. But it is not. Strangely enough, mythography and etymology both suggest that, just like the name "Caesar", the name "Rome" travelled from East to West, rather than the other way. *Romos*, latinized in *Romus* or *Remus*, is a Greek word meaning "strong" or, according to Jerome in *Adversus*

Joviniarum, "courage" (*fortitudo*). The Italian Romans were Etruscans from Lydia in Asia Minor. They were well aware of their eastern origin, the memory of which was preserved in their legends. According to the tradition elaborated by Virgil in his epic *Aeneid,* Rome was founded by Aeneas from Troy, in the immediate vicinity of the Bosphorus. According to another version, Rome was founded by Romos, the son of Odysseus and Circe.[72] The historian Strabo, supposedly living in the first century BC (but quoted only from the fifth century AD), reports that "another older tradition makes Rome an Arcadian colony," and insists that "Rome itself was of Hellenic origin" (*Geographia* V, 3). Dionysius of Halicarnassus in his *Roman Antiquities*, declares "Rome is a Greek city." His thesis is summed up by the syllogism: "The Romans descend from the Trojans. But the Trojans are of Greek origin. So the Romans are of Greek origin." The same Dionysius claimed that "the language spoken by the Romans" derives from Aeolic Greek, a theory called "Aeolism" and later taken up by Renaissance scholar Janus Lascaris.[73]

Rome was actually the city with the largest Greek-speaking population after Alexandria before the founding of Constantinople, and we should remember that many cultured Romans, such as Hadrian (nicknamed *Graeculus*) and Marcus Aurelius, spoke and wrote in Greek.[74]

Greek-speaking Roman historian Herodian (c. 170-240 AD) tells a revealing story about the Romans' attachment to the goddess Cybelle, "mother of the gods", and their kinship with the Phrygians from Anatolia:

> "When Roman affairs prospered, they say that an oracle prophesied that the empire would endure and soar to greater heights if the goddess were brought from Pessinus [in the heart of Anatolia] to Rome. The Romans therefore sent an embassy to Phrygia and asked for the statue; they easily got it by reminding the Phrygians of their kinship and by recalling to them that Aeneas the Phrygian was the ancestor of the Romans." (Book 1, chapter 10)

The famous legend of Romulus and Remus, told by Titus Livy (I, 3), is generally considered of later origin. It could very well be an invention of the late Middle Age. Anatoly Fomenko, of whom we will have more to say later on, believes that its central theme, the simultaneous foundation of two cities, one by Romulus on the Palatine Hill, and the other by Remus on the Aventine, is a mythical reflection of the struggle for ascendency between the two Romes. As we shall see, the murder of Remus by Romulus is a fitting allegory of the events unfolding from the Fourth Crusade.[75] It is also interesting to note that Remus and Romulus bear some resemblance to the brothers Valens and Valentinian, who are said to have reigned respectively over Constantinople and Rome from 364 to 378. Their story is known only from Ammianus Marcellinus, and it happens that *valens* is a Latin equivalent for the Greek *romos*.

I have started this chapter by suggesting that much of the history of the Western Roman Empire is of Renaissance invention. But as we progress in our investigation, another complementary hypothesis will emerge: much of the history of the Western Roman Empire is borrowed from the history of the Eastern Roman Empire, either by deliberate plagiarism, or by confusion resulting from the fact that the Byzantines called themselves Romans and their city Rome. The process can be inferred from some obvious duplicates. Here is one example, taken from Latin historian Jordanes, whose *Origin and Deeds of the Goths* is notoriously full of anachronisms (the manuscript was discovered in 1442): in 441, Attila crossed the Danube, invaded the Balkans, and threatened Constantinople, but could not take the city and retreated with an immense booty. Ten years later, the same Attila crossed the Alps, invaded Italy, and threatened Rome, but couldn't take the city and retreated with an immense booty.

The mysterious origin of Latin

Another objection against questioning the existence of the Western Roman Empire is the spread of Latin throughout the Mediterranean world and beyond. It is admitted that Latin, originally the language spoken in the Latium, is the origin of French, Italian, Occitan, Catalan, Spanish and Portuguese, that is, "Western Romance Languages".

However, this filiation, which became dogma in the middle of the nineteenth century (under the strong influence of Émile Littré and his *Histoire de la langue française*, 1862) is now questioned with very strong counter-arguments. In his book *Le Français ne vient pas du latin. Essai sur une aberration linguistique,* French latinist Yves Cortez shows that, although the general public is unaware of it, the divergence between Latin and the Romance languages has always puzzled linguists. In 1940, the Danish linguist Louis Hjelmslev came to the conclusion that: "the mother tongue that we are led to reconstruct is not the same Latin as that which has been transmitted to us by literature." In 1953, the French linguist Jean Perrot also observed that the mother tongue that can be reconstructed from the different Romance languages "does not correspond to the state of Latin that we know." In 1985, the great Latinist Jozsef Herman acknowledged at an international congress :

> "We Romanists, with perhaps historians of the Latin language, are the only ones aware that with regard to the very process of transformation of Latin into the Romance languages we have more hypotheses and controversies than certainties."

As Yves Cortez explains, for Latin to be the origin of the Romance languages would mean that all the Romance languages have produced the same disappearances of grammatical forms and the same appearances of new grammatical forms, as well as the disappearance of the same Latin words and the appearance of the same non-Latin words. It defies all logic. Why are the Romance languages so similar to each other and so different from Latin? And why, during the same period, did Latin freeze?[76]

The same points are made by amateur historian and linguist M. J. Harper:

"The linguistic evidence mirrors the geography with great precision: Portuguese resembles Spanish more than any other language; French resembles Occitan more than any other; Occitan resembles Catalan, Catalan resembles Spanish and so forth. So which was the Ur-language? Can't tell; it could be any of them. Or it could be a language that has long since disappeared. *But the original language cannot have been Latin.* All the Romance languages, even Portuguese and Italian, resemble one another more than any of them resemble Latin, and do so by a wide margin."[77]

To bypass this difficulty, linguists postulate that "Romance languages" do not derive directly from Latin, but from Vulgar Latin, the popular and colloquial sociolect of Latin spoken by soldiers, settlers, and merchants of the Roman Empire. What was Vulgar Latin, or proto-Romance, like? No one knows.

In *Romance Did Not Begin in Rome: A Critic of the Latin Origin of Romance languages,* Spanish philologist Carme Jiménez Huertas highlights the same problems as does Yves Cotez, and seeks a solution in the easternmost Romance language, namely Romanian:

"Romance languages share a high percentage of phonetic, lexical, morphosyntactic and semantic characteristics, showing a close kinship to a linguistic typology that relates them to each other but distances them from Latin. … The structural, lexical, phonetic and conceptual similarities between Romanian and the rest of Western Romance languages — distant languages whose people have not been in direct contact for at least two thousand years — suggests an earlier common language which must be much older than Latin. Therefore, the characteristics of the Romance languages might have evolved directly from this common, previous language, without having to justify this development through Latin. The relationship between Romance languages and Latin would then be of kinship and not filiation. The evidence is increasingly conclusive: Romance languages do not originate in Latin."[78]

The language that most resembles Latin is Romanian, which, although divided in several dialects, constitutes the only member of the "Eastern branch of Romance languages". It is the only Romance language that has maintained such archaic traits of Latin as the case system (endings of words depending on their role in the sentence) and the neutral gender.[79]

But how did Romanians come to speak Vulgar Latin? That is another mystery. Part of the linguistic area of Romanian, we are told, was conquered by Emperor Trajan in 106 AD, and formed the Roman province of Dacia for a mere 165 years. (Dacian prisoners, wearing a Phrygian hat, figure on victory monuments in Rome, particularly the column of Trajan and the Arch of Constantine.) One or two Roman legions were stationed in the South-West of Dacia, and, although not Italians, they are supposed to have communicated in Vulgar Latin and imposed their language to the whole country, even north of the Danube, where there was no Roman presence. What language did people speak in Dacia before the Romans conquered the south part of it? No one has a clue. The "Dacian language" "is an extinct language, ... poorly documented. ... only one Dacian inscription is believed to have survived."[80] Only 160 Romanian words are hypothetically of Dacian origin. Dacian is believed to be closely related or identical to Thracian, itself "an extinct and poorly attested language."[81]

Let me repeat: The inhabitants of Dacia north of the Danube adopted Vulgar Latin from the non-Italian legions that stationed on the lower part of their territory from 106 to 271 AD, and completely forgot their original language, to the point that no trace of it is left. Yet the Romans hardly ever occupied Dacia (on most textbook maps of the Roman Empire, Dacia is not even included). The next part is also extraordinary: Dacians, who had so easily given up their original language for Vulgar Latin, then became so attached to Vulgar Latin that the German invaders, who caused the Romans to retreat in 271, failed to impose their language. So did the Huns and, more surprisingly, the Slavs, who dominated the area since the seventh century and left many traces in the toponymy. Less than ten percent of Romanian words are of Slavic origin (but the Romanians adopted Slavonic for their liturgy).

One more thing: although Latin was a written language in the Empire, Romanians are believed to have never had a written language until the Middle Ages. The first document written in Romanian goes back to the sixteenth century, and it is written in Cyrillic alphabet.

Joseph Solodow highlights the enigma of the Rumanian language in *The Survival of Latin in English and the Romance Languages:*

> "once linguists were certain of Rumanian's ancestry, they faced a puzzle that has not yet been solved. How did a Latin-based language come to be the speech of so large a population in that area? One theory is that Latin persisted north of the Danube, in the province called Dacia, just as it did in Spain and Gaul. But the Romans occupied Dacia for only about 170 years before abandoning it, in 271 C.E. This does not look like a long enough period for Latin to have taken hold so firmly. ... Because w know so little about Rumanian's early history—the first preserved text dates only from the sixteenth century—we may never be in a position to decide the question."[82]

Obviously, there is room for the following alternative theory: Latin is a language originating from Dacia; ancient Dacian did not vanish mysteriously but is the common ancestor of both Latin and modern Romanian. This is the thesis presented in the Romanian documentaries: "Dacians: Unsettling Truths,"[83] and "Dacians: Unsettling Truths".[84]

Dacian, if you will, is Vulgar Latin, which preceded Classical Latin. The reason why Dacia is also called Romania is because Dacia—rather than Italy—was the original home of the Romans who founded Constantinople.[85] That is consistent with the fact that Constantine the Great was a native Dacian. It is also consistent with the notion that the Roman language (Latin) remained the administrative language of the Eastern Empire until the sixth century AD, when it was abandoned for Greek, the language spoken by the majority of its subjects. That, in turn, is consistent with the character of Latin itself. M. J. Harper makes the following remark:

"Latin is not a natural language. When written, Latin takes up approximately half the space of written Italian or written French (or written English, German or any natural European language). Since Latin appears to have come into existence in the first half of the first millennium BC, which was the time when alphabets were first spreading through the Mediterranean basin, it seems a reasonable working hypothesis to assume that Latin was originally a shorthand compiled by Italian speakers for the purposes of written (confidential? commercial?) communication. This would explain:

a) the very close concordance between Italian and Latin vocabulary;

b) the conciseness of Latin in, for instance, dispensing with separate prepositions, compound verb forms and other 'natural' language impedimenta;

c) the unusually formal rules governing Latin grammar and syntax;

d) the lack of irregular, non-standard usages;

e) the unusual adoption among Western European languages of a specifically vocative case ('Dear Marcus, re. you letter of...')."[86]

Steven Runciman once noted that, "while Greek is a subtle and flexible tongue, admirably suited to express every shade of abstract thought, Latin is far more rigid and inelastic; it is clear, concrete, and uncompromising, a perfect medium for lawyers."[87]

The hypothesis that Latin was a "non-demotic" language, a *koine* of the empire, a written artifact developed for the purpose of administration, was first proposed by Russian researchers Igor Davidenko and Jaroslav Kesler in *The Book of Civilizations* (2001). But in truth, it goes back to the great

Italian poet Dante Alighieri. In *De vulgari eloquentia* (1303), the earliest treatise on European linguistics, he assumes that Latin (which he calls *grammatica*) was an artificial and synthetic language created "by the common consent of many peoples."[88] As Stefano Corno writes:

> "Even if today the fact that Romance languages descend from Latin seems obvious to us, this was not the case for Dante, because in his time Latin appeared like an artificial language, the only one endowed with a true grammar, which had been created to save men from *confusio linguarum*."[89]

A final note on the Dacian hypothesis: since, as will become clearer in chapter 4, the Dacians, also known as the Getae, are identical to the Goths, the search for a new ethnolinguistic paradigm for Europe will have to include the Goths, who mysteriously left so little trace of their supposedly German language—apart from the highly suspicious silver-lettered pages from Ulfila's Bible discovered in the 17th century.

Although I was unable to read it, I must mention a German book from 1830 that defends the thesis of "the Germanic origin of the Latin language and of the Roman people": Ernst Gottlob Jäkel, *Der germanische Ursprung der lateinischen Sprache und des römischen Volkes*. The origin of Latin as an administrative *lingua franca* conceived by the Franks in the Early Middle Ages, is a hypothesis that cannot be rejected out of hand, especially since Germanic languages are the only Indo-European languages that share with Latin a system of declension and a neutral gender.

How old is ancient Roman architecture?

The strongest objection against the theory that ancient Imperial Rome is a fiction is, of course, Rome's many architectural vestiges. This subject will be more fully explored in chapter 4, but a quotation from James Bryce's influential work, *The Holy Roman Empire* (1864), will point to the answer:

"The modern traveller, after his first few days in Rome, when he has looked out upon the Campagna from the summit of St. Peter's, paced the chilly corridors of the Vatican, and mused under the echoing dome of the Pantheon, when he has passed in review the monuments of regal and republican and papal Rome, begins to seek for some relics of the twelve hundred years that lie between Constantine and Pope Julius the Second. 'Where,' he asks, 'is the Rome of the Middle Ages, the Rome of Alberic and Hildebrand and Rienzi? the Rome which dug the graves of so many Teutonic hosts; whither the pilgrims flocked; whence came the commands at which kings bowed? Where are the memorials of the brightest age of Christian architecture, the age which reared Cologne and Rheims and Westminster, which gave to Italy the cathedrals of Tuscany and the wave-washed palaces of Venice?' To this question there is no answer. Rome, the mother of the arts, has scarcely a building to commemorate those times."[90]

Officially, there is hardly a medieval vestige in Rome, and the same applies to many other Italian cities believed to have been founded during Antiquity. (But some cities of Roman Antiquity like Avignon, on the other hand, have mysteriously lost all trace of their pre-medieval past.) François de Sarre, a French contributor to the field of research here presented, was first intrigued by the magnificent palace of the Roman emperor Diocletian (284-305 AD), in the center of the city of Split, today in Croatia. The Renaissance constructions are integrated to it in such a perfect architectural ensemble as to be almost indistinguishable. It is hard to believe that ten centuries separate the two stages of construction, as if the ancient buildings had been left untouched during the whole Middle Ages.[91]

Also puzzling is the little-known fact that ancient Roman architects used advanced technologies such as concretes of remarkable quality. Roman concretes came in many variations, including "highly specialized marine concrete" for structures built in the sea (J. P. Oleson, ed., *Building for Eternity: The History and Technology of Roman Concrete*

Engineering in the Sea, Oxbow Books, 2014). The most outstanding Roman concrete structures were the domes (Lynne Lancaster, *Concrete Vaulted Construction in Imperial Rome: Innovations in Context,* Cambridge UP, 2005), such as the Pantheon's beautifully preserved dome.

Roman concretes continue to bewilder scientists, as can be read in a long article published by *Science Advances,* which starts like this: "Ancient Roman concretes have survived millennia, but mechanistic insights into their durability remain an enigma." The authors report on the chemical analysis of 2000-year-old Roman concrete samples obtained from the archaeological site of Privernum, Italy.

"In contrast to their modern counterparts, ancient Roman mortars and concretes have remained durable in a variety of climates, seismic zones, and even in direct contact with seawater, as in the case for maritime concrete. Because of this proven longevity on the order of millennia, these ancient construction materials are attractive model systems for the design of sustainable, durable cementitious composites for modern engineering applications."[92]

Some of the secrets of fabrication of Roman concrete are described in Vitruvius' multi-volume work entitled *De architectura* (first century BC), in which he also explains how to draw the perspective view, which he calls *scenographia*.[93] Medieval men, we are told, were totally ignorant of the technologies documented by Vitruvius, because, Wikipedia informs us, "Vitruvius' works were largely forgotten until 1414, when *De architectura* was 'rediscovered' by the Florentine humanist Poggio Bracciolini in the library of Saint Gall Abbey." Him again!

SPQR

The Commune of Rome was founded in 1144 as a Republic with a consul and a senate, in the wake of other Italian cities (Pise in 1085, Milano in 1097, Gene in 1099, Florence in 1100). It defined itself by the acronym SPQR, which is taken to mean *senatus populusque romanus* ("the Senate and the Roman people"). Beginning in 1184 and until the early sixteenth century, the city of Rome struck coins with these letters.

But, we are also told, SPQR was already the mark of the first Roman Republic founded in 509 BC and, more incredibly, it was preserved by emperors, who apparently didn't mind being left out and continued to display SPQR abundantly on coins, buildings and banners.

As outrageous as it sounds, one cannot easily brush aside the suspicion that the ancient Roman Republic, known to us thanks to Petrarch's "piecing together" Titus Livy's *History of Rome*,[94] is an imaginative portrait of late medieval Rome in antique garb. Petrarch, let us recall, was deeply involved in Roman politics, and "involved in a great quarrel against the papacy of Avignon."[95]

The hypothesis that ancient Rome was, to a large extent, a fabulation of late medieval Rome, is an alternative explanation of the strong affinity of the two, the reverse explanation, in fact, to the one suggested by French medievalist Robert Folz:

> "In 1143, the Capitol became the residence of the Council of the Commune of Rome. Its foundation is part of the movement which carried the Italian cities towards the emancipation of their lords: Rome follows, with a lag of

more than half a century, the example of the cities of Italy of the North. But in Rome, the enterprise was singularly perilous, because of the exceptional importance of the city's lord, the pope, capable of asserting venerable texts in his support, and of mobilizing powerful alliances against the city. Moreover, in an environment where the past was the object of such a passion as in Rome, any attempt at new creation had necessarily to take the aspect of a restoration of the past: the council of the commune was called senate, the senatorial era was used in the dating of acts, while the sign SPQR also reappeared. It all happened as if we were returning to the tradition of republican Rome."[96]

There is an additional mystery about this SPQR acronym. Although we are told that it means *senatus populusque romanus* ("the Senate and the Roman people"), contemporary evidence of that is lacking. In 1362, the Roman poet Antonio Pucci believed it stood for the Italian words *Sanato Popolo Qumune Romano* ("The Senate and People of the Commune of Rome").[97] Forty-two other medieval Italian cities used the acronym SPQ followed by the Initial of the city's name, as SPQP for Pisa, SPQT for Tusculum, or SPQL for Lucera.[98] This raises the strong suspicion that SPQR was never used in Rome before the founding of the Commune of Rome in the twelfth century. In that case, the ancient Roman Republic and its imperial glory are, to some extent, a fiction of the Middle Ages, as many other clues in literature, art and architecture suggest.

As Robert Folz mentions, the Commune of Rome was always in conflict with the pope, who was repeatedly expelled, and moved to Viterbo in 1257, then to Avignon in 1309. So "the idea of Empire was inseparable from it [the Roman Republic]: the complex symbolism of the Capitol teaches this well. This explains why, almost immediately, the Romans had to take a position with regard to the Empire."[99] Here Folz refers to the alliance of the Commune of Rome with the Hohenstaufen emperors against the popes, in the most intense conflict of the Middle Ages, which would evolve into the endless wars between the Guelphs and the Ghibellines.

To be clear, the hypothesis I am suggesting here is that the mirage of the ancient Roman Republic and Empire was produced, not by the twelfth-century founders of the Commune of Rome, but rather by later Roman humanists and patriots of the fourteenth and fifteenth century, such as Petrarch, through their exaltation of the immemorial antiquity of their city's glory (because, remember, prestige rests primarily on antiquity).

As a temporary conclusion: all the oddities that we have pointed out are like pieces of a puzzle that do not fit well within our conventional representation. We will later be able to assemble them into a more plausible picture. But before that, in the next chapter, we will focus on ecclesiastical literature from Late Antiquity to the Middle Ages, for it is the original source of the great historical distortion that later took a life of its own before being standardized as the dogma of modern chronology and historiography.

CHAPTER 2
How fake is Church history?

In the previous chapter, I have argued that the forgery of ancient books during the late Middle Ages and the Renaissance was more widespread than usually acknowledged, so that what we think we know about the Roman Empire — including events and individuals of central importance — rests on questionable sources. (I have not claimed that all written sources on the Roman Empire are fake.)

I have also argued that the traditional perspective of the first millennium is distorted by a strong bias in favor of Rome, at the expense of Constantinople. The common representation of the Byzantine Empire as the final phase of the Roman Empire, whose capital was transferred from the Latium to the Bosphorus, is today recognized as a falsification. Politically, culturally, linguistically, and religiously, Byzantium owes nothing to Rome. "Believing that their own culture was vastly superior to Rome's, the Greeks were hardly receptive to the influence of Roman civilization," states a recent *Atlas de l'Empire Romain,* mentioning only gladiator combats as a possible, yet marginal, debt.[100]

The assumption that Western civilization originated in the Italian Rome rests partly on a misunderstanding of the word "Roman". What we now call "the Byzantine Empire" (a term that appeared in the sixteenth century and became customary in the nineteenth century) was then called *Basileía tôn Rhômaíôn* (the kingdom of the Romans), and for most of the first millennium, "Roman" simply meant what we understand today as "Byzantine".

Our perception of Rome as the origin and center of Western civilization is also linked to our assurance that Latin is the mother of all Romance languages. But that filiation, which became a dogma in the mid-nineteenth century, is under severe attack. It seems that Dante was correct when he assumed in *De vulgari eloquentia* (c. 1303), the first treatise on the subject, that Latin was an artificial, synthetic language created "by the common consent of many peoples" for written purposes.[101]

The distortions that produced our textbook history of the first millennium have both a geographical and a chronological dimension. The geographical distortion is part of that Eurocentrism that is now being challenged by scholars like James Morris Blaut (*The Colonizer's Model of the World,* Guilford Press, 1993), John M. Hobson (*The Eastern Origins of Western Civilization,* Cambridge UP, 2004), or Jack Goody (*The Theft of History,* Cambridge UP, 2012). The chronological distortion, on the other hand, is not yet an issue in mainstream academia: historians simply do not question the chronological backbone of the first millennium. They don't even ask when, how and by whom it was created.

So far, we have formulated the working hypothesis that the Western Roman Empire is, to some extent, a phantom duplicate of the Eastern Roman Empire, conjured by Rome in order to steal the birthright from Constantinople, while concealing its debt to the civilization that it conspired to assassinate. The Roman Empire, in other words, was a dream rather than a memory, exactly like the ancient empire of King Solomon, that archaeologists are now compelled to call a fantasy.[102] But, one will instantly object, while archaeologists have found no trace of Solomon's empire, the vestiges of Augustus' empire are plentiful. True, but are these vestiges really from Antiquity, and if so, why are medieval vestiges nowhere to be found in Rome? If Rome was the beating heart of medieval Western Christendom, it should have been busy constructing, not just restoring.

In the first chapter, I have questioned the objectivity and even the probity of those late-Middle-Age and Renaissance humanists who claimed to resurrect the long forgotten splendor of Republican and Imperial Rome. In this second article, we turn our attention to ecclesiastical historians of earlier times, who fashioned our vision of Late Antiquity and the Early Middle Ages. Their history of the Christian Church, peopled with miracle-performing holy men and diabolical heretics, is hard to connect with political history, and secular historians specialized in Late Antiquity are generally happy to leave the field to "Church historians" and teachers of faith. And so the credibility of this literature has largely gone unchallenged.

The papal forgery factory

"Arguably the most distinctive feature of the early Christian literature is the degree to which it was forged." So Bert Ehrman begins his book *Forgery and Counterforgery: The Use of Literary Deceit in Early Christian Polemics.* Throughout the first four centuries AD, he says, forgery was the rule in Christian literature, and genuine authorship the exception. Forgery was so systemic that forgeries gave rise to counterforgeries, that is, forgeries "used to counter the views of other forgeries."[103] If forgery is part of the DNA of Christianity, we can expect it to persist throughout the Middle Ages.

The German specialist of medieval *diploma* Harry Breslau (1848-1926) estimated that almost fifty percent of documents from the Merovingian period were forgeries. He concludes :

> "It is undeniable that even the most eminent men of the Church, clergymen whose piety and virtuous conduct are highly praised … have resorted to theft and lying to come into possession of venerated and miraculous relics, even that they resorted to falsification and fraud when it came to increasing or defending the property, rights and reputation

of their churches. ... Often entire series of acts have been fabricated for such purposes."[104]

The most famous medieval forgeries is the "Donation of Constantine." By this document, Emperor Constantine is supposed to have transferred his own authority over the Western regions of the Empire to Pope Sylvester. This forgery of outrageous audacity is included in a collection of about a hundred counterfeit decrees and acts of Synods, attributed to the earliest popes or other Church dignitaries, and known today as the *Pseudo–Isidorian Decretals*, whose aim was to set forth precedents for the exercise of sovereign authority of the bishop of Rome over the universal Church.

These forgeries did not exercise any major influence on the legal tradition until the eleventh century, and it is not before the twelfth century that they were incorporated by Gratian into his *Decretum,* which became the basis of all canon law. Yet the scholarly consensus is that they date back from the time of Charlemagne. For that reason, Professor Horst Fuhrmann, president of Monumenta Germaniae Historica, classifies them as "forgeries with anticipatory character,"

> "Sylvester legend, Constantinian Donation, Symmachian Forgeries, Pseudo-Clemens letters, Pseudo-Isidorian Forgeries: let us stop at that list. All these forgeries have the characteristic that at the time they were written, they had hardly any effect. At the time of their creation, they had anticipatory character."

According to him, these fakes had to wait, depending on the case, between 250 and 550 years before being used. Heribert Illig and Hans-Ulrich Niemitz have protested against this theory of forgeries allegedly written by clerics who had no use of them and did not know what purpose their forgeries could serve centuries later. Forgeries are produced to serve a project, and they are made on demand when needed. Therefore these forgeries are wrongly dated. Their "anticipatory character" is an illusion created by one of the chronological distortions that we have set out to correct.[105] The Donation of Constantine must date from the tenth century, when it first came into use. The first attested legal document where it is mentioned is the "Ottonian Privilege" (*Privilegium Ottonianum*), issued by Otto the Great on February 3, 962, after his coronation by Pope John XII. This document grants the pope a long list of domains, including "the city of Rome with its duchy", "the entire exarchate of Ravenna", as well as Venetia, Corsica, and Sicily (then occupied by the Saracens). It mentions the Donation of Constantin, but also a Donation made by Pepin, king of the Franks, to Pope Stephen II, later confirmed by Pepin's son Charlemagne to Pope Sylvester II. So the Donation of Constantine is the basis for the Donation of Pepin, supposedly confirmed by Charlemagne, which is the basis for the Ottonian Privilege. Doubts have always hung over the existence of the "Donation of Pepin", because no authentic act is known, nor is Charlemagne's confirmation attested by any legal diploma.[106] It is most probable that the Donation of Constantine and the Donation of Pepin were both fabricated during the same period, as an inextricable legal *mise en abyme*. In fact, there is no confirmation that the "Ottonian Privilege" itself, whose original is jealously kept in the Vatican archives, is not itself a forgery.

Other false decretals probably date from the early stages of the Gregorian Reform, which started with the accession of Pope Leo IX in 1049. The Gregorian Reform was a continuation of the monastic revival launched by the powerful Benedictine Abbey of Cluny, which a century after its foundation in 910 had developed a network of more than a thousand monasteries all over Europe.[107] The Gregorian Reform can be conceived as a monkish coup over Europe, in the sense that celibate monks, who used to live at the margin of society, progressively took the leadership.

It is worth insisting on the revolutionary character of the Gregorian Reform. It was, wrote Marc Bloch in *Feudal Society*, "an extraordinarily powerful movement from which, without exaggeration, may be dated the definite formation of Latin Christianity."[108] More recently, Robert I. Moore wrote in *The First European Revolution, c. 970-1215*: "The 'reform' which was embodied in the Gregorian program was nothing less than a project to divide the world, both people and property, into two distinct and autonomous realms, not geographically by socially." The reform triumphed at the Fourth Lateran Council convened by Innocent III in 1215. The world created by Lateran IV was "an entirely different world — a world pervaded and increasingly moulded by the well-drilled piety and obedience associated with the traditional vision of 'the age of faith', or medieval Christianity." Yet in a sense, Lateran IV was only a beginning: in 1234, Innocent III's cousin Gregory IX instituted the Inquisition, but the great period of witch-hunting — the last battle against paganism — was still two centuries away.[109]

In his book *Law and Revolution, the Formation of the Western Legal Tradition* (Harvard UP, 1983), Harold Berman also insists on the revolutionary character of the Gregorian Reform, by which "the clergy became the first translocal, transtribal, transfeudal, transnational class in Europe to achieve political and legal unity." "To speak of revolutionary change within the Church of Rome is, of course, to challenge the orthodox (though not the Eastern Orthodox) view that the structure of the Roman Catholic Church is the result of a gradual elaboration of elements that had been present from very early times. This was, indeed, the official view of the Catholic reformers of the late eleventh and early twelfth centuries: they were only going back, they said, to an earlier tradition that had been betrayed by their immediate predecessors."[110] The reformers, in other words, established a new world order under the pretense of restoring an ancient world order. They invented a past in order to control the future.

For that, they employed an army of jurists who elaborated a new canonical legal system to supersede customary feudal laws, and they made their new legal system appear as the oldest by producing forgeries on a massive scale. Besides the *Pseudo–Isidorian Decretals* and the false Donation of Constantine, they crafted the Symmachian forgeries, destined to produce legal precedents to make the pope immune from legal condemnation or trial. One of these documents, the *Silvestri constitutum,* takes up from the Donation of Constantine the legend of Pope Sylvester I curing Constantine the Great of leprosy with the waters of baptism, and receiving in gratitude Constantine's imperial insignia and the city of Rome. Charlemagne's father was also made to contribute with the false Donation of Pepin. It is now admitted that the vast majority of legal documents supposedly established before the ninth century are clerical forgeries. According to French historian Laurent Morelle, "two thirds of the acts entitled in the name of the Merovingian kings (481-751) have been identified as false or falsified."[111] It is very likely that the real proportion is much higher, and that many documents which are still deemed authentic are forgeries. For example, it is our view that the wording of the foundation charter of the Abbey of Cluny, by which its founder William I (the Pious) renounced all control over it, cannot possibly have been dictated or endorsed by a medieval duke of Aquitaine (virtually a king).[112]

These forged documents served the popes on several fronts. They were used in their power struggle against the German emperors, as a justification for their extravagant claim that the pope could depose emperors. They were also powerful weapons in the geopolitical war waged against the Byzantine church and empire. By bestowing on the papacy "supremacy over the four principal sees, Alexandria, Antioch, Jerusalem and Constantinople, as also over all the churches of God in the whole earth," the false Donation of Constantine justified Rome's claim for precedence over Constantinople, which led to the Great Schism of 1054 and ultimately the sack of Constantinople by the Latins in 1204. By a cruel irony, the spuriousness of the Donation of

Constantine was exposed in 1430, after it had served its
purpose. By then, the Eastern Empire had lost all its
territories and was reduced to a depopulated city besieged by
the Ottomans.

It is little known, but of great importance for
understanding medieval times when ethnicity played a major
role in politics, that the Gregorian reformers were Franks,
even before Bruno of Egisheim-Dagsburg gave the first
impulse as pope Leo IX. That is why Orthodox theologian
John Romanides blames the Franks for having destroyed the
unity of Christendom with ethnic and geopolitical
motivations.[113] In Byzantine chronicles, "Latin" and "Frank"
are synonymous.

The fake autobiography of the Latin Church

It should now be clear that the very concept of a
Gregorian "Reform" is a disguise for the revolutionary
character of the reformers' project; "the idea that Gregorians
were rigorous traditionalists is a serious oversimplification,"
argue John Meyendorff and Aristeides Papadakis; "the
conventional conclusion which views the Gregorians as
defenders of a consistently uniform tradition is largely
fiction." In fact, before the twelfth century, "the pope's
fragile hold upon Western Christendom was largely
imaginary. The parochial world of Roman politics was
actually the papacy's only domain."[114] Aviad Kleinberg
even argues that, "until the twelfth century, when the pope's
status was imposed as the ultimate religious authority in
matters of education and jurisdiction, there was not really an
organization that could be called 'the Church'."[115] There
certainly were no "popes" in the modern sense before the
end of the eighth century: this affectionate title, derived
from the Greek *papa,* was given to every bishop. Even
conventional history speaks of the period of the "Byzantine
papacy," ending in 752 with the conquest of Italy by the
Franks, and teaches that civil, military and even
ecclesiastical affairs were then under the supervision of the

exarch of Ravenna, the Greek representative of the Byzantine Emperor.[116]

This means that the first-millennium history of the Western Church written by itself is a complete sham. One of its centerpieces, the *Liber Pontificalis,* a book of biographies of the popes from saint Peter to the ninth century, is today recognized as a work of imagination. It served to ascertain the pope's claim to occupy the "the throne of saint Peter" in an unbroken chain going back to the first apostle — the "rock" on which Jesus built his kingdom (Matthew 16,18).

As the story goes, in the second year of Claudius, Peter went to Rome to challenge Simon Magus, the father of all heresies. He became the first Catholic bishop and was crucified head downwards in the last year of Nero, then buried where St. Peter's Basilica now stands (his bones were found there in 1968). That story appears in the works of Clement of Rome, the fictional traveling companion and successor of Peter, whose prolific literature in Latin contains so many improbabilities, contradictions and anachronisms that most of it is today recognized as apocryphal and renamed "pseudo-clementine". Peter's story is also the theme of the *Acta Petri,* supposedly written in Greek in the second century but surviving only in Latin translation.

It is interesting to note that while Rome claimed the apostle Peter as first bishop, Constantinople responded, not by denying the story, but by claiming Peter's brother as the founder of its bishopric. For, explained Heinrich Fichtenau, "In the gospel, Andrew appears as the first to be invited by Christ to be his disciple; it was Andrew who brought his brother Peter to Christ. Thus he had temporal priority and with it a higher rank."[117] Andrew's prestige, however, is far outmatched by Peter's in the Gospels, and Constantinople lost the competition.

The point is that there is no reason to take the story of Peter's trip to Rome as reliable history. It is, anyway, inconsistent with the New Testament, which says nothing of Peter's travel to Rome, and assumes that he simply remained the head of the Jerusalem church. Paul's Epistle to the Romans, written around 57, makes clear that he had no knowledge that any apostle, let alone Peter, had preceded him in Rome. The "discovery" of the bones of Peter in St. Peter's Basilica in the 1940s, officialized in 1953 by Pius XII, only adds to the suspicion, since the tomb does not bear any distinctive Christian sign. In the final analysis, the legend of saint Peter in Rome tells us nothing about real events, but informs us about the means deployed by the Roman curia to steal the birthright from the Eastern Church. It is fake currency minted to overbid on Constantinople's genuine claim that the unity of the Church had been achieved in its immediate vicinity, at the so-called "ecumenical" councils (*Oikouménê* designated the civilized world under the authority of the *basileus*), whose participants were exclusively oriental. Christopher Dawson makes a good point in *Religion and the Rise of Western Culture* (1950):

> "we must remember that at the time of the fall of the Roman Empire in the West the main centres of Christian culture and the majority of the Christian population were still non-European. The mother tongue of the Church was Greek and its theological development was mainly due to Asiatic Greek councils and Asiatic Greek theologians, at a time when in the Latin West paganism was still strong, and the ruling classes, and, far more, the rural population, were still largely non-Christian in culture and tradition. ... Thus, unlike Christian Byzantium, Christian Rome represents only a brief interlude between paganism and barbarism. There were only eighteen years between Theodosius' closing of the temples and the first sack of the Eternal City by the barbarians. The great age of the Western Fathers from Ambrose to Augustine was crammed into a single generation, and St. Augustine died with the Vandals at the gate."[118]

Although we cannot delve here into the editorial history of the New Testament, it is interesting to note that the story of Paul's travel to Rome also bears the mark of falsification.

If we remember that the Byzantines called themselves "Romans", we are intrigued by the fact that, in his "Epistle to the Romans" (written in Greek), Paul calls the Romans "Hellenes" to distinguish them from Jews (1:14-15; 3:9). Moreover, if we look up on a map the cities addressed by Paul in other epistles — Ephesus, Corinth, Galata, Philipae, Thessaloniki (Salonica), Colossae — we see that Italian Rome was not part of his sphere of influence. Paul's trip to Rome in Italy in Acts 27-28 (where Italy is explicitly named) belongs to the "we section" of Acts, which is recognizably foreign to the first redaction.

Our main source for the early history of the Church is Eusebius' *Ecclesiastical History* in ten volumes. Like so many other sources (e.g., Irenaeus of Lyon), it was supposedly written in Greek, but was known in the Middle Ages only in Latin translation (from which it was later translated back into Greek). Its Latin translation was attributed to the great saint and scholar Jerome (Hieronymus). Saint Jerome also produced, at the request of Pope Damasus, the Latin Bible known as the *Vulgate*, which would be decreed the sole authorized version at the Council of Trent in the mid-sixteenth century.

Eusebius tells us of Constantine's conversion to Christianity. But two panegyrics of Constantine have been preserved, and they make no mention of Christianity. Instead, one contains the story of a vision Constantine had of the sun-god Apollo, "with Victory accompanying him." From then on, Constantine placed himself under the protection of *Sol invictus,* also called *Sol pacator* on some of his coins.[119] What Eusebius writes in his *Life of Constantine* about the battle of the Milvian Bridge is obviously a rewriting of that earlier pagan legend. When marching on Rome to overthrow Maxentius, Constantine "saw with his own eyes in the heavens a trophy of the cross arising from the light of the sun, carrying the message, 'by this sign, you shall win'." The following night, Christ appeared to him in his dream to confirm the vision. Constantine had all his

troops paint the sign on their shields and won the battle —
making Christ a victorious military god.

Our author swears he got this story from Constantine
himself:

> If someone else had reported it, it would perhaps not be
> easy to accept; but since the victorious Emperor himself
> told the story to the present writer a long while after, when
> I was privileged with his acquaintance and company, and
> confirmed it with oaths, who could hesitate to believe the
> account, especially when the time which followed provided
> evidence for the truth of what he said? (I,28)[120]

Does that inspire your trust or your suspicion? Are these
the words of a genuine biographer, or of an unscrupulous
liar? The main problem with this account is that the arch
built by Constantine to commemorate this victory in Rome
contains numerous representations of pagan deities, and
especially of the sun god Apollo, but not a single reference
to Christ. Can there be a stronger proof that "Eusebius"
invented Constantine's encounter with Christ?

The same author has this to say about the sign adopted
by Constantine as a military standard (now called the
labarum):

> This was something which the Emperor himself once saw
> fit to let me also set eyes on, God vouchsafing even this. It
> was constructed to the following design. A tall pole plated
> with gold had a transverse bar forming the shape of a cross.
> Up at the extreme top a wreath woven of precious stones
> and gold had been fastened. On it two letters, intimating by
> its first characters the name 'Christ', formed the monogram
> of the Saviour's title, *rho* being intersected in the middle by
> *chi*. These letters the Emperor also used to wear upon his
> helmet in later times. (I,31)[121]

This Chi-Rho sign is today the coat of arms of the
papacy. But archeology and numismatics have proven that it
predates Christianity. It is found, for example, on a drachma
of Ptolemy III Euergetes (246-222 BC). It also appears on a
coin minted by Maxentius, whom Constantine is said to
have defeated precisely by this sign. It is clear that the Chi-

Rho — or *chrismon* or christogram — was a pre-Christian talisman stolen by the Church. It is unclear, however, what it stood for before Christianity. Egyptologist Flinders Petrie speculated that it originally denoted the god Horus, but became a symbol of good fortune. Being often surrounded by a vegetal wreath, it may have referred to a cosmic principle associated to the resurrection of Nature at Easter time, a symbol of *Anastasis*. Since the Chi-Rho appears behind the head of Constantine in a mosaic in Hinton St Mary, Dorset, England, and since Constantine liked to be portrayed with a solar or radiant crown, it is likely that Chi-Rho has a solar significance.[122]

Some see it as a symbol borrowed from the cult of Mithras, closely associated with the cult of *Sol Invictus*. The analogies between Mithras and Jesus are so numerous that Justin and Tertullian accused Mithras of *imitatio diabolica*. We also know that several Italian churches, including Saint Peter's Basilica, were built on Mithraic crypts. Note on the frontispiece of Saint Peter's that the P comes before the X, suggesting an acronym beginning with P. One possibility is that the sign was originally a Latin short for PAX, but I find it unlikely, because of its frequent association with the Greek letters α and ω.

We actually do not have a single archaeological clue that Constantine claimed or even promoted the Christian faith. We do know, however, that he had himself represented as the sun god Apollo in Rome as well as in Constantinople, where there stood a 100-feet-high column topped with a statue of himself as Sun God Apollo. *Sol Invictus* was publicly celebrated on December 25. Since the earliest reference to December 25 as the date of Christ's birth does not come before 354 (in the *Depositio Martyrum*), seventeen years after Constantine's death, and since it was Emperor Theodosius I who in 380 banned the cult of *Sol Invictus* to make December 25 a Christian holiday, we have evidence that Christianity usurped elements of the cult of *Sol Invictus* which Constantine was promoting throughout his life. The evergreen wreath of Christmas is a likely legacy from that time (and remember that the Chi-Rho is often associated to this evergreen wreath).

I hope to have shown that there is much cause for radical skepticism regarding the autobiography of the Roman Church. It is not just legal documents that were forged. The whole underlying narrative could be phony. In the late seventeenth and early eighteenth century, one man, Jesuit librarian Jean Hardouin (1646-1729), spent a lifetime researching and questioning Church history, until he came to the conclusion of a massive fraud originating in Benedictine monasteries in the thirteenth century. His conclusions were published posthumously in *Ad Censuram Veterum Scriptorum Prolegomena* (1766). According to Hardouin, all the works ascribed to Augustine, Jerome, Ambrose of Milan, and Gregory the Great, were in fact written just decades before the cunning Boniface VIII (1294-1303) promoted them as the "Latin Fathers of the Church." Eusebius' history translated by Jerome is a web of fiction according to Hardouin.

The Prolegomena of Jean Hardouin were translated in English in the nineteenth century by Edwin Johnson (1842-1901), who built up on Hardouin's insights in his own works, starting with *The Rise of Christendom* (1890), followed one year later by *The Rise of English Culture*. Johnson argued for a medieval origin of most literary sources ascribed to Antiquity or Late Antiquity, and insisted that the whole first-millennium history of the Roman Church was fabricated by the Roman curia in its effort to impose its new world order.

The medieval origin of these texts, Johnson says, explains why their supposed authors are fighting heresies that so much resemble the later heresies fought by the medieval Church. The Manicheans and Gnostics attacked by Tertullian, Augustine and Irenaeus of Lyon are like the ghosts of those attacked under the same denominations by twelfth and thirteenth-century popes. According to Patricia Stirnemann, the oldest manuscript of Augustine's *Contra Faustus,* written and preserved in the abbey of Clairvaux, is the witness of the struggle against "the resurgence of a neo-manicheism in the 12th century." She doesn't question the authorship of the work, but gives us additional reason to do so.[123] However, Hermann Detering claims that Augustine's *Confessions* are a medieval forgery, probably from the hand of Anselm of Canterbury (1033-1109).[124]

The medieval background of the Latin colonization of the East by the crusaders is transparently clear in many spurious sources from Late Antiquity, according to Johnson. Jerome's biography is a case in point: "he is made to travel from Aquileia to Rome, and from Rome to Bethlehem and to Egypt. He settles at Bethlehem, is followed by Roman ladies, who found there a nunnery, and there he dies. This is a reflection of something that was happening during the later Crusades."[125] The same goes for Constantine: the legend of his military conquest by the sign of the Crucified bears the mark of the age of the crusades, "when military men came under monkish influence."[126]

If all first-millennium Church history is bogus, how can we reconstruct the real history of the Church before the Gregorian Reform? Johnson says there was no Western Christianity then: the Western Church was "a purely Mediaeval institution, without either literary or oral links with the past," and its fables "were not heard of in the world until the epoch of the Crusades."[127] A less radical hypothesis is that Christianity only became a dominant force in the West with the Gregorian Reform. And there is plenty of evidence that it imposed its religious hegemony not so much by the destruction of pagan traditions as by their assimilation. The cult of Notre Dame promoted by Bernard de Clairvaux (1090–1153), was super-imposed on the cult of Isis, whose representations with the child Horus (Harpocrates) are conspicuous in the Mediterranean world. Above is a cultic figurine of Isis breastfeeding Horus found in Antipolis and dated from the 4th century AD.

What the Gregorian reformers did was rewrite history in order to create the illusion that Christianity was 1000 years old in Europe. Not all sources were written from scratch. Many were simply heavily edited. One example is the *Ecclesiastical History of the English People* by Bede the Venerable (672-735). James Watson has shown that it was originally a *History of the English People* with no mention of Christianity; it was heavily interpolated during the tenth century, Watson says, when "most of the ecclesiastical notices in the work have been engrafted with the original history."[128] Another case is Boethius (c. 480-524), turned into a Christian theologian and martyr at the time of Abélard, although his famous *Consolation of Philosophy,*

written while awaiting execution, makes no mention of his supposed Christian faith.

As for the *History of the Franks,* supposedly written at the end of the sixth century by Gregory of Tours, and virtually our only source on Clovis' conversion to Catholicism, it is most probably a clerical forgery from the Gregorian period, possibly using earlier sources. At the very least, according to historian Leo Wiener, it "has come down to us highly interpolated."[129] It is interesting to note that our pseudo-Gregory of Tours (perhaps Odilo of Cluny, who wrote a *Life of Gregory*) believed it possible for a medieval power to orchestrate the systematic rewriting of all books: he writes that King Childeric introduced new signs into the Latin alphabet, and "wanted all the old manuscripts to be erased with pumice stone, to make other copies, where the new signs would be used" (chapter IV).[130]

Chroniclers of the eleventh century are important sources for understanding the Christianization of Europe. Thietmar of Merseburg spoke in his *Chronicon* of a new dawn illuminating the world in 1004, and the French monk Rodulfus Glaber wrote:

> "At the approach of the third year after the year 1000, in almost all the earth, especially in Italy and in Gaul, the churches were rebuilt. Although they were in a good state and did not need it, the whole Christian people competed for possession of the most beautiful churches. And it was as if the world itself, shaking the rags of its old age, covered itself on all sides with a white mantle of churches. Then, at the initiative of the faithful, almost all the churches, from the cathedrals to the monasteries dedicated to the various saints, and down to small village oratories, were rebuilt, only more beautifully" (book III, §13).[131]

Since Rodulfus writes under Cluniac supervision (he dedicates his work to the abbot of Cluny, Odilo), we must be wary of his claim that what appeared new was in fact old, for this was exactly the pretense of the Gregorian "reformers". Because he says the churches were "in a good state", their "rebuilding" may be an understatement for their rededication to a new cult. Gregory the Great (590-604), who may be a duplicate of Gregory VII (ordinal numbers are later inventions), recommended that pagan temples be exorcised and reused for Christian worship.[132] The name of the "basilicas" from a Greek word designating a chamber of justice under the authority of the *basileius*. Textbook history teaches that, as the Roman Empire adopted Christianity, the basic architectural plan of the *basilica* was adopted for major church buildings throughout Europe, but that explanation has the ring of a flinch.

In reality, Western Christianity was in its infancy in the year 1000 AD. We have now reached a point where one of the working hypotheses of our first chapter can be reconsidered: although French scholar Polydor Hochart was fully justified to question the prevailing theory that Christian monks copied pagan books on precious parchments,[133] we must consider the alternative theory that those who, between the ninth and eleventh centuries, copied the manuscripts that humanists discovered in the fourteenth century were actually not Christians. This will become clearer in chapter 4.

The theft of Constantinople's birthright

Where shall we go from here? Assuming that the history of the first millennium is heavily distorted by the forgeries of pontifical scribes and later humanists, can we evaluate the degree of that distortion and reconstruct a credible picture? The best we can do is to position ourselves in the eleventh century, the earliest period for which we have a good amount of chronicles. For that period, we can perhaps trust historians to give us a generally accurate picture of the European, North-African, and Near-Eastern world, and, looking back a couple of centuries away, we can try to discern the movements of history that led to that world. Beyond that, everything is blurry.

Geographically, we might as well position ourselves at the center of the world we are seeking to understand. That center was not Rome. Despite Roman propaganda praising the *Mirabilia Urbis Romae* ("the wonders of the city of Rome") in the tenth and eleventh centuries, the political, economic, cultural and religious center of the civilization that included Rome, was Constantinople (with Alexandria in second position).

In the eleventh century, the walls of Constantinople could have contained the ten largest cities of the West. Its size, architectural masterpieces, and wealth so impressed Western visitors that, in the French novel *Partonopeu de Blois*, Constantinople is the name of paradise. The economic prosperity of Constantinople rested on its situation at a crossroads of the great trade routes, on a monopoly in the trade of luxury products like silk, on a considerable gold money supply, and on an efficient tax administration (the *kommerkion* was a ten-percent tax on any transaction in the city's port).

Greek culture was radiating from Constantinople to the four corners of the world, from Persia and Egypt to Ireland and Spain. Klaus Oehler, specialist of Hellenistic Greek thought, wrote :

> "It should first be remembered that all of the literature of ancient Greece that has come down to us, with very few exceptions, has remained available to the modern world only through copyists in Byzantine schools and cloisters. For it was in Byzantium, not in the Latin West, that the river of the tradition of ancient Greece found its natural extension. It is here, not in the West, that the great works of the ancient Greeks were once again read, studied, commented on and copied."[134]

Anthony Kaldellis also stresses that the West owes its Renaisance to the rediscovery of the Greek classical tradition preserved in Constantinople: "The classical tradition was never lost in Byzantium, which is why it could not be rediscovered."[135]

In the eleventh and twelfth centuries, there was a vast movement of translation from Greek to Latin of philosophical and scientific works (medicine, astronomy, etc.). Greek books were also translated into Persian and Syriac, and, from there, into Arabic. In his book *Aristote au mont Saint-Michel. Les racines grecques de l'Europe chrétienne*, Sylvain Gouguenheim defeats the common idea that the spread of philosophy and science in the Middle Ages was due mainly to Muslims. In reality, the Greek heritage was transmitted to Italian cities directly from Constantinople, that is, in the opposite direction of the fictitious *translatio imperii* of Constantine.[136]

The *basileus* maintained good relations with the Fatimid caliphate of Egypt, which had conquered Jerusalem and lower Syria from the Abbasids in the 960s. In the early 1070s, the alliance between Byzantines and Fatimids was reinforced by a common threat: the incursions of the Seljukid Turks, who had taken control of the caliphate in Badhdad. In 1071, they defeated the Byzantine army at the Battle of Manzikert and established in Anatolia the Sultanate of Rum, with their capital city in Nicaea, just one hundred kilometers from Constantinople. Then they took a part of Syria, including Jerusalem, from the Fatimids.

Until recently, it was commonly believed that the crusades were the generous response of the Roman Church to a desperate plea for help from Byzantine Emperor Alexios Komnenos. This is how Western contemporary chroniclers presented it, using a forged letter of Alexios to the count of Flanders, in which the former confessed his powerlessness against the Turks and humbly begged for rescue.[137] In fact, the emperor was in no desperate situation, and his request was just for mercenaries to fight under his command and help him reconquer Anatolia from the Seljukids. The Byzantines had always drawn in warriors from foreign nations to serve under their banner in return for imperial largesse, and Frankish knights were highly appreciated in that quality.

Instead, Urban II (a former abbot of Cluny), wanted to raise an army that would immediately set out to conquer Jerusalem, a city on which Alexios had no immediate claim, and that he would have happily given back to the Fatimids. An army of crusaders under the order of a papal legate was never what Alexios had called for, and the Byzantines were worried and suspicious when they saw it coming. "Alexios and his advisers saw the approaching crusade not as the arrival of long-awaited allies but rather as a potential threat to the *Oikoumene*," writes Jonathan Harris. They feared that the liberation of the Holy Sepulcher was a mere pretext for some sinister plot against Constantinople.[138]

The first crusade succeeded in establishing four Latin states in Syria and Palestine, which formed the basis of a Western presence that was to endure until 1291. At the end of the twelfth century, Jerusalem having been recovered by Saladin, Pope Innocent III proclaimed a new crusade, the fourth in modern numbering. This time, the Byzantines' fear of a hidden agenda proved fully justified. Instead of going to Jerusalem via Alexandria, as officially announced, the Frankish knights, indebted by the tricky Venetians (and mainstream historians do speak here of a "Venetian conspiracy"), moved toward Constantinople. The huge army of the crusaders penetrated into the city in April 1204 and sacked it during three days. "Since the creation of this world, such great wealth had neither been seen nor conquered," marveled the crusader Robert de Clari in his chronicle.[139] Palaces, churches, monasteries, libraries were systematically pillaged, and the city became a shambles.[140]

The new Franco-Latin Empire, built on the smoking ruins of Constantinople, lasted only half a century. The Byzantines, entrenched in Nicaea (Iznik), slowly regained part of their ancient territory, and, in 1261, under the commandment of Michael VIII Palaiologos, chased the Franks and Latins from Constantinople. But the city was but the shadow of its past glory: the Greek population had been slaughtered or had fled, the churches and the monasteries had been profaned, the palaces were in ruins, and international trade had come to a stop. Moreover, Pope Urban IV ordered that a new crusade be preached throughout Europe to retake Constantinople from the "schismatics".[141] There were few volunteers. But in 1281 again, Pope Martin IV encouraged the project of Charles of Anjou (brother of King Louis IX) to take back Constantinople and establish a new Catholic empire. It failed, but the Fourth Crusade and its aftermath had inflicted on the Byzantine civilization a mortal wound, and it collapsed one century and a half later, after one thousand years of existence, when the Ottoman Sultan Mehmet II took Constantinople in 1453. The renowned medieval historian Steven Runciman wrote:

> "There was never a greater crime against humanity than the Fourth Crusade. Not only did it cause the destruction or dispersal of all the treasures of the past that Byzantium had devotedly stored, and the mortal wounding of a civilization that was still active and great; but it was also an act of gigantic political folly. It brought no help to the Christians in Palestine. Instead it robbed them of potential helpers. And it upset the whole defense of Christendom."[142]

How Roman were the Byzantines?

As I hinted before, there is an enduring controversy about the use of the term "Romans" (*Rhomaioi*) by which the "Byzantines" called themselves, and this controversy is symptomatic of a deeper cognitive dissonance. Let me illustrate this with a recent book by Greek-American historian Anthony Kaldellis, *Romanland: Ethnicity and Empire in Byzantium* (2019). The author takes issue with the habit among Byzantinist scholars to underestimate the significance of the Byzantines' self-identity as "Romans". In reaction to one typical statement by those he calls "denialists" that, despite their "shrunken circumstances," the Byzantines "found it difficult to abandon their sense of being *Rhomaioi*, 'Romans',"[143] Kaldellis writes: "This sounds instead like a displaced metaphor for what is going on in modern scholarship: We would like to abandon the term *Roman* in dealing with the Byzantines, but we cannot quite do so, because it is written all over the sources."[144]

Kaldellis shows that the Byzantines understood their Romanness in an ethnic sense: in Constantinople and in its surrounding provinces lived a majority of "Romans" together with minorities such as Slavs, Rus', Jews, Armenians, Persians, Arabs, Franks, Bulgars, Goths, who were citizens of the Empire, but were not regarded as "Romans". Having convincingly established that "the Romans of Byzantium saw themselves as an ethnic group or nation," Kaldellis asks:

> "Did the Byzantine Romans believe that they were collectively descended from the ancient Romans too? / This is harder to document. It probably formed only a vague aspect of Romanness in Byzantium; I doubt many people thought about it in explicit terms. But it was presupposed in many discursive practices. Merely by calling themselves Romans they asserted a continuity between themselves and the ancient Romans, whose default, unreflexive mode in traditional societies was generic."[145]

Kaldellis' insistence that Byzantines were implicitly referring to their ancestors from Italy when calling themselves "Romans", coupled with his inability to give any evidence of it, shows that it is an unsubstantiated presupposition. Among the eight "snapshots" Kaldellis provides to "highlight the ethnic aspects of Romanness in Byzantium," none of them indicate that Byzantines thought they descended from Italian or even Western immigrants, and three of them indicate the exact opposite:

1. In a story from the *Miracles of Saint Demetrios of Thessalonike,* we hear about people captured in the Balkans by the Avars and resettled in Pannonia, on the south bank to the Danube. Although they married local women, sixty years later, "each child received from his father the ancestral traditions of the Romans and the impulse of their *genos*," and "this large people longed to return to its ancestral

cities." By their ancestral cities, these "Romans" meant the Greek-speaking Balkans.[146]

2. In 1246, the population of Melnik wanted to be ruled by the Roman *basileus* rather that the Bulgarian tsar because, they said, "we all originate in Philippopolis and we are pure Romans when it comes to our *genos*." Philippopolis is a Greek city founded by Philip II of Macedon, about 200 miles west of Constantinople, in today's Bulgaria.[147]

3. Basileios I (867-886) settled people from Herakleia in his newly founded city of Kallipolis (Gallipoli) on the coast of southern Italy. A twelfth-century addition to the history of Ioannes Skylitzes comments: "This explains why that city still uses Roman customs and dress and a thoroughly Roman social order, down to this day." Herakleia, or Heraclea Pontica, is a Greek city on the Black Sea coast, about 200 miles east of Constantinople.[148]

In the first two instances, we have people equating their being Roman to their origin in the Balkans, not in Italy. In the third instance, we have people living in Italy calling themselves Romans specifically because they originate from Asia Minor—and presumably regarding their Italian neighbors as non-Romans.

There in another example in Kaldellis' book *Hellenism in Byzantium*: To attack his theological opponent Gregorios of Cyprus in the 1280s, Ioannes Bekkos argued that while he himself "had been born and raised among Romans and from Romans," Gregorios "was born and raised among Italians, and not only that, he merely affects our dress and speech."[149] Here a Byzantine asserts that he is a true Roman, while Italians are not.

So Kaldellis reads in his sources the exact opposite of what they say, because he takes as an unquestionable postulate that "Roman" means "from Rome, Italy", or in a vaguer sense, "of Western descent." If he had been consistent and unprejudiced in his quest for the ethnicity of the Byzantine Romans, he would have noticed that they referred to Italians not as Romans, but as Latins. (He should also have taken note that even the inhabitants of today's Greece, from Late Antiquity throughout the Middle Ages, called themselves either "Romans" or "Hellenes", never "Greeks".[150])

Kaldellis himself documents that the Byzantines not only called themselves Romans, but called their Greek language Romaic: "for most of their history the Byzantines did not think that their language made them Greek; to the contrary, their ethnicity as Romans made their language 'Roman,' or Romaic." Still, Kaldellis accepts the premise that "they were Romans who had lost touch with the Latin tradition," and concludes, "The Byzantines had *two* Roman languages, one the language of their ancestors (Latin) and another their language in the present (Romaic)," without even trying to solve the mystery of how they forsook their ancestors' language, despite their strong ethnic sense of identity.[151]

These embarrassing facts, and many more mentioned in the previous chapter, point to a very fundamental misunderstanding which can easily be traced back to a sleight of hand by the medieval papacy, who tried to copyright the name "Roman" by erasing its eastern origin, and, with a fabricated legend of saint Peter, usurped Constantinople's prestige as being the cradle and the capital of Christian civilization.

I do not mean here to disparage the work of Professor Anthony Kaldellis. On the contrary, I wish to stress that his revisionist Byzantine scholarship points to major fallacies in the Western narrative of the relationship between Rome and Constantinople, and I suggest that the fallacies may be greater than he is willing to admit. Before showing, in *Romanland,* that the Byzantines thought of themselves as more Romans than those we call Romans, Kaldellis had shown, in *The Byzantine Republic* (2015), that politically too, they were more Roman than the Romans, in the sense that the Roman republican ideal was more developed in Constantinople than it has ever been in Rome. "Byzantium was probably more republican than its predecessors, the

Principate and the Dominate." If this contradicts the common image, it is because of a longstanding Western prejudice: "An imaginary modern construct labeled 'Byzantium,' identified with theocracy and absolutism, has come to stand between us and the vibrant political culture of the east Romans."[152]

Procopius' Secret History

As I have mentioned earlier, what prevents Classical scholars from breaking through the thick layers of papal propaganda is their unwarranted trust in second-hand sources, by which I mean Latin or Greek literature supposedly written in Antiquity or Late Antiquity, but only available in supposedly medieval manuscripts miraculously discovered in the Renaissance. Anthony Kaldellis is no exception here. One case in point is a book attributed to Procopius, known as the *Anecdota*, or *Secret History*, meant to destroy the reputation of Byzantine emperor Justinian, his wife Theodora, and his general Belisarius, and through them to smear Byzantium as a whole. As Kaldellis writes:

> "Its effect on Justinian's reputation has been devastating. It is worth considering what that reputation might have been had the works of Prokopios not survived, or not been written. Justinian would surely be remembered and even celebrated as one of history's great rulers: a builder of magnificent churches on an unparalleled scale, especially the cathedral of Hagia Sophia in Constantinople; a codifier of Roman law and major legislator in his own right; an emperor who reconquered provinces that had been lost to the barbarians, chiefly North Africa and Italy, temporarily reversing the empire's "decline"; and an ascetic Christian monarch who worked tirelessly to restore the Church to unity, contributing personally to the theological debates."[153]

According to the *Secret History*, however, Justinian and his wife Theodora were moved by an inhuman delight in evil-doing and destruction. Justinian is portrayed as cruel, venal, prodigal, and incompetent. He was, literally, a demon in human disguise, whose mystical powers were even responsible for natural disasters, ranging from floods and earthquakes to the plague of the 540s. As for Theodora, she had been a prostitute in a Constantinopolitan brothel, would often stand naked in the street and have sex with more than thirty men in one night. Her lifestyle hardly changed after she became Empress.

Was this book really written by Procopius, secretary to Justinian's general Belisarius and author of *Justinian's Wars,* as well of *The Buildings,* "a panegyric glorifying Justinian's constructions"[154]? Byzantine scholars almost unanimously accept the authenticity of the *Secret History,* yet they all see it as a collection of extravagant rumors, without explaining why Procopius, a highly respected historian, would ruin his reputation with such a book. Kaldellis follows the consensus and accepts it as authentic, without discussion. I think he is wrong. Just consider the circumstances of this text's discovery. It was unknown until it was discovered in 1623 in the Vatican library, in a manuscript dated from the 14th century. The man who discovered it and immediately got it printed is Niccolò Alamanni (1583-1626), an antiquarian of Byzantine origin, who taught Greek to persons of rank, was ordained priest according to the Latin rite, appointed secretary to Cardinal Borghese, then custodian of the Vatican Library, where he made his discovery. Consider now the scenario suggested for its writing (here in the words of John Bagnell Bury):

> "It was a document which he [Procopius] must have preserved in his most secret hiding-place, and which he could read only to the most faithful and discreet of his friends. It could never see the light till Justinian was safely dead, and if he were succeeded by as nephew or cousin, its publication even then might be impossible. As a matter of fact we may suspect that his heirs withheld it from circulation, and that it was not published till a considerable time had elapsed. For it was unknown to the writers of the

next generation, unless we suppose that they deliberately ignored it."[155]

What are the odds that such a work would reach us? Scholars believe that a small portion of the books preserved in Constantinople's imperial library survived the two major calamities of 1204 and 1453. We have, for example, only thirty percent of the 280 books cited by Photios in his *Bibliotheca*. By what miracle would a copy of the *Secret History* have found its way into a 14th-century Byzantine scriptorium, and for what purpose would it be copied? By what additional miracle would this copy end up in the Vatican, only to be discovered by an apostate Greek scholar on the pope's payroll? That's simply too many miracles for me to believe. There are other formal reasons to consider the *Secret History* a forgery made in the very place where it was discovered, some time between the fourteenth and the seventeenth century. First, its opening paragraph reproduces word for word the opening paragraph of Book VIII of *Justinian's Wars* — the signature of an imitator. Secondly, the author gives two contradictory indications for the date of his writing (after Justinian's death, and 32 years after the beginning of Justinian's rule), and both dates are considered impossible: it is surmised that he wrote it in 550, when Justinian had still 15 years to live, which contradicts the author's claim that he had to wait for Justinian's death to write the truth about him.

The arguments in favor or authenticity strike me as very weak. First, it is said that "No imitator could have achieved the Procopian style of the *Secret History*" (John Bagnell Bury).[156] But imitation was the foundation of Byzantine scholarship (Procopius himself imitated Thucydides), and based on Kaldellis' description of Procopius' style, I cannot fathom why it would be especially hard to imitate: "the individual sentences that make up *The Secret History* are short and blunt and their syntax is usually uncomplicated. The same syntactical forms are repeated often and there are almost no rhetorical flourishes."[157] The other arguments in favor of authenticity are based on corroboration from other sources. But this is grossly underestimating the intelligence of forgers, who, as a rule, create the illusion of "corroboration" by inserting bits of informations found in others sources, and when possible, chose to write books that are reported lost.

In conclusion, the *Secret History* should be counted as part of the anti-Byzantine papal propaganda that Kaldellis himself takes pain to dispel.

How ancient is Classical Greece?

For the West, and Italy in particular, the conquest and looting of Constantinople in 1204 kicked off an astounding economic growth, fed initially by the vast quantities of plundered gold. In the early thirteenth century the first gold coins appeared in the West, where only silver coinage had been issued so far (except in Sicily and Spain).[158] The cultural benefits of the Fourth Crusade were also impressive: in subsequent years, whole libraries were pillaged, which Greek-speaking scholars would then start to translate into Latin. It can be said without exaggeration that the rise of humanism in Italy was an indirect effect of the fall of Constantinople.

The Council of Florence in 1438, the last attempt to reunite the Catholic and Orthodox churches, is an important date in the transfer of Greek culture to the West. Byzantine Emperor John VIII Paleologus and the Patriarch Joseph II came to Florence with a retinue of 700 Greeks and an extraordinary collection of classical books yet unknown in the West, including manuscripts of Plato, Aristotle, Plutarch, Euclid, and Ptolemy. "Culturally, the transmission of classical texts, ideas, and art objects from east to west that took place at the Council was to have a decisive effect on the art and scholarship of late 15th-century Italy."[159] And when, after 1453, the last bearers of Constantinople's high culture fled Ottoman rule, many came to contribute to the blooming of the Italian Renaissance. In 1463, the Florentine court of Cosimo de' Medici made acquaintance with the Neoplatonic philosopher George Gemistos, known as Pletho, whose discourses upon Plato so fascinated them that they decided to refound Plato's Academy in Florence.[160] They named Marsilio Ficino as its head, supplying him with Greek manuscripts of Plato's work, whereupon Ficino started translating the entire corpus into Latin.

At the same time as they appropriated the Greek heritage, the Italian humanists affected to ignore their debt to Constantinople. As a result, until very recently, medieval studies overlooked the Byzantine influence on the West, and even the importance of the Byzantine Empire in the Middle Ages. An aggravating factor is that "practically all the archives of the imperial and patriarchal chanceries of Byzantium perished either in 1204, when the city was sacked by the Crusaders, or in 1453, when it fell under the Turks."[161] Byzantium was killed twice: after taking it then losing it again (1260), the Latin West strove to erase it from its collective memory. As Steven Runciman writes:

> "Western Europe, with ancestral memories of jealousy of Byzantine civilization, with its spiritual advisers denouncing the Orthodox as sinful schismatics, and with a haunting sense of guilt that it had failed the city at the end, chose to forget about Byzantium. It could not forget the debt that it owed to the Greeks; but it saw the debt as being owed only to the Classical age."[162]

It must be emphasized, however, that at this stage, scholars did not possess a consistent global chronology to date precisely the Greek classical age; that would be a project of the Jesuits in the sixteenth century, as we will document in the next article. French byzantinist Michel Kaplan makes the interesting remark that Western humanists who studied the Greek literature imported from Constantinople from the fourteenth century, "did not distinguish between the works of classical and Hellenistic Greece and those of the Byzantine era."[163] The implicit assumption is that modern scholars are now able to clearly make that distinction. But are they really?

The same questions I have raised about Latin sources in the previous chapter can be applied to Greek sources. What proof do we have that the works ascribed to Plato, for instance, date from about 2500 years ago? It has been solidly established that all of Plato's known manuscripts derive from a unique archetype, dated from the period of the great Patriarch Photios (c. 810-895). It was then that Byzantine emperor Leo the Philosopher "rediscovered" and promoted knowledge of Plato, as well as of his disciples Porphyry, Iamblichus and Plotinus, whom we now call Neoplatonists and ascribe to seven centuries later than Plato. Then there is the linguistic issue: Greek scholars such as Roderick Saxey II of Ohio State University notes "how little the language had changed, even in well over three millennia."[164] According to Harvard professor Margaret Alexiou, "Homeric Greek is probably closer to demotic [modern Greek] than twelfth-century Middle English is to modern spoken English."[165] If we assume that the evolution of languages follows universal laws, Homeric Greek should not be much older than Middle English.

There are also, as with Rome, architectural issues. According to our textbook chronology, the Parthenon was built 2,500 years ago. Its current state may seem consistent with such old age, but few people know that it was still intact in 1687, when it was blown up by a bomb shot by a Venetian mortar. The French painter Jacques Carrey had made some fifty-five drawings of it in 1674 (next page).

In ancient times, we are told, the Parthenon housed a gigantic statue of *Athena Parthenos* ("Virgin"), while in the sixth century it became a church dedicated to the Virgin Mary and a major site of Christian pilgrimage until it was turned into a mosque by the Ottomans. In *The Christian Parthenon,* Anthony Kaldellis highlights the continuity: "the adoration of the Theotokos in Byzantium continued many of the same themes as had that of Athena in antiquity, especially that of the Virgin patron of war."

> "When the Theotokos replaced Athena in the Parthenon, she took over the pagan goddess' place as the patron deity and protectress of the city, its *poliouchos*. ... Thus the role that the monument played in the topography and civic ideology of Athens was preserved, among both Christians and pagans. One patron 'saint' took over from another just as elsewhere healing gods were replaced by healing saints."[166]

Byzantine authors such as Theodoros Prodromos argued that the ancient Athenians had been worshipping the Theotokos "before they fully recognized her."[167]

Strangely enough, historian William Miller tells us in his *History of Frankish Greece* that the Parthenon is not mentioned in Western literature before around 1380, when the King of Aragon describes it as "the most precious jewel that exists in the world." The Acropolis was then known as "the Castle of Athens."[168]

In the framework of our hypothesis that between the eleventh and the fifteenth century Rome invented or embellished its own Republican and Imperial Antiquity in the context of a competition with Constantinople for the elder's birthright of Roman civilization and Christendom, it makes sense that Rome would also emphasize the pre-byzantine Greek civilization as the origin of her own Greek heritage, rather than acknowledging her debt to Constantinople. In that case, much of what has passed in the Latin world as Greek art and science was in reality Byzantine. To explain how this Greek legacy had filled the world before reaching Rome, Alexander the Great was summoned. But how real is he?

He is known in Arabic and Persian as Iskandar, while the city he founded is Al-Iskandariyah, which contains *rihadh,* "garden". It is therefore tempting to suppose that the Greek form Alexander is derived from the Arabic name of the city, and that the Greek stories about him are legendary. In Syriac sources, echoed in sura 18 of the Qur'an, Iskandar is given as a Roman and a Christian subduing Persia, like Byzantine emperor Heraclius.[169]

In the literary genre that scholars call collectively "the Alexander Romance," born in Alexandria in the third century AD, Alexander's life "features such vivid episodes as Alexander ascending through the air to Paradise, journeying to the bottom of the sea in a glass bubble, and journeying through the Land of Darkness in search of the Water of Life (Fountain of Youth)."[170]

The existence of Alexander as a historical character rests entirely on a few ancient Greek sources which were unknown in the West before the Renaissance, and whose date of writing is a matter of guesswork. According to Plutarch, Alexander's most sober biographer, at the age of 22, this Macedonian prince (educated by Aristotle) set out to conquer the world with about 30,000 men, founded seventy cities, and died at the age of 32, leaving a fully formed Greek-speaking civilization that stretched from Egypt to Persia. Sylvain Tristan remarks, after Anatoly Fomenko, that the Seleucids (*Seleukidós*), who ruled Asia Minor after Alexander, bear almost the same name as the Seljukids (*Seljoukides*) who controlled that same region from 1037 to 1194.[171] Is the Hellenistic civilization another phantom image of the Byzantine commonwealth, pushed back in the distant past in order to conceal Italy's debt to Constantinople? Such questions are legitimate, given the historical obscurity surrounding Alexander. We must admit that, if today Wikipedia tells us that Alexander was born on July 21, 356 BC and died on June 11, 323 BC, it is because some sixteenth-century scholar declared it so, using arbitrary guesswork and a biblical measuring tape. However, with the recent progress in archaeology, the problems met by our received chronology have accumulated into a critical mass.

Here is one example: the "Antikythera mechanism" is an analogue computer composed of at least 30 meshing bronze gear wheels, used to predict astronomical positions and eclipses for calendar and astrological purposes decades in advance. It was retrieved from the sea in 1901 among wreckage from a shipwreck off the coast of the Greek island Antikythera. It is dated from the second or first century BC. According to Wikipedia, "the knowledge of this technology was lost at some point in Antiquity" and "works with similar complexity did not appear again until the development of mechanical astronomical clocks in Europe in the fourteenth century." This technological chasm of 1,500 years is perhaps believable for someone who already believes that the heliocentric model developed by Greek astronomer Aristarchus of Samos in the third century BC was totally forgotten until Nicolaus Copernicus reinvented it in the sixteenth century AD. But skepticism is here less extravagant that the scholarly consensus.

The number of skeptics has grown in recent years, and several researchers have set out to challenge what they call the Scaligerian chronology (standardized by Joseph Scaliger in his book *De emendatione temporum*, 1583). Most of these "recentists," whom I will introduce in the next chapters, focus on the first millennium AD. They believe that it has been counted too long, in other words, that Antiquity is closer to us than we think. They actually find themselves in agreement with the Renaissance humanists who, according to historian Bernard Guenée, thought of the "middle age" between Antiquity and their time (the term *media tempestas* first appears in 1469 in the correspondence of Giovanni Andrea Bussi) as "nothing but a parenthesis, an in-between."[172] In 1439, Flavio Biondo, the first archaeologist of Rome, wrote a book about this period and titled it: *Decades of History from the Deterioration of the Roman Empire*. Giorgio Vasari thought of it as a mere two centuries when he wrote in his *Life of Giotto* (1550), that Giotto (1267-1337) "brought back to life the true art of painting, introducing the drawing from nature of living persons, which had not been practised for *two hundred years*."[173]

Have Roman Antiquity and the Middle Ages been artificially stretched? When, how, and why? By how many centuries? Does that mean that the history of these added centuries is pure fiction? We will try to answer these questions in the next chapters.

Chapter 3
Twin events and phantom times

Scientific dating methods

The claim that our standard chronology contains non-existing years immediately raises the objection of scientific methods of dating events and things. One of these methods is quite old: comparing astronomical retrocalculations with historical records of cosmic events such as eclipses has been done for many centuries. Since the celestial bodies move like a clockwork mechanism, don't they give us a precise measuring rod?

There are indeed very ancient astronomical records, as astronomy is one of the oldest sciences. The Babylonians left astronomical observations on clay tablets, and were even able to make predictions about conjunctions and eclipses. Today, a computer program such as NASA Eclipse Explorers and Eclipse Search Engines freely available on the NASA Eclipse Web Site makes possible a true astronomical projection of the real time line.[174] So in theory, matching astronomical events recorded in chronicles with their real time should be easy. In practice, it is hardly the case. Richard Stephenson writes in *Historical Eclipses and Earth's Rotation*, regarding ancient Greek and Roman sources:

> "Although numerous descriptions of both solar and lunar obscurations are preserved in these sources, commencing as early as the seventh century BC, most accounts are too vague to be suitable for investigating the Earth's past rotation. The majority of writings which mention eclipses are literary rather than technical, and include historical works, biographies and even poems."[175]

As a result, astronomical records are only used to fine-tune the existing chronology. An eclipse recorded in a first-millennium-AD Latin text can be dated precisely if we already know the span of a few decades when to look for it. The best match will be adopted, and whatever inconsistency is found will be ascribed to the imprecision of the source. When no match is found, the source will be considered faulty. Let us take as an example Titus Livy, who in his *History of Rome from Its Foundation,* Book 37, reported the following astronomical event that had taken place many years earlier:

> "When the consul [Publius Africanus] left for the war, during the games celebrated in honour of Apollo, on the fifth day before the ides of July, in a clear sky during the day, the light was dimmed since the Moon passed before the circle of the Sun."

The best match that has been found in accordance with the time ascribed to Livy (59 BC-17 AD) is March 14, 190 BC. But, as Florin Diacu comments in *The Lost Millennium*: "Fomenko, broadening the search by surveying all the eclipses from 600 BC to AD 1600, found only one that matched both the text's description of the eclipse and its reference to July: AD July 10, 967."[176]

The layman — like myself — has no means of checking who is right, so the only point I am making here is that correlating ancient chronicles with astronomical retrocalculations always implies reliance on a pre-existing chronology, that is, circular reasoning. As a matter of fact, it has never led to a significant revision of the standard chronology, except by mavericks like Fomenko.

Even more to the point, approximations and errors are common—the rule rather than the exception. For example, Scaliger relied intensely on astronomy, but, as his contemporary critics already complained, he refused to take into account the phenomenon of "precession" (the slow wobbling of the Earth's axis through the poles), believing that those who affirmed its existence, including Copernicus, were wrong. This affected his calculations, since the precession advances the calendar of by one day every seventy-one years.[177]

German researchers Uwe and Ilya Topper use astronomical records to challenge the consensual chronology. Believing that the earth's axis has known several jerks in past centuries, they calculate that the period between the last two jerks (in Caesar's time and in the fifteenth century), was not 1,400 years long, but only 700 years long. I have no confidence in their calculation, and only mention it to hammer home the point that astronomy is a double-edged sword in the chronological controversy. (The Toppers, nevertheless, have some very interesting articles in English on their blog www.ilya.it/chrono/en).

The unreliability of using astronomy to confirm the existing chronology has been involuntarily demonstrated by astronomer Robert Russell Newton who, in his book *The Moon's Acceleration* (1979), surveyed astronomical events recorded in history (as conventionally dated), and concluded that the moon knew periods of unexplained acceleration. Fomenko believes he should have rather concluded that events were wrongly dated. Conversely, the same Newton argued, in *The Crime of Claudius Ptolemy* (1977), that "Ptolemy certainly fabricated many of the aspects of the lunar eclipses, and he may have fabricated all of them,"[178] but here again, Fomenko and other chronology revisionists disagree: they believe that Ptolemy lived at a different time.[179]

The appearances of comets, which are among the most reported events in the annals, are a case in point that astronomy can be a challenge to conventional chronology. Unlike eclipses, their periodicity is either imprecise or unknown, and therefore cannot serve as a chronological marker. We can convince ourselves of this by reading, for example, on the site cometography.com the contradictory opinions concerning the comet reported in February 1106, described in great detail in the *Chronica* of Sigebert of

Gembloux (1030-1112).[180] On the other hand, the comets are rare enough to allow their accounts to be synchronized, but again, synchronization can bring surprising results. Gunnar Heinsohn, whose theory will be presented in the next chapter, has used the famous Comet of Justinian in 536 as a marker for synchronizing Antiquity, Late Antiquity and the Early Middle Ages, thus reducing the first millennium CE by two thirds.

What about modern, scientific methods of dating like radiocarbon and dendrochronology? Are they as reliable as their inventors pretend? Radiocarbon laboratories rarely make their calculations available for independent corroboration, and there have been so many cases of misdating that early enthusiasm has now cooled down. As we can read in an article from Cornell University, "new research shows that commonly accepted radiocarbon dating standards can miss the mark — calling into question historical timelines."[181] Besides its restriction to organic materials, and in addition to errors due to contamination — as one author said, "the radiocarbon date, that's the date the last dog pee-ed on it" — the more fundamental problem comes from the false assumptions on which the whole method is based. The basic principle is that when an organism dies, it ceases exchanging carbon atoms with the surrounding, and its ratio between carbon 14 (^{14}C or C14)

and carbon 12 (^{12}C or C12) decreases exponentially, so that it is possible to calculate the time passed since its death from the measure of that ratio. But that is based on the assumption that the C14/C12 ratio is perfectly constant in the atmosphere everywhere on Earth and throughout history, and unaffected by any cosmic event. It is most probably false, since C14 is formed from cosmic rays hitting the Earth's atmosphere, and cosmic conditions are affected by multiple factors.[182] As Lars-Åke Larsson and Petra Ossowski Larsson explain:

"the $^{14}C/^{12}C$-ratio in the atmosphere turned out to be anything but stable. ^{14}C is generated in the upper atmosphere by cosmic radiation, which is highly variable. Moreover, 'old' carbon from the oceans, tundras and from volcanoes is injected into the atmosphere at a changing rate, not to mention the burning of fossil fuels. Soon after this unpredictable behaviour had been understood, the necessity of a calibration procedure when converting measured '^{14}C-ages' into true calendar ages was realized. For this calibration the radiocarbon content of many samples of known ages had to be measured."[183]

Because of its imprecision, radiocarbon dating is rarely used for the first millennium AD. As the British archaeologist Alex Bayliss wrote in 2009: "[radiocarbon] studies in the Roman period remain extremely rare as there is a perception that artifact-based dating is more precise (and less expensive!)."[184] As regarding its use for dating more ancient artefacts, Peter James writes in *Centuries of Darkness,* prefaced by Cambridge archaeology professor Colin Renfrew:

"when a radiocarbon date agrees with the expectations of the excavator it appears in the main text of the site report; when it is slightly discrepant it is relegated to a footnote; if it seriously conflicts it is left out altogether."[185]

This leaves us with dendrochronology, or tree-ring dating. Each time period creates typical sequences of tree rings so that, by overlapping sequences of different trees from archaeologically dated wood samples, it is possible in theory to construct a standard sequence that reaches back centuries for a given region. Dendrochronology has proved very useful for dating Roman sites, since there are considerable amounts of well replicated tree-ring sequences from construction oak wood of Roman origin from Germany, France and England. Ernst Hollstein, one of the earliest and most active dendrochronologists in Germany, produced in 1980 an absolute reference for oak going back from our time to 716 BC.[186] In 1984, a joint venture by the dendro-labs in Belfast, Köln and Stuttgart Hohenheim, produced a continuous oak tree-ring chronology for Western Europe, which spanned more than 7000 years.

To come up with this impressive result, dendro-chronologists use a big amount of math. Here is the list by Ernst Hollstein himself: "Transformation of the ring-width into logarithmic differences, preferential treatment of the correlating arithmetic, theoretical derivation of congruent patterns, distance regression of similarity, regional analysis, test function with scope of dating, statistics of sapwood and lost tree rings, distribution of centered differences between dating of art styles and dendrochronological dating."[187]

Such a complicated method can be fine-tuned to reach the desired results without anyone noticing. Some historians have complained about a lack of transparency. There are also potential sources of errors, such as: "Some tree species tend to form false rings. For instance, in 1936 and 1937, a Texas yellow pine grew five rings because of early spring frosts."[188]

What is even more important to understand it that tree-ring dating is relative by definition, because any tree-ring sequence is "floating" until someone decides where to fit it. And the decision always rests on a preconceived idea. Any sample is first attributed an approximate place in time based on historical and archaeological information, then an acceptable match is searched for, which will circularly reinforce the original assumption.

Moreover, the strength of dendrochronology depends on the amount of overlapping samples available for any given time: since tree-rings are not as precise as bar-codes, only a great number of samples can give certainty against error. But since the dating of one sequence depends on the dating of other sequences, a weakness somewhere in the chain can totally invalidate the whole chain.

Such a weakness has been identified by Lars-Åke Larsson and Petra Ossowski Larsson, Swedish scientists specialized in the analysis of dendrochronological data. As the inventors of Cdendro, a program for dendro-chronological crossdating and data quality tests, they developed a critical view of the way dendrochronological data are sometimes bent to fit preconceived ideas.

Much of what I have written so far in this chapter is borrowed from their articles, and I will now focus on the conclusions they have drawn from their extensive research.

In a series of articles published from 2010, they first underscored a weakness in the European dendro record. "There is a severe shortage of ring width data within the 'Migration gap' centred around AD 350."[189] As a result, "there is a weak period of about two hundred years in virtually all published European oak chronologies between Roman time and early medieval time." In 2016, the authors explained in more detail:

> "Building with oak becomes uncommon after RomAD 250 [250 according to standard chronology] and ceases completely around the time of Constantine. New activity starts first in the 7th century. For the intermediate period not even oaks in the river beds could be found which left a hardly bridgeable gap in the European oak tree-ring chronologies."[190]

To artificially bridge this "Roman gap", "it had been necessary to 'calibrate' the Roman complex of the Middle European oak chronology with historical considerations."[191] This means that dendrochronological measurements are adapted to the chronological consensus rather than used to test it.

Twin events in Constantine's and Justinian's times

In 2010 the Larsson couple focused on one of the centerpieces of Ernst Hollstein's oak-tree chronology: a single stem from the basement of the Roman amphitheater of Trier, built in the first century AD, that had been well preserved because the basement had remained filled with water for centuries. Based on the 227 rings identified in the stem, Ernst Hollstein dated its felling year as around AD 694. But Lars-Åke and Petra Larsson noticed that a sequence of 100 years in that stem "matches perfectly not only to AD 670 but *also* to the Hollstein data 207 years earlier." "The match implies, that when we are looking at data of the periods AD 236-336 and AD 443-543, then we are looking at data from the *same* time!" This means that "207 invented years" have crept into Hollstein's curve.[192] The authors conclude: "all dendrochronological datings done on West Roman time wood is wrong by some unknown number of years!"[193]

In the following years, the Swedish scholars refined they analysis and in February 2015 confirmed: "we see the growth pattern of Hollstein's data for the period AD 203-336 being repeated 207 years later in the period AD 410-543." This means that "current tree ring curves for middle Europe connecting the period around AD 100 to AD 1000 are built on sand!" "Is the current paradigm of exactly 1000 years between AD 1 and AD 1000 too solid to be at all questioned?"[194]

The Larssons expanded their investigation by examining how dendrochonologists have tried to bridge the continental "Migration gap" by using Irish and Scandinavian data, but could not confirm the optimistic claims of the community. They published their result in April 2015, under the title "Dendrochronological Dating of Roman Time":

"we have found a distinct correlation between a long north-west European oak curve anchored archaeologically in Roman time, and the Scandinavian pine curves, but 218 years later than expected. There is no correlation at or near to the expected point of match."

"the match of the European Roman oak complex extended with Irish late BC collections against the absolute Scandinavian pine masters does not confirm the conventional dating. Instead there is a significant match 218 years later than expected."[195]

In February 2016, they published an additional article titled "Astronomical dating of Roman time," in which they correlated their earlier findings with astronomical data, leading them to conclude that our first millennium chronology is too long by 232 years. "Our results indicate that the Christian era was inflated with 232 years already when it was invented. This was done by back-dating West-Roman and related history by means of astronomical retrocalculation after the western part of the Roman empire had declined."[196]

One of the clues that led them to this conclusion was drawn from Pliny the Elder (c. 61-113 AD), who has left us with precise indications of eclipses that he witnessed himself. In Book II of his *Natural History*, Pliny mentions:

a. "the eclipse of both sun and moon within 15 days of each other … in the year of the third consulship of the elder Emperor Vespasian and the second consulship of the younger."

b. "The eclipse of the sun which occurred the day before the calends of May, in the consulship of Vipstanus and Fonteius a few years ago, … visible in Campania between the seventh and eighth hour of the day but … reported by Corbulo commanding in Armenia as observed between the tenth and eleventh hour."

Larsson & Ossowski Larsson show that the commonly agreed corresponding eclipses in 71 AD is a very approximate match, while a perfect match can be found (with the NASA Eclipse Web Site) exactly 232 years later, in 303 AD.

In August 2016, the couple published their longest and most synthetic article titled "Redating West-Roman history," in which they documented two sets of "twin events" separated by 232 years. These are "major incisive events which were dated or reported multiple times in different historical contexts so that it seems that they happened twice."

> "With our hypothesis that 232 years were invented for some reason at the transition between Late Antiquity and Early Medieval time, we have searched and found two 'twin events', i.e. events where parts of the historical and scientific evidence are dated in different context. This means more explicitly that part of the evidence is dated with West-Roman dating methods and thus has been dated 232 years before the other part of the evidence which is dated with East-Roman dating methods which are correctly synchronized with our own Christian era."[197]

The first event is the natural disaster documented by ancient historians of the Eastern Roman Empire such as Procopius of Caesarea, Cassiodorus, or John of Ephesus. Procopius writes that in the tenth year of Justinian (536), "the sun gave forth its light without brightness, like the moon, during this whole year" (Book IV, chapter 14). This led to a plague from around 541 till the end of Justinian's reign in 565: "During these times there was a pestilence, by which the whole human race came near to being annihilated" (Book II, chapter 22). Scientists have long suspected that the disease was the bubonic plague caused by the pathogen *Yersinia pestis,* and this was confirmed in 2013 by DNA analysis of samples collected from a graveyard in Aschheim, Germany. Larsson & Ossowski Larsson write:

> "The Justinian plague was such a traumatic event that it apparently resulted in multiple reports. Moreover, it dates to the very beginning of the European chronology section which is secured by scientific methods, that means it dates to the younger edge of the Roman gap ... Therefore we

may now challenge our hypothesis and see if there are reports of "twin events" on the older edge of the Roman gap. That means we could look for events reported around 542 minus 232 = 310 in Roman context (RomAD 310)."

They find what they are looking for in the *Church History* by Eusebius of Caesarea (c. 263-339), who writes of an epidemic in the year AD 310 or 311, with symptoms consistent with the bubonic plague (Book IX, chapter 8):

> "The usual winter rains and showers were denying the earth its normal downpour when famine struck, as well as plague and an epidemic of another sort of disease: an ulcer that was called a carbuncle because of its fiery appearance. It spread very dangerously over the entire body but attacked the eyes in particular, blinding countless men, women, and children ... Countless numbers died in the cities and even more in the villages and countryside ... Death, waging war with the two weapons of plague and famine, quickly devoured whole families, so that two or three bodies might be removed for burial in a single funeral procession."

Larsson & Ossowski Larsson comment: "the description of two episodes of plague and famine in the written sources with 232 years in between is of course a 'through ball' for our hypothesis."

If the two events are one and the same, then the intervening years may be invented. The authors find confirmation in the *Liber Pontificalis,* a collection of biographies of the bishops of Rome from saint Peter up to the fifteenth century, edited by several authors at different times. Based on internal evidence, it is admitted that the earliest lives, up to Sylvester I (314-335) in Constantine's days, were composed around 535-540. In a recent article, Eivind Heldaas Seland argues that:

> "The names and dates up to 354 seem to be derived from a chronicle of that year called the "Liberian Catalogue" after Pope Liberius, who held the papacy from 352 to 366. Most of the other information contained in the biographies up to the period from which the author had personal experience

or information, that is until the late 5th century onwards, is
either impossible to confirm, apparently misinformed and
in some cases even plainly invented."[198]

According to the Larssons' hypothesis, both Eusebius
and Procopius described the same pandemic because they
are contemporaries. Since Eusebius writes about the time of
Constantine and Procopius writes about the time of
Justinian, this would mean that Constantine and Justinian
are also contemporaries.

Eusebius and Procopius happen to come from the same
city of Caesarea Palestinae. Eusebius was a Christian
historian and theologian and became the bishop of Caesarea
around 314. Procopius was a secular historian and lawyer
who was close to Justinian and his chief military
commander Belisarius. Strangely, Procopius supposedly
wrote some 160 years after Christianity became the state
religion of the Roman empire, yet he mentions Christianity
only in passing remarks such as: "At the opening of spring,
when the Christians were celebrating the feast which they
call Easter ..." (Book IV, chapter 14). Moreover, he
consistently calls the capital of the empire Byzantium,
although it had been refounded and renamed Constantinople
200 years earlier.

Could Constantine and Justinian be the same person?
"Maybe his name was Constantine as emperor in the west,
and Justinian after he founded his Nova Roma and became
emperor of the whole empire." That sounds very
implausible, as it is contradicted by Procopius, who makes
references to Constantine as clearly distinct and much earlier
than Justinian.

Yet Larsson & Ossowski Larsson draw attention to a
mosaic in Hagia Sophia depicting the Virgin Mary with
Child flanked to her left by Constantine offering his Nova
Roma and to her right by Justinian offering his Hagia
Sophia. The two emperors are clad identically, but appear of
different ages: "while Constantine is depicted as a young

man with brown hair and rosy cheeks, Justinian is an old
man with grey hair and wrinkles."

It is reported by Socrates Scholasticus of Constantinople
(c. 380-439) that Constantine's son Constantius built "a
great church called *Sophia*" around 346. This church is said
to have been destroyed by fire fifty years later, while the
present building was inaugurated by Justinian in 537, then
rededicated in 562. "Interesting with our hypothesis in
mind," write the authors, "is that 562, the date for the
rededication of the present Hagia Sophia, would be the same
year as RomAD 330, the year of the dedication of
Constantinople by Constantine."

The hypothesis that Justinian, like Constantine, lived and
ruled in a period of transition from paganism to Christianity
is consistent with the very name of Hagia Sophia, as I
pointed out earlier: Sophia is the goddess of pagan
philosophers, not Christian priests.

Eusebius' and Procopius' different perspectives on the
same events reflect their standing on the opposite sides of
the widening gap between the old pagan world and the new
Christian one. The connecting dots between their two
narratives is all the more significant. Procopius reports for

the year 539 the appearance of a comet "at first about as long as a tall man, but later much larger. And the end of it was toward the west and its beginning toward the east, and it followed behind the sun itself." Although Eusebius does not mention a natural cosmic event triggering the famine and the plague in his *Church History*, he does include a *supernatural* cosmic event in his *Life of Constantine*, for the year 312 (= 539 − 227):

> "He said that about noon, when the day was already beginning to decline, he saw with his own eyes the trophy of a cross of light in the heavens, above the sun, and bearing the inscription, Conquer by this. At this sight he himself was struck with amazement, and his whole army also, which followed him on this expedition, and witnessed the miracle."

In the hypothesis of the contemporaneity — or perhaps identity — of Constantine and Justinian, the first Council of Nicaea presided by Constantine in 325 is the same as the second Council of Constantinople convened by Justinian in 553 (= 325 + 228), or at least part of the same endeavour to dogmatize and centralize the Church. Elaborating on their hypothesis that Constantine and Justinian are one and the same person, the Larssons write:

> "Constantine becomes Augustus in the West after turbulent years with famine, plague and civil war, which convinced him about monotheism. He starts supporting the Christians who already have communities in the empire. When he becomes the Emperor of the whole empire, he drops old pagan Rome and moves the capital city to the new-founded Constantinople. At the same time he changes name to Justinian and starts a new life building churches throughout the empire. After his death there are again emperors in the west and in the east simultaneously who 'produce' parallel history. First after Justinian the Roman empire starts to crumble."

Shortening Late Antiquity

The second case of "twin events" that Larsson & Ossowski Larsson document in their groundbreaking article of August 2016, "Redating West-Roman history," is the end of the city of Petra in Jordan, presumably after a major earthquake which crippled the city's water managing system. Such an earthquake, which devastated the Roman cities of Palestine from Haifa in the north to Petra in the south, happened on the night between the 18 and 19 May 363 in standard chronology (RomAD 363).

> "Nabataean/Roman infrastructure was never rebuilt after the earthquake, it is thought that the post-363 inhabitants dwelt for more than two and a half centuries in a city affected by flash floods and with a primitive economy. Petra suddenly and mystically disappears from the sources after that period."

However, archaeological evidence, including papyri found in Petra, shows that the city was still prosperous — and partly Christian — up to the second half of the sixth century. Based on radiocarbon dating, epigraphy and the Petra papyri, the authors hypothesize a large earthquake in the southern part of the Dead Sea Fault around 595, which happens to be exactly 232 years after the documented earthquake of 363. At that time, Petra had passed from West-Roman domination to Byzantine domination, but "With our hypothesis, Roman Petra and Byzantine Petra existed side by side, maybe in separated quarters, and were destroyed in the same earthquake in 595."

In that case, "the time between RomAD 363 and 595 would collapse to nothing." The Christian era counts 232 years too many between the beginning of the 5th century and the middle of the 7th century. This period coincides with the so-called "Migration period". The authors make an interesting connection to the work of Belgian historian Henri Pirenne, who in *Mohammed and Charlemagne* (1939) has developed an alternative theory about the collapse of the Western Roman Empire. According to Pirenne, the empire did not collapse at all in the 5th century, but in the 7th century, and not because of the Barbarian invasions, but because of the Arab-Muslim conquest of Syria and North Africa, which destroyed the Roman unity of the Mediterranean world and brought a stop to the trade between East and West. Pirenne's thesis has suffered the paradoxical fate of being largely corroborated (being firmly based on an impeccable use of primary sources), yet ignored because it puts too much pressure on the conventional narrative. Larsson & Ossowski Larsson's revised chronology makes full sense of it: "According to our hypothesis, the crash of the West-Roman empire came with the start of the Arabian expansion after 630. This has been postulated by Henri Pirenne." In that shortened perspective, the much-speculated affinity between the Barbarians' Arianism and Islam would have to considered in a new light.

Other unsolved mysteries in the early relationship between the Roman-Christian world and the Arab-Islamic world can begin to find a solution, as "the development of Christianity within the Roman empire ... becomes a much more dynamic process." The authors write in "Astronomical dating of Roman time":

> "With the hypothesis that RomAD 412 in Alexandria is the same year as 644 in Constantinople, Arianism gets a quite dynamic development. It took only about one hundred years until Islam emerged possibly as the result of a theological controversy. The Christian church reacted with a sharp persecution of all kinds of heresy, and with a strict consolidation of the scriptures."[199]

What Larsson & Ossowski Larsson are really doing is condense Late Antiquity, a period so elusive that it had gone unnoticed until Peter Brown drew attention to it in 1971.[200] They believe this period of about 350 years has to be drastically reduced to just over one century of "clustered natural catastrophes." As they write in the concluding section of their article "Redating West-Roman history":

"while the mainstream historians count about 350 years during this period, we count just slightly more than 100 years which unarguably adds a dynamic touch to the 'dark ages'. Because in the end it is the time frame given by the scientific consensus which allows the historians to spread the known historical events over the available time span. Do you dispose of 350 years, you will have to write history for 350 years. This means for example that in mainstream history the early Byzantine period always comes after the late Roman period, never parallel with it, which might be problematic as in the case of Petra. Byzantine Petra seems to exist for 232 more years among the ruins of Roman Petra.

The same is valid for the advance of Christianity in the Roman empire. Initiated under Constantine, the process seems still not finished under Justinian though Christianity has been the state church for almost 200 years. Prominent chroniclers contemporary with Justinian write in a 'classic style' which evokes the question if they are already Christians or still pagans. Pagan festivals are still observed in Constantinople as reported by Agathias.

… In our short version of Late Antiquity, Constantine and Justinian are at least contemporaries. Byzantine Petra is destroyed in the same earthquake as Roman Petra. Christianity is new to the Romans and there are a lot of people, especially the intellectuals like Procopius and Agathias, who still follow classic ideals. Byzantium is the name used for the capital city until the end of the reign of Justinian, after his death Constantinople is used instead. …

The cold period which is called the Late Antique Little Ice Age is in our version not only a part of Late Antiquity, it is *pari passu* with Late Antiquity. This means that climatic coincidences most probably started the course of events which hundred years later led to the fall of the West-Roman empire and the transformation of the East-Roman empire, simultaneously and not after each other with 232 years in- between."[201]

The authors added new arguments to their theory in August 2019, in an article about the famous "coin collection" found in the grave of Childeric, an early

Merovingian king believed to have reigned from 458-481 AD. His grave contained a large amount of old Roman *denarii* that had stopped being circulated around 240, more than two hundred years before Childeric's death. Rather than being evidence of a dynastic heirloom (the dynasty had hardly begun), this treasure shows that Childeric was contemporary with Severus Alexander (AD 222 to 235).

> "The period of instability which allowed Childeric to gain power in parts of Gaul thus was not the time after the fall of the West-Roman empire as conventionally assumed, but the Crisis of the Third Century. Childeric did not live more than hundred years after, but 60 years before Constantine the Great (whoever that was). Therefore his pagan style burial with a stunning sacrifice of 21 horses was fully acceptable also by Roman standards. His son Clovis was the first Merovingian king to become a Christian as narrated by Gregory of Tours (book II), in a manner very similar to the conversion of Constantine I as narrated by Eusebius. We will have to reconsider which of the stories is the original and which is the copy. / This also explains why there are no 'western' coins of the Tetrarchy and the Constantinian and Valentinian dynasties (RomAD 284 to 392) in Childeric's treasure. These dynasties would have reigned after 518, long after Childeric's death."[202]

The Coptic calendar

If the standard historiography of the first millennium counts two or three centuries too many, removing those centuries is not a simple task. The difficulty is to find the correct synchronization between East and West. The Western dendrochronological data corrected by Larsson and Ossowski do not tell us when, in the Byzantine timeline, ghost centuries must be removed. Erasing the historical block between Constantine and Justinian is neither the only nor the best solution. Based on the considerations presented earlier, I am rather inclined to consider as non-existent the obscure period of Byzantium before Constantine—or, more precisely, before Diocletian. This means that we can move forward Western Roman history without touching Eastern Roman history. That brings Augustus much closer to Constantine. The fake timespan between the foundations of Western and Eastern empires can be attributed to Rome's obsession to claim precedence over Constantinople.

Whatever the precise solution, the notion that there are two and a half or three centuries too many in the history of Christianity has many arguments in its favor. One of them is the Coptic calendar, which is shorter by 284 years. I am told that

> "Polish independent historian Arthur Lalak has been saying for years that the only unaltered calendar is the Coptic calendar and currently according to this calendar the year is 1739. Our calendar was artificially extended by the 6th – 9th centuries and the evidence shows contradictions between various chronicles. Unfortunately, most of his works have not been translated into English."[203]

The details of Lalak's theory remain inaccessible to me, but it has also been pointed to me that he believes in cyclical great epidemics every 676 years (the last one in 1348 and the next one in 2024).[204] Regardless, I find the observation that "Coptic years are counted from 284 AD" (Wikipedia) extremely interesting.

Copts are Egyptian Christians who, like the Syrian Jacobites, adhere to the Monophysite Christology. Despite its condemnation at the Council of Chalcedon in 451, Monophysitism remained strong even in Constantinople. Empress Theodora, Justinian' wife (527-565), was a declared supporter of the Monophysite Church. Yet, their unfavorable condition in Syria and Egypt later led them to welcome the Muslim conquerors, under whom they were treated on an equal footing with the Orthodox Christians, known then as Melkites (from the Semitic root for "king", because they recognized themselves as subjects of the Byzantine *basileus*).

How can we explain that the Coptic Church preserved a calendar shorter by 284 years than the calendar adopted universally by other Christians? The standard explanation is that 284 AD is "the year Diocletian became Roman Emperor, whose reign was marked by tortures and mass executions of Christians, especially in Egypt" (Wikipedia). This explanation smacks of a secondary justification to cover up the original cause of the discrepancy. It is inconceivable that the ancient churches of Syria and Alexandria would count years from any other date than their own reckoning of the birth of Jesus. No matter how severe was the Diocletianic persecution, it is highly improbable that it could gain a higher symbolic value than the year of God's Incarnation, and the probability is even reduced if we take into account that its severity is now believed to have been greatly exaggerated by ecclesiastical historians and hagiographers.[205] Therefore, the Coptic calendar is akin to a fossil: the tangible proof of an earlier stage of the Christian comput, which has been lengthened by roughly 300 years at some indeterminate date.

Charlemagne's ghost

Without surprise, but nevertheless with disappointment, the stimulating work of Lars-Åke Larsson & Petra Ossowski Larsson has so far been met with contempt within the dendro community, despite their scientific credentials. In a paper published in 2019 by the academic journal *Dendrochronologia* under the title "Missing link in Late Antiquity?" Andreas Rzepecki and his co-authors acknowledge weak matches in the dendrochronological record for Roman times, but conclude that they must be correct anyway because "criticism of the general accepted medieval timeline has already been disproved by various scientific disciplines."[206]

On their side, Lars-Åke Larsson & Petra Ossowski Larsson respectfully acknowledge the work of Heribert Illig and Hans-Ulrich Niemitz, who together with other German scholars (known as the *Zeitenspringers* or "time jumpers") argue that our conventional chronology of the first millennium AD is too long by some 300 years. (We have already met them in chapter 1, for their critic of the notion of "forgeries with anticipatory character.") Since Illig and Niemitz are, to my knowledge, the only members of this group who have published accounts of their theory in English, and since, to my shame and frustration, I do not read German, I will rely on their two articles respectively titled "Anomalous Eras – Best Evidence: Best Theory," and "Did the Early Middle Ages Really Exist?"[207]

The German discussion originally focused on Charlemagne. Sources on this Karolus Magnus are often contradictory and unreliable. His main biography, Eginhard's *Vita Karoli* (written, Eginhard tells us, "for the benefit of posterity rather than to allow the shades of oblivion to blot out the life of this King, the noblest and greatest of his age, and his famous deeds, which the men of later times will scarcely be able to imitate"), is recognizably modeled on Suetonius' Life of the first Roman emperor Augustus.

The concept of an empire lasting only 45 years, from 800 to its dislocation in three kingdoms, defies reason. Ferdinand Gregorovius, in his *History of the City of Rome in the Middle Ages* in 8 volumes (1872), writes: "The figure of the Great Charles can be compared to a flash of lightning who came out of the night, illuminated the earth for a while, and then left night behind him."[208] Is this shooting star just an illusion, and the legends about him devoid of relation to history?

The main problem with Charlemagne is with architecture. Charlemagne's residence in Ingelheim was built in the Roman style of the 2nd century, with materials supposedly recycled from the 2nd century. On the opposite, his Palatine Chapel in Aachen (today Aachen Cathedral) exhibits a technological advance of 200 years, with arched aisles not seen before the 11th century. Its central octagonal dome, 15 meters in diameter, assembled from carefully hewn stones, is the most anachronistic. As Illig notes,

"Aachen stands as a masterpiece with no precursor, no successor, as an erratic within the so-called Carolingian Renaissance." There are no Roman domes after AD 400, and therefore "no building tradition that could have transported this knowledge to the Franks more than 400 years later."

"Neither does it have a successor, for there is no Carolingian building with a dome after 820. The technology appears to have been totally forgotten. In the Occident, buildings with domes started up again only around 970, but the first domes had a span of only 3.5 meters (about 11 1/2 feet). From that point onward, the span of the vaults was increased inch by inch. Around 1050, it was possible to construct vaults over the aisle of the imperial cathedral at Speyer on the Rhine: with 7.5 meters(approx. 25 feet) they were the largest vaults of their time. Then started the building of the large Romanesque domes at Toulouse, Cluny, Santiago de Compostela, and again in Speyer. Shortly after 1100, in that city, the central nave and the transept were also given vaults. As in Aachen, the transept is an octagonal dome with a diameter of around 15 meters (approx. 50 feet)."

Another oddity is that Carolingian archaeological items are conspicuously lacking around Aachen. Illig quotes German art historian and archaeologist Matthias Untermann:

"Amazingly, there has not been an archeological dig or review of a building site within and outside the old city of Aachen that produced clear settlement remains of the Carolingian era, though the historical tradition points to the presence of merchants and numerous inhabitants as well as the existence of high-ranking noblemen and their courts, of whose buildings and physical remains there ought to be quite a lot in the ground. Everything that has so far been said about the road system, the structure of the settlement and its extent rests exclusively on written sources and theoretical considerations."

In other words, to the archaeologist, the imperial capital city of Aachen looks like a ghost town. To Illig and Niemitz, this raises the possibility that the Carolingian Empire itself was a phantom empire, a literary half-fiction born out of the needs of later Germanic emperors. While the Palatine Chapel itself probably dates from shortly after 1100, the political events and acting personnel of Charlemagne's *gesta* are "either pure invention or duplicating projections from other periods."

> "Needless to say, someone must have carried out this artificial and deliberate interpolation. I have shown that there was a small window of opportunity between 990 and 1009 during which the three most important powers of the occident — the Byzantine emperor, the German emperor, and the Pope — were able to cooperate. I therefore designated Emperors Constantine VII and Otto III and Pope Sylvester II as the authors of this interpolation."

Illig's conclusion is that "Charlemagne has no historical background. He is an invented figure." Since the "cult of Charlemagne" started under Otto III, who in 1000 miraculously discovered the tomb of his illustrious predecessor, with the enthroned sitting corpse miraculously preserved, it is suspected that the legend of Charlemagne's unlikely empire (and its regretable split between his grandchildren) was fabricated by the Ottos' propagandists. If the "Ottonian Privilege" issued by Otto III's grandfather in 962 is authentic, then Charlemagne was already in "existence" at that time.

More details were added to his life and reign in the second half of the 12th century, under the rule of Frederick I Barbarossa, who had Charlemagne canonized in Aachen in 1165. Many false diplomas attributed to Charlemagne or his heirs were also fabricated as justification of Church property ownership after the Concordat of Worms, signed on September 23, 1122 by Emperor Henry V and Pope Callixtus II. An important issue in that Concordat was the many domains that Henry V and his father Henry IV had seized from the Church in Italy and Germany, including whole duchies, which the emperor promised to return. In this context, the Roman curia fabricated a vast number of false diplomas in order to claim lands for which it possessed no genuine legal document.

But according to Illig and Niemitz, the first step in the addition of three centuries to the first millennium happened under Otto III. Niemitz writes:

> "Otto III didn't live accidentally around the year 1000 AD; he himself had defined this date! He wanted to reign in this year, because this suited his understanding of Christian milleniarism. He defined this date with the help of his famous and well-versed friend Gerbert de Aurillac, later Pope Sylvester II. ... Consequently chroniclers had to invent 300 years of history. To fill up empty periods — what a great occasion for dynasties and kings!"

Byzantine emperor Constantine VII (905-959), Otto III's contemporary, is also on the list of suspects. Thanks to byzantinists like Peter Schreiner, we know that he organized a complete rewriting of the whole Byzantine history. In Niemitz's words,

> "beginning in the year 835 AD monks rewrote piece by piece all texts which had been written in Greek *maiuscula*, in the new form of writing hence called *minuscula*. Schreiner postulates that each text was produced only once. Then the originals were destroyed. This means that all existing texts of the then leading culture nation had been changed or rewritten completely in new script in the lifetime of two generations, or even faster."

Although it may seem that the theory of Lars-Åke Larsson et Petra Ossowski and the theory of Heribert Illig and Hans-Ulrich Niemitz end up with comparable results in terms of the shortening of the first millennium, this is hardly the case. The time-blocks they delete are different. For the Larssons, it has to be taken from Late Antiquity, from around 300 to 550, while for Illig and Niemitz, the phantom period belongs to the Early Middle Ages, roughly between 610 and 910. But the Larssons are confident about this later period, if I interpret correctly their statements:

"European oak chronologies containing archaeologically significant timbers are continuous from today back to about 400. They are multiple replicated, which means that their continuity has been verified by comparing them towards each other. They are also regarded as correctly synchronized with history ... tree-ring and ice core chronologies are at the present synchronized worldwide back to 774. / This means that we can regard European tree-ring chronologies back to about 500 as a true projection of the real time line."[209]

Yet in 2010 the same authors stated that the "Roman gap" is not the only weak point in the dendro-chronology: "also the 'Carolingian gap' (or 'Merovingian gap') centred around AD 750 is problematic."[210] The great Ernst Hollstein himself expressed a similar view:

"All attempts to get enough tree ring sequences from timber of the Carolingian times have failed ... It is strange, but it proved as extremely difficult to connect the Merovingian wood samples from excavations with the above mentioned chronologies. ... After two years of intensive studies I can name at last the right dates and put in order all samples of the early Middle Ages."[211]

Why the Larssons later concluded that "Hollstein bridged the 'Carolingian gap' correctly!" escapes me. But I note that, in the same article, they add: "the closing of the Carolingian gap does not imply a proof against the theory of invented years during Carolingian time!"[212]

In the end, is it possible that Illig-Niemitz and the Larssons are both right about, respectively, the "Migration gap" of Late Antiquity and the "Carolingian gap" of the Early Middle Ages? If so, our first-millennium chronology would have to be shortened by not just one period comprising 2 to 3 centuries, but by two such periods. Not only would Constantine and Justinian be contemporaries, but the birth of the Ottonian "Roman Empire" would be much closer to Justinian (as close as Charlemagne is in our textbook chronology). In that case, the Western Roman Empire, the Eastern Roman Empire, and the Northern

Roman Empire are all overlapping. This leads us to the theory of Gunnar Heinsohn, which will be the focus of the next chapter.

CHAPTER 4
How long was the first millennium?

Anatoly Fomenko and the two Romes

In the previous chapters, I examined a series of fundamental problems in our standard history of the greater part of the first millennium AD. These problems have led some researchers to advocate a paradigm shift in first millennium chronology.

The best-known of these revisionists is perhaps the Russian mathematician Anatoly Fomenko (born 1945). With his associate Gleb Nosovsky, he has produced tens of thousands of pages in support of his "New Chronology." In my view, Fomenko and Nosovsky have signaled a great number of major problems in conventional chronology, and provided plausible solutions to many of them, but their global reconstruction is extravagantly Russo-centric. Their confidence in their statistical method is also exaggerated.[213] Nevertheless, Fomenko and Nosovsky must be credited for having provided stimulus and direction for many others. For a first direct approach to their work, I recommend volume 1 of their series *History: Fiction or Science*, especially chapter 7, "'Dark Ages' in Mediaeval History", pp. 373-415.[214]

One major discovery of Fomenko and Nosovsky is that our conventional history is full of doublets, produced by the arbitrary end-to-end alignment of chronicles that tell the same events, but are "written by different people, from different viewpoints, in different languages, with the same characters under different names and nicknames."[215]

It is easy enough to understand. Imagine that someone, a thousand years from now, discovers a brief account of World War II written by Hitler. Then someone else discovers the five thousand pages of the same war written by Churchill, who always places himself at the center of events. Assuming Hitler writes *die Deutschen, die Engländer* and *die Sowjets* when Churchill writes "the British", "the Germans" and "the Russians", and supposing that each uses different chronological markers, and of course totally different viewpoints, the first historian to exploit these sources could see there two different wars, and the following ones would follow suit. In such a way ancient wars and whole periods of history were duplicated.

For example, drawing from the work of Russian Nikolai Mozorov (1854-1946), Fomenko and Nosovsky bring attention to a striking parallel between the sequences Pompey/Caesar/Octavian and Diocletian/Constantius/Constantine, leading to the conclusion that the Western Roman Empire is, to some extent, a phantom duplicate of the Eastern Roman Empire.[216] According to Fomenko and Nosovsky, the capital of the one and only Roman Empire was founded on the Bosporus some 330 years before the foundation of its colony in the Latium. Starting from the age of the crusades, Roman clerics, followed by Italian humanists, produced an inverted chronological sequence, using the real history of Constantinople as the model for their fake earlier history of Italian Rome. A great confusion ensued, as "many mediaeval documents confuse the two Romes: in Italy and on the Bosporus," both being commonly called Rome or "the City".[217] A likely scenario is that the prototype for Titus Livy's *History* was about Constantinople, the original capital of the "Romans". The original Livy, Fomenko conjectures, was writing around the tenth century about Constantinople, so he was not far off the mark when he placed the foundation of the City (*urbs condita*) some seven centuries before his time. But as it was rewritten by Petrarch and reinterpreted by later humanists, a chronological chasm of roughly one thousand year was introduced between the foundation of the two "Romes" (from 753 BC to 330 AD).

However, even the dates for Constantinople are wrong, according to Fomenko and Nosovky, and the whole sequence happened much more recently: Constantinople was founded around the tenth or eleventh century AD, and Rome, 330 or 360 years later, i.e. around the fifteenth or sixteenth century AD. Here, as often, Fomenko and Nosovsky spoil their best insights by exaggeration and overconfidence in the infallibility of their mathematical and statistical tools. These tools are very difficult for the layman to judge, but it is easy to see from their prose that their trust in them is unreasonably unshakable, and their openness to historians' critic very low. An excellent and balanced appraisal of the work of Fomenko and his team is Florin Diacu's book, *The Lost Millennium: History's Timetables Under Siege,* published by the John Hopkins University Press. "Fomenko's chronological results," he writes, "seem to fall into three categories: good, mediocre, and blunders," with his linguistic speculations as examples of blunders.[218]

In the mid-1990s, independently from the Russian school, German scholars Heribert Illig, Hans-Ulrich Niemitz, Uwe Topper, Manfred Zeller, Angelika Müller and a few others also became convinced that something is wrong with the accepted chronology of the Middle Ages. I have introduced their general approach in the previous chapter.

Illig and Niemitz challenge the existence of Charlemagne and argue that he is a mythical predecessor invented by the Ottonian emperors to legitimate their claim to the Roman *imperium.* They argue that all Carolingians of the 8th and 9th and their wars are also fictitious, and that the timespan of roughly 600-900 CE, is a phantom era.

Gunnar Heinsohn objects to this theory on numismatic ground: about 15,000 coins have been found bearing the name Karlus (alternatively Karolus or Carlus) Magnus.

Gunnar Heinsohn's breakthrough

Gunnar Heinsohn, from the University of Bremen, is one of the most interesting and prolific scholar in the field of chronological revisionism. His recent articles in English are posted on q-mag.org or academia.edu,[219] and for an introduction, I recommend his 2016 conference in Toronto.[220] Heinsohn focuses on hard archaeological evidence, and insists that stratigraphy is the most important criterion for dating archaeological finds. He shows that, time and again, stratigraphy contradicts history, and that archaeologists should have logically forced historians into a paradigm shift. Unfortunately, "In order to be consistent with a pre-fabricated chronology, archaeologists unknowingly betray their own craft."[221] When they dig up the same artifacts or building structures in different parts of the world, they assign them to different periods in order to satisfy historians. And when they find, in the same place and layer, mixtures of artifacts that they have already attributed to different periods, they explain it away with the ludicrous "heirloom theory," or call them "art collections."

> "Archaeologists are particularly confident of correctly dating finds from 1st-millennium excavation sites when they find coins associated with them. A coin-dated layer is considered to be of utmost scientific precision. But how do scholars know the dates of the coins? From coin catalogues! How do the authors of these catalogues know how to date the coins? Not according to archaeological strata, but from the lists of Roman emperors. But how are the emperors dated and then sorted into these lists? Nobody knows for sure."[222]

Quite often, archaeologists unearth coins of supposedly widely different dates in the same settlement strata or the same tombs. One example is the famous leather purse of Childeric, a Frankish prince reigning from 458-481 AD. For Heinsohn, these coins are not a "coin collection" but "indicate the simultaneity of Roman Emperors artificially dispersed over two epochs — Imperial Antiquity and Late Antiquity."[223]

Heinsohn's work is not easy to summarize, because it is a work in progress, because it covers virtually all regions of the globe, and because it is abundantly illustrated and referenced with historical and archaeological studies. Nothing can replace a painstaking study of his articles, completed with personal research. All I can do here is try to reflect the scope and the depth of his research and the significance of his conclusions. Rather than paraphrase him, I will quote extensively from his articles and borrow a couple of his illustrations. In this chapter and the next, only quotations from other authors will be indented.

The best starting point is his own summary, "Heinsohn in a nutshell": "According to mainstream chronology, major European cities should exhibit — separated by traces of crisis and destruction — distinct building strata groups for the three urban periods of some 230 years that are unquestionably built in Roman styles with Roman materials and technologies (Antiquity/**A**>Late Antiquity/**LA**>Early Middle Ages/**EMA**). None of the ca. 2,500 Roman cities known so far has the expected three strata groups super-imposed on each other. ... Any city (covering, at least, the periods from Antiquity to the High Middle Ages [**HMA**; 10th/11th c.]) has just one (**A** or **LA** or **EMA**) distinct building strata group in Roman format (with, of course, internal evolution, repairs etc.). Therefore, all three urban realms labeled as **A** or **LA** or **EMA** existed simultaneously, side by side in the Imperium Romanum. None can be deleted. All three realms (if their cities continue at all) enter **HMA** in tandem, i.e. all belong to the 700-930s period that ended in a global catastrophe. This parallelity not only explains the mind-boggling absence of technological and archaeological evolution over 700 years but also solves the enigma of Latin's linguistic petrification between the 1st/2nd and 8th/9th c. CE. Both text groups are contemporary."[224]

In other words: "The High Middle Ages, beginning after the 930s A.D., are not only found — as would be expected — contingent with, i.e., immediately above the Early Middle Ages (ending in the 930s). They are also found — which is

chronologically perplexing — directly above Imperial
Antiquity or Late Antiquity in locations where settlements
continued after the 930s cataclysm."[225] "There is — in any
individual site — only one period of some 230 years (all of
them with Roman characteristics, such as imperial coins,
fibulae, millefiori glass beads, villae rusticae etc.) that is
terminated by a catastrophic conflagration. Since the
cataclysm dated to the 230s shares the same stratigraphic
depth as the cataclysms dated to the 530s or the 930s, some
700 years of 1st millennium history are phantom years."[226]
The first millennium, in other words, lasted only about 300
years. "Following stratigraphy, all earlier dates have to come
about 700 years closer to the present, too. Thus, the last
century of Late Latène (100 to 1 BCE), moves to around 600
to 700 CE."[227]

All over the Mediterranean world "three blocks of time
have left — in any individual site — just one block of strata
covering some 230 years." Wherever they are found, the
strata for Imperial Antiquity and Late Antiquity lie just
underneath the tenth century and therefore really belong to
the Early Middle Age, that is, 700-930 AD. The distinction
between Antiquity, Late Antiquity and Early Middle Age is
a cultural representation that has no basis in reality.
Heinsohn proposes contemporaneity for the three periods,
because they "are all found at the same stratigraphic depth,
and must, therefore, end simultaneously in the 230s CE
(being also the 520s and 930s)."[228] "Thus, the three parallel
time-blocks now found in our history books in a
chronological sequence must be brought back to their
stratigraphical position."[229] In this way, "the early medieval
period (approx. 700-930s AD) becomes the epoch for which
history can finally be written because it contains Imperial
Antiquity and Late Antiquity, too."[230]

As a result of stretching 230 years into 930 years, history
is now distributed unevenly, each time-block having most of
its recorded events localized in one of three geographical
zones: Roman South-West, Byzantine South-East, and

Germanic-Slavic North. If we look at written sources, "we have [for the 1st-3rd century] a spotlight on Rome, but know little about the 1st-3rd century in Constantinople or Aachen. Then we have a spotlight on Ravenna and Constantinople, but know little about the 4th-7th century in Rome or Aachen. Finally, we have a spotlight on Aachen in the 8th-10th century, but hardly know any details from Rome or Constantinople. I turn on all the lights at the same time and, thus, can see connections that were previously considered dark or completely unrecognizable."[231]

Each period ends with a demographic, architectural, technical, and cultural collapse, caused by a cosmic catastrophe and accompanied by plague. Historians "have identified major mega-catastrophes shaking the earth in three regions of Europe (South-West [230s]; South-East [530s], and Slavic North [940s]) within the 1st millennium."[232] "The catastrophic ends of (1) Imperial Antiquity, (2) Late Antiquity, and (3) the Early Middles Ages sit in the same stratigraphic plane immediately before the High Middle Ages (beginning around 930s AD)."[233] Therefore these three devastating collapses of civilization are one and the same, which Heinsohn refers to as "the Tenth Century Collapse."

700	930
Northern Roman Empire (Aachen)	
300	530=640
Eastern Roman Empire (Constantinople)	
0	230
Western Roman Empire (Rome)	

Heinsohn's identification of three time-blocks that should be synchronized is not to be taken as an exact parallelism: "This assumption does not claim a pure 1:1 parallelism in which events reported for the year 100 AD could simply be supplemented with information for the year 800 AD."[234] Stratigraphic identity only means that all real events that are dated to Imperial Antiquity or Late Antiquity happened in fact during the Early Middle Ages — in other words, in the recent past of the Central Middle Ages.

Moreover, all three time-blocks do not have the same length. That is because Late Antiquity (from the beginning of Diocletian's reign in 284 to the death of Heraclius in 641) is some 120 years too long, according to Heinsohn. The Byzantine segment from the rise of Justinian (527) to the death of Heraclius (641) was in reality shorter and overlapped with the period of Anastasius (491-518). This means that not only the first millennium as a whole, but Late Antiquity itself has to be shortened. Duplicates account for its phantom years. Thus the Persian emperor Khosrow I (531-579) fought by Justinian is identical to the Khosrow II (591-628) fought by his immediate successors — regardless of the fact that archaeologists decided to ascribe the silver drachmas to Khosrow I and the gold dinars to Khosrow II.[235]

Other duplicates suggested by Heinsohn within Late Antiquity include the Roman emperor Flavius Theodosius (379-395) being identical to the Gothic ruler of Ravenna and Italy Flavius Theodoric (471-526), who bears the same name, only with the additional suffix *riks,* meaning king. "At some point in the half millennium with manipulations of the original texts that can no longer be counted or reconstructed, two names of one person have become two persons with different names placed one behind the other." The Gothic wars have also been duplicated: with the war fought by Odoacer and his son Thela in the 470, and the one fought by ToTila in the 540s, "we are not dealing with two different Italian wars, but with two different narratives about the same war, which were connected chronologically one after the other."[236]

The strength or Heinsohn's approach, as compared to Illig and Niemtiz's, is that he doesn't really delete history: "If one removes the span of time that has been artificially created by mistakenly placing parallel periods in sequence, only emptiness is lost, not history. By reuniting texts and artifacts that have been chopped up and scattered over seven centuries, meaningful historiography becomes possible for the first time."[237] In fact, "a much richer image of Roman history emerges. The numerous actors from Iceland (with Roman coins) to Baghdad (whose 9th c. coins are found in the same stratum as 2nd c. Roman coins) can eventually be drawn together to weave the rich and colourful fabric of that vast space with 2.500 cities, and 85.000 km of roads."[238]

Rome

Applied to Rome, Heinsohn's theory solves a conundrum that has always puzzled historians: the absence of any vestige datable from the late third century to the tenth century (mentioned in chapter 1): "Rome of the first millennium CE builds residential quarters, latrines, water pipes, sewage systems, streets, ports, bakeries etc. only during Imperial Antiquity (1st-3rd c.) but not in Late Antiquity (4th-6th c.) and in the Early Middle Ages (8th-10th c.). Since the ruins of the 3rd century lie directly under the primitive new buildings of the 10th century, Imperial Antiquity belongs stratigraphically to the period from ca. 700 to 930 CE."[239] "The heart of the *Imperium Romanum* has no new construction for the seven centuries between the 3rd and the 10th c. CE.

As shown above, the urban material of the 3rd c. is stratigraphically contingent with the early 10th in which it was wiped out."[240] In the illustration below, the floor of Trajan's Forum (Piano Antico 2nd/3rd c. AD) is directly covered by the dark mud (*fango*) layer of the cataclysm that sealed Roman Civilization (more on it later).

In order to fill up their artificially stretched millennium, modern historians often have to do violence to their primary sources. As Fomenko already pointed out, the Getae and the Goths were considered the same people by Jordanes — himself a Goth — in his *Getica* written in the middle of the 6th century. Other historians before and after him, such as Claudian, Isidore of Seville and Procopius of Caesarea also used the name Getae to designate the Goths. But Theodor Mommsen has rejected the identification: "The Getae were Thracians, the Goths Germans, and apart from the coincidental similarity in their names they had nothing whatever in common."[241] Yet archaeologists are puzzled by the fact that the Getae and the Goths inhabit the same area at 300 years distance, and there is no explanation for how the Getae disappeared before the Goths appeared, and for the lack of demography during the 300-year interval. Besides, contrary to what Mommsen claims, there is evidence of great resemblance between their culture, including in clothing, as Gunnar Heinsohn points out: Goths in the 3rd/4th centuries "made great efforts to dress, from head to toe, like their mysteriously missing predecessors" (the 1st/3rd-c. Getae), and continued "to manufacture 300-year older ceramics, rolling back technological evolution to pre-Christian La Tène earthenware."[242] Compare the Getian prisoner and the Gothic warrior below, represented with the same clothing, including the Phrygian hat.

According to Heinsohn, "The identity of Getae and Goths can help to solve some of the most stubborn enigmas of Gothic history," such as the remarkable parallel between Rome's Getic/Dacian wars in the first century AD and Rome's Gothic wars some 300 years later. According to the

Chronicle of Theophanes the Confessor, in 374 the war against the Goths was led by a general named Trajan sent by Rmperor Valens. Emperor Trajan fighting the Dacians/Getae around 103 AD may be identical to this general Trajan, and this could explain why he appears after Constantine on the Arch of Constantine. The Dacian leader Decebalus (meaning "The Powerful") may also be identical to the Goth Alaric (meaning "King of all"). By such processes, "different sources dealing with the same events have been split (and altered) in such a way that the same event is described twice, albeit from different angles, thereby creating a chronology that is twice as long as the actual course of history that can be substantiated by archaeology."[243]

I cannot even begin to clarify the many mysteries which surrounds the Goths, their origin, language, religion, etc. The Byzantine historian Jordanes, our only source on the origin of the Goths, makes them come from Scandinavia, and his theory has long been taken for granted, but it is now disputed, and for good reasons.[244] Walter Goffart writes in "Jordanes's 'Getica' and the Disputed Authenticity of Gothic Origins from Scandinavia":

> "Great efforts have gone into the defense of Gothic origins from Scandinavia. This has been a matter of urgent concern to well-intentioned persons, a way of affirming continuity and identity with a precious part of the supposed past. But

Jordanes, Goth though he claimed to be, is not a
spokesman for that past. He was, on the contrary, one of
the obedient agents of Justinian's campaign of destruction.
For the true end of [Jordanes' *History of the Goths*] was the
affirmation that they (and their barbarian cousins) belong
outside, not within, the world of Rome in which they had
lived and striven to exist enduringly for close to two
centuries. That is the message of exclusion that
Constantinople would propagate, via Jordanes and others,
including Procopius, so that it might be more secure—even
in a barbarous present—in claiming for itself alone the
great heritage of imperial and Christian Rome."[245]

History is written by the victors, and of the history of the
Goths we know only what their enemies let us know.
Justinian's war against the Goths is presented in standard
history as a war against their Arian "heresy". This is where
the mystery of the Goths is interwoven with the mystery of
Constantine. For despite all his efforts to make Constantine
the guardian of Nicene orthodoxy, Eusebius of Caesarea, his
biographer, acknowledged that Constantine died an Arian,
baptized by the Arian Eusebius of Nicomedia that he had
installed as Patriarch of Constantinople. And if the Goths
were Arians, it is because Constantine's son and successor,
Constantius II, was himself an Arian and had sent the Arian
Ulfila to convert them. How can we reconcile this with the
story of Constantine convening and presiding the Council of
Nicaea, and forcing all bishops to sign the anti-Arian Nicene
Creed, under threat of exile or worse? It makes little sense,
and the odds are that the Council of Nicaea, of which no
record survives, is a fiction fabricated long after
Constantine's death, perhaps under Theodosius.

Constantinople

"While no new residential areas with latrines, water
systems and streets were built in Rome during Late
Antiquity and the Early Middle Ages, they are missing in
Constantinople during Imperial Antiquity and the Early
Middle Ages. ... Both cities have these basic components of

urbanity in only one of the three epochs of the first millennium. Although in Rome they are dated to Imperial Antiquity, whilst in Constantinople they are dated to Late Antiquity, from the point of view of architecture and building technology they are nearly indistinguishable."[246] That is because, in reality, they "share the same stratigraphical horizon."[247]

The Early Middle Ages are known as Byzantium's Dark Ages, beginning in 641 after the reign of Heraclius, and ending with the Macedonian Renaissance under Basil II (976-1022 AD).[248] In the words of historian John O'Neill, "About forty years after the death of Justinian the Great, from the first quarter of the seventh century, [for] three centuries, cities were abandoned and urban life came to an end. There is no sign of revival until the middle of the tenth century."[249] For Heinsohn, this period, like most other "dark ages", is a phantom age. The Justinian dynasty starting with Justin I (AD 518-527) is identical to the Macedonian dynasty, which we can count from Constantine VII (913-959), initiator of the Macedonian Renaissance. The 400-year period between Justinian (527-565 AD) and Basil II lasted in reality only 70 years, corresponding to the Tenth Century Collapse.

Besides archaeology, there are also "anachronisms and puzzles in the development of the laws of Justinian (527-535 CE)," written in 2nd-c. Latin. "Not a single jurist from the 300 years between the Severan early 3rd century and Justinian's 6th century textbook date is included in the *Digestae*. Moreover, no post-550s jurist put his hand to the *Digestae*." So that "There are, from the Severans to the end of the Early Middle Ages, some 700 years without comments by Roman jurists." In addition: "It is a mystery why Justinian's Greek subjects had to wait 370 years [until the 900s CE], only to receive a version of the laws in Koine Greek of the 2nd c. out of use since 700 years." It all "looks bizarre only as long as the stratigraphic simultaneity of Imperial Antiquity, Late Antiquity, and the Early Middle

Ages is denied."[250] The simultaneity of the Severan and Justinian dynasties explains that both fought a Persian emperor named Khosrow.

According to Heinsohn, the foundation of Imperial Rome and Imperial Constantinople are roughly contemporary. It is "a geographical sequence from west to east ... turned into a chronological sequence from earlier to later."[251] "Diocletian did not reside in ruins, but lived at the same time as Augustus. His capital was not Rome. He had residences in Antioch, Nicomedia, and Sirmium. From there he worked tirelessly for the protection of Augustus' empire."[252] Heinsohn's hypothesis of the contemporaneity of Diocletian in the East and Octavian Augustus in the West (ruling in concert) distinguishes him from Fomenko, who believes that Augustus is a fictitious duplicate of the Roman Emperor residing in Constantinople. Heinsohn also differs from Fomenko in the way he sees the relationship between the two Roman capitals: he accepts Rome's precedence and assumes that Diocletian was a subordinate of Octavian Augustus. Fomenko, on the other hand, considers that Constantinople was the original center of the empire. This is consistent with Diocletian's position as the superior of his Western counterpart Maximian. Diocletian was an Eastern Emperor from the beginning. He was born in today's Croatia, where he built his palace (Split), and hardly ever set foot in Rome. Maximian, sent to rule in Rome, was himself from the Balkans.

Ravenna

Ravenna is a special case, because it stands between Rome and Constantinople: it was long under Byzantine control, yet was the "capital of the Occident in Late Antiquity" (Friedrich Wilhelm Deichmann). Ravenna has been called a "palimpsest" for the reason explained by historian Deborah Mauskoppf Deliyannis (*Ravenna in Late Antiquity,* Cambridge UP, 2014), quoted by Heinsohn:

"Ravenna's walls and churches were usually built of reused brick. Scholars disagree over whether the use of these *spolia* was symbolic (triumph over Roman paganism, for example) or whether their use simply had to do with the availability and expense of materials. In other words, was their use meaningful, or practical, or both? Did it demonstrate the power of the emperors to control construction of preexisting buiidings, or the power of the church to demolish them? Or, by the time Ravenna's buildings were constructed, were Roman *spolia* simply considered *de rigueur* for impressive public buildings. / One striking feature to all these [5th-century; GH] buildings is that, like the city walls they were made of bricks that had been reused from earlier [2nd/3rd-century; GH] Roman structures. ... It was expected that a noble church would be built of *spolia*."[253]

One senses here a desperate effort to force into the accepted chronological framework a situation that doesn't fit. Heinsohn's revisionism solves this problem: the buildings and their materials are, of course, contemporary, rather than separated by 300 years.

There is also a problem with Ravenna's civil and military port, which could harbor 240 ships according to Jordanes, with its lighthouse praised by Pliny the Elder as rivaling with the Pharos of Alexandria. "However, what is considered strange is that — after all port activities ceased around 300 AD — it is still being celebrated by a mosaic supposedly created in the 5th/6th century" in the Basilica of Sant'Apollonare Nuove. "Even Agnellus in the 9th century knows the lighthouse, although the city had supposedly fallen into ruins in the late 6th century."[254]

Andrea Agnellus (ca. 800-850) was a cleric from Ravenna who wrote the history of Ravenna from the beginning of the Empire to his time. After Vespasian (69-79 AD), the emperor of the martyrdom of Peter, Agnellus doesn't report anything before events dated 500 years later. He writes about saint Apollinaris being sent to Ravenna by saint Peter to found the church of Ravenna, then about the construction of Ravenna's first church (Sant'Apollinare dated 549 AD), without apparently being aware that half a millennium separated the two. Again, we see here how historians do violence to their sources by inserting phantom times into their chronicles. According to Heinsohn, only approximately 130 years passed between Vespasian and Agnellus.

Charlemagne and the European Dark Ages

In the footsteps of Illig and Niemitz, Heinsohn notes that Charlemagne's residence at Ingelheim is built like a Roman villa dating from the 2nd and not from the 9th century CE. As noticed in a website dedicated to the building, it "was not fortified. Nor was it built on a naturally protected site, which was usually necessary and customary when building castles." Heinsohn comments: "It was as if Charlemagne did not understand the vagaries of his own period, and was behaving like a senator still living in the Roman Empire. He insisted on Roman rooftiles but forgot the defenses. Was he not just great but also insane?"[255] No medieval fortification has been found that could be attributed to Charlemagne or any of the Carolingians.

Archaeologists excavating Ingelheim, we are told, were "staggered by a building complex that — down to the water supply, and up to the roofing — was 'based on antique designs', and, therefore, appears to be a reincarnation of 700-year-older Roman outlines from the 1st to 3rd c. CE."[256] The same is true of his Aachen residence (chapel excluded): "Excavators are realizing that Aachen's Imperial Antiquity and Aachen's Early Middle Ages cannot have followed each other at a distance of 700 years, but must have existed simultaneously. This seems incredible, but the material findings, down to the floor tiles, speak with unmistakable clarity: Aachen's Roman sewer system is so well intact that the early medieval Aacheners 'tied themselves to the Roman sewer system.' The same applies to transport routes: 'A continuous use from Roman times also applies to large parts of the inner city road and path network. ... The Roman road, which has already been documented in the Dome-*Quadrum* [Palatinate ensemble] in northeast-southwest orientation, was used until the late Middle Ages'."[257]

As mentioned earlier, Heinsohn objects to Illig and Niemitz's conclusion of the non-existence of Karlus Magnus, on the ground of the great number of coins bearing his name. However, he adds, "These coins are sometimes surprising because they may be found lumped together with Roman coins that are 700 years older."[258] Deleting 700 years solves this problem, and at the same time matches Charlemagne's palaces with 2nd/3rd century Roman architecture. The Carolingian era that precedes immediately the Tenth Century Collapse is the era of the Roman Empire. "Today's researchers see Charlemagne as the promoter of a restoration of the Roman Empire (*restitutio imperii*). They see his time as an ingenious and conscious renaissance of a perished civilization. Charlemagne himself, however, knows nothing about such notions. ... Nowhere does he proclaim that he lives many centuries after the glories of imperial Rome."[259]

Just like "Carolingian architects erected buildings and water pipes in the early Middle Ages that were similar in form and technology to those of Imperial Antiquity," so "Carolingian authors wrote in the early Middle Ages in the Latin style of Imperial Antiquity." Thus, Alcuin of York (*Flaccus Albinus Alcuinus*, 735-804 AD) brought back to life at the court of Charlemagne the classical Latin of Imperial Antiquity (1st-3rd century), down to calligraphic style, after many dark centuries.[260] Alcuin also wrote *Propositiones ad acuendos iuvenes,* which is seen as the earliest general survey of mathematical problems in Latin. "We do not understand how Alcuin could learn mathematics and write it down in Ciceronian Latin after the crises of the 3rd and 6th century, when there were no more teachers from Athens, Constantinople and Rome to instruct him."[261]

Even Charlemagne's biography, Eginhard's *Vita Karoli,* imitates the style of Suetonius (1st-2nd century), in form and in substance, borrowing at least 112 narrative motifs from Suetonius' Life of Augustus. Louis Halphen, scholar and editor of this text, writes that Eginhard wanted to "give us, as much as possible, feature for feature, a replica of the details of the Roman historian," only improved at Charlemagne's advantage. He followed Suetonius "so faithfully" and took up "with such servility the expressions familiar to the Latin historian that the *Life of Charlemagne* often appears more as the thirteenth 'Life of the Caesars' than as an original work."[262] Consequently, even if the existence of Charlemagne is attested, the value of his biography is highly questionable. More importantly, one must ask whether the *Vita Karoli* and the *Vita divi Augusti* were not written during the same period. It seems all the more likely since Suetonius' earliest surviving manuscript, dated from "late in the 8th century or very early in the 9th," has been determined to be "the archetype of all the extant manuscripts," and therefore plausibly the original work.[263]

Heinsohn shows that many Carolingian "Charles" appear to have the same signature and may be one and the same, although Heinsohn "has not come to a final view on how many Carolinginan Carolus rulers have to be retained."[264] Below are two signatures of Charlemagne on the left, two signatures of Charles the Simple on the right, and coins with signatures of Charles the Bald and Charles the fat.

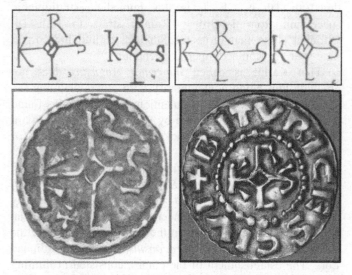

It must be noted that Karlus is the Latin form of Karl, a Slavic noun meaning "king", hardly a personal name. Heinsohn remarks: "There have been, we are told, two Frankish lords by the name of Pepin in the territory of *Civitas Tungrorum* (roughly the diocese of Liège). Each had a son named Charles. One was Charles Martel, the other Charlemagne. Each Charles waged one war against the Saracens on the French-Spanish border, and ten wars against the Saxons. ... This author sees both Pepins, as well as both Charles', as *alter egos*."[265] Moreover, Heinsohn recently suggested that: "Stratigraphically ..., Charlemagne and

Louis [the Pious] do not belong to the 8th/9th century, but to the 9th/10th century. They live through the turmoil of the plague of Marcus Aurelius and Commodus of the late 2nd century."[266]

According to Heinsohn, Charlemagne, known as Flavius Anicius Carolus to Alcuin,[267] belongs to Roman Antiquity. He was not the architect of a Roman and Latin *renovatio*, but "blossomed within the Roman realm of the later 2nd c. CE that, stratigraphically, is succeeded by the Ottonians in the 10th/11th c. CE. It is this immediate stratigraphic succession from 1st-3rd c. Roman strata to 10th/11th Ottonian strata that turns the 8th-10th c. into the correct time-span for Rome's imperial splendour."[268]

That Karlus is called *Imperator Augustus* does not preclude him being contemporary with others claiming the same title in Italy. Heinsohn mentions that gold coins found in Ingelheim "caused surprise by the imperial diadem worn by Charles making him look like a junior partner of Rome."[269]

In any case, the objection that there could not have been several emperors reigning at the same time is easily overcome: *imperator* was a military title bestowed by legions to victorious commanders. "During the Republican period, many persons received the *imperium:* they were the army generals in chief, the *proconsuls*," explains Ferdinand Lot. "The establishment of the empire consisted in limiting to one person only to whom was conferred the *imperium,* and to confer it for the rest of his life."[270] But that was the theory; in practice, the title was often claimed by several chiefs with local authority. Even the title *Augustus,* which had a quasi religious meaning, was overused. In a 124-page article date 2021, Heinsohn lists ten self-proclaimed emperors during the same period as Diocletian (284-305 AD) — Carinus, Sabinus Iulianus, Caius Amandus, Lucius Domitianus, Achilleus, Eugenius, Maximinian, Carausius, Alectus, Iulianus, Constantius I — and twenty during the time of Constantine the Great (306-337 AD) — Valerius

Constantinus, Galerius, Valerius Severus, Maxentius, Maximinian, Romulus, Lucius Alexander, Licinius, Candidianus, Bassianus, Licinius II, Galerius Daia, Valerius Valens, Crispus, Constantinus Iunior, Marcius Martinianus, Constantius II, Calocaerus, Dalmatius, Hannibalianus.[271]

Saxon England

Throughout his articles, Heinsohn mentions many European cities where archaeologists fail to find urban structures for 700 years between Imperial Antiquity and the Early Middle Ages leads. For Turicum (Zürich/Switzerland), for example, it is claimed by Reinhold Kaiser: "Due to the archaeological findings, a destruction of the settlement structures in Zurich can be ruled out. The Roman settlement [of the 2nd century] probably hasn't changed much until the early Middle Ages [of the 9th century]. Roman roads, buildings and infrastructure continued to be used" 700 years later. Heinsohn comments: "Respect must be paid to the Zürich excavators for being straightforward about the absence of building activities for 700 years."[272]

Saxons are said to start taking over England in 410 AD, yet archaeologists cannot find any trace of them in that period. Saxon houses and sacral buildings are missing; there is no trace of their agriculture, and not even of their pottery.[273] Heinsohn solves this problem by suggesting that the earliest Anglo-Saxons of the Early Middle Ages (8th-10th century) were contemporaries of Roman Imperial Antiquity (1st-3rd century); "that would mean that Romans and Anglo-Saxons had fought simultaneously and in competition with each other for control of Celtic Britain."[274]

Although the Anglo-Saxons are recognized, from the written sources they left, to have had a highly educated elite, they have failed to leave any material trace between about 400 AD and the 10th century, that is, for 700 years. Heinsohn quotes medieval historian Robin Fleming, from a 2016 lecture titled "Vanishing Plants, Animals, and Places: Britain's Transformation from Roman to Medieval":

"Roman conquerors introduced many — perhaps as many as 50 — new and valuable food plants and animals (such as the donkey) to its province of Britannia, where these crops were successfully cultivated for some 300 years. ... Following the collapse of Roman rule after 400 AD, almost all of these food plants vanished from Britain, as did Roman horticulture itself. Post-Roman Britons ... suddenly went from gardening to foraging. Even Roman water mills vanished from British streams. But similar mills came back in large numbers in the 10th and 11th centuries, along with Roman food plants and farming techniques."[275]

In Winchester, the city of Alfred the Great (871-899 AD), no archaeology remains has been found that match his reign. "Nobody knows where the Anglo-Saxon king was able to hold court. Although some scholars try to resort to the idea of a mobile court with no fixed capital anywhere on the British Isles in the 8th to early 10th c. period, the sources give no hint of such homeless rulers. They describe Venta Belgarum/Winchester as the unchallenged capital of Wessex. Since there are no building strata in 9th c. Venta Belgarum/Winchester, the mobile court theory would have to be expanded to a mobile nation theory because Afred's bureaucrats as well as his subjects are without fixed homesteads, too. Yet, is it possible that entire nations have always been on the move without leaving traces?"[276]

Archaeologists do find an abundance of buildings in Winchester, but they are in typical 2nd-century Roman style, and, unlike in Charlemagne's case, archaeologists see them as genuinely 2nd century rather than imitations of 2nd century. "Yet, the Roman period 2nd/3rd c. building stratum with Roman town houses (domus), temples, and public buildings on a forum with Jupiter column ... is contingent with Winchester's 10th/11th c. building stratum." "There are no strata anywhere between the 3rd and the 11th c. to accommodate the king's 9th c. palace. Yet, there is a 2nd/3rd c. Roman period palace in Winchester for which no one claims ownership."[277] Therefore, according to Heinsohn, the 2nd/3rd c. building stratum belongs to the period of

Alfred. This is also consistent with the Roman style of Alfred's coins (as is the case with Charlemagne's).

The city of London offers Heinsohn another opportunity to show the absurdity of the conclusions that archaeologists adopt, in contradiction to the evidence, only to satisfy historians. The archaeological site of Lundenwic was an agrarian settlement located 1.5 kilometers from Londinium (in today's London's Covent Garden area). Both sites are stratigraphically at the same depth, and both are buried under a black earth that testifies to the same catastrophic end. And yet, historians separate their destructions by 700 years: Lundenwic disappeared in the 930s, they say, but Londinium in the 230s. No trace of settlement is identified in Lundenwic before 700, but the road that connects Lundenwic to the Roman city of Londinium, although intact, is believed to be of Roman times. According to Heinsohn, the two sites were destroyed at the same time, possibly following the passage of comet Swift-Tuttle.[278] "The most amazing thing about Lundenwic is that, like Londinium, but 700 years later, it collapses under dark earth. ... It is also astonishing that in Lundenwic the dark earth layers from Londinium's 3rd century cannot be found, while in Londinium the dark earth layers of Lundenwic from the early 10th century left no traces."[279] "If our textbook chronology did not forbid it, then the earliest Lundenwic Anglo-Saxons of the Early Middle Ages (8th-10th century) could have lived at the same time as the Romans of Imperial Antiquity (1st-3rd century)."[280] This is the only possible conclusion in view of the physical evidence, according to Heinsohn. Textbook chronology, therefore, is wrong.

Heinsohn's theory of the contemporaneity of the Early Middle Ages and Roman Antiquity solves the riddle of the legendary King Arthur: "The Celtic ruler Arthur of Camelot, active in a time when Saxons and Romans are simultaneously and competitively at war to conquer England, finds his *alter ego* in *Aththe-Domaros of Camulodunum*, the finest Celtic military leader in the period of Emperor Augustus, whose archeological evidence moves to a stratigraphy-based date of c. 670s-710s AD." "Camelot, Chrétien de Troyes' [c. 1140-1190 AD] name for Arthur's Court, is derived directly from Camelod-unum, the name of Roman Colchester."[281] Thus both Arthur of Camelot and Aththe of Camulodunum, by reuniting, come out of obscurity. This is a good illustration of the way Heinsohn, rather than extinguishing parts of history, brings them into the light of history.

The Vikings of the 8th century were contemporary with the Franks and Saxon invaders: "1st-3rd as well as 4th-6th c. Scandinavians were the same people we call Vikings today. The evidence that stratigraphically belongs only to their 8th-10th c. period has been spread over the entire 1st millennium to fill a 1,000 year time span whose construction is neither understood nor challenged."[282] "Viking 9th c. longboats with square sails are in actual fact found at the same stratigraphic depth as Roman longboats with square sails. The latter are wrongly dated 700 years too early to the 2nd c. CE. Therefore, the Scandinavians' supposed 700 year delay in all major fields of development, like towns, ports, breakwaters, kingship, coinage, monotheism, and sailing ships, is derived from chronological ideas that make the Roman period some 700 years older than stratigraphy allows."[283]

Similar problems are found throughout the lands of Franks, Saxons and Slavs — that is, in the regions where archaeological finds are generally dated to the Early Middle Ages. Thus, the cities of Pliska and Preslav in Bulgaria, supposedly built in the 9th century, are entirely consistent with 1st-3rd century Roman architecture and technology. "The eternal controversies between different Bulgarian schools of archaeology about whether Pliska and Preslav belong to Antiquity, Late Antiquity or the Early Middle Ages could never come to a conclusion because all of them are right."[284]

Heinsohn's shortened chronology of the first millennium can potentially solve fundamental inconsistencies in the history of many regions of the globe. It explains, for example, "why the invention of hand-made paper takes about 700 years to spread from China to east and west." "The enigmatic absence of paper in Japan, so close to China, up to the 8th century AD, when it was suddenly produced in 40 provinces, can be explained, too, by taking into account that the Han stratigraphically are some 700 years younger than in textbook chronology."[285] Other problems include the fact that Han and Tang art are hardly indistinguishable.

The Cataclysmic hypothesis

Heinsohn links with the cataclysmic paradigm pioneered by Immanuel Velikovsky, a Russian-born scientist, author in 1950 of *Worlds in Collision* (Macmillan), followed by *Ages in Chaos* and *Earth in Upheaval* (Doubleday, 1952 and 1956). Although Velikovsky's books were then severely attacked by the scientific community, his hypothesis of a major cataclysm caused by the tail of a giant comet about ten thousand years ago has been vindicated. Even his theory that the comet settled as planet Venus now sounds less farfetched than it first appeared, for it has been reported recently that "Venus sports a giant, ion-packed tail,"[286] and that it "behaves like a comet."[287] Velikovsky is given due credit by astronomer James McCanney in *Planet-X, Comets & Earth Changes.*[288]

There is a growing consensus that the sudden drop of global temperatures that marked the beginning of the geological era of the Younger Dryas 12,000 years ago started with a comet impact that blew large amounts of dust and ashes into the atmosphere, eclipsing the sun for years. This catastrophic comet and later ones may have formed the basis for the worldwide myths about flying and fire-breathing dragons (read here).

For the first millennium AD, Heinsohn gathers evidence of three major civilization collapses caused by cosmic catastrophe followed by plague, in the 230s, the 530s and the 930s, and argues that they are one and the same, described differently in Roman, Byzantine, and Medieval sources.[289]

The first of these cataclysms caused the "Crisis of the Third Century" that started in the 230s. Textbook history defines it primarily as "a period in which the Roman Empire nearly collapsed under the combined pressures of barbarian invasions and migrations into the Roman territory, civil wars, peasant rebellions, political instability" (Wikipedia). Disease played a major role, most notably with the Plague of Cyprian (c. 249-262), originating in Pelusium in Egypt. At the height of the outbreak, 5,000 people were said to be dying every day in Rome (Kyle Harper, *The Fate of Rome: Climate, Disease, and the End of an Empire,* Princeton UP, 2017). Although Latin sources make no mention of it, the massive damage observed by archaeologists in several cities suggest that the crisis was triggered by a cosmic cataclysm. In Rome, "Trajan's market — the commercial heart of the known world — was massively damaged and never repaired again. All eleven aquaeducts were destroyed. The first was not repaired before 1453."[290] As illustrated above, thick layers of so-called "dark earth" are found immediately above the 3rd century, with no new construction above before the 10th century. This situation, which is repeated in many other Western cities such as London, is generally interpreted as proof that the land was converted to arable and pastoral use or abandoned entirely for seven centuries. But it is more likely that the mud resulted primarily from a cosmic cataclysm.

Three hundred years after the Third Century Crisis in Italy, the Easter Empire was impacted by identical phenomena, whose effect, notes historian of Late Antiquity Wolf Liebeschuetz, "was like the crisis of the third century."[291] A climatic disaster is documented by ancient historians of that period, such as Procopius of Caesarea, Cassiodorus, or John of Ephesus. Procopius (already quoted in the previous chapter) writes that in the tenth year of Justinian (536), "the sun gave forth its light without brightness, like the moon, during this whole year." This led to "a pestilence, by which the whole human race came near to being annihilated." John of Ephesus writes: "the sun became dark and its darkness lasted for eighteen months. ... As a result of this inexplicable darkness, the crops were poor and famine struck." To explain this *Late Antique Little Ice Age (LALIA),* some scientists like David Keys hypothesize massive volcanic irruptions (*Catastrophe: An Investigation into the Origins of the Modern World,* Balanine, 1999, and the Channel 4 documentary based on it, titled "The Mystery of 536 AD: The Worst Climate Disaster in History").[292] Others see "a comet impact in AD 536" causing a plunge in temperatures by as much as 5.4 degrees Fahrenheit for several years, leading to the crop failures that brought famine to the Roman Empire. Its weakened inhabitants soon became vulnerable to diseases.[293] In 541, bubonic plague struck the Roman port of Pelusium, exactly like Cyprian's Plague 300 years earlier, this time spreading to Constantinople, with some 10,000 people dying daily in Justinian's capital alone, according to Procopius. In the words of John Loeffler, "How Comets Changed the Course of Human History": "The terrified citizens and merchants fled the city of Constantinople, spreading the disease further into Europe, where it laid waste to communities of famished Europeans as far away as Germany, killing anywhere from a third to a half of the population"[294] (watch also Michael Lachmann's BBC documentary "The Comet's Tale").[295]

According to Heinsohn, the Western collapse of the third century and the Eastern collapse of the sixth century are both identical with the "Tenth Century Collapse" starting in the 930s.[296] This civilizational collapse is documented by archaeology in peripheral parts of the Empire: "Widespread destructions from Scandinavia to Eastern Europe and the Black Sea are dated to the end of the Early Middle Ages (930s CE). The disaster struck in territories where no devastations appear to have occurred during the 'Crisis of the Third Century', or the 'Crisis of the Sixth Century'.[297] Archaeology shows that Austria, Poland, Hungary, Bulgaria were also hit in the early 10th century, as well as Slovak and Czech territories. Bulgarian metropolis Pliska basically disappeared, strangled by a considerable amounts of erosion material (colluvium), also known as "black earth". All Baltic ports suddenly and mysteriously "undergo discontinuity."[298]

What Heinsohn calls the "Tenth Century Collapse" is well known to historians of the Middle Ages, but generally attributed to invasions. Mark Bloch wrote about it in his classic work *Feudal Society* (1940):

> "From the turmoil of the last invasions, the West emerged covered with countless scars. The towns themselves had not been spared — at least not by the Scandinavian — and if many of them, after pillage or evacuation, rose again from their ruins, this break in the regular course of their life left them for long years enfeebled. ... Along the river routes the trading centres had lost all security ... Above all, the cultivated land suffered disastrously, often being reduced to desert. ... Naturally the peasants, more than any other class, were driven to despair by these conditions. ... The lords, who derived their revenues from the land, were impoverished."[299]

This upheaval marked the end of the ancient world and was followed by the emergence of the feudal world. Heinsohn remarks: "The Tenth Century Collapse ran its lethal course closer to the present than any other world-shaking event in human history. However, it is the least researched, too. ... We do not yet know what could have been powerful enough to bring about such a mind-boggling transformation of our planet. Though it must have been enormous we still cannot reconstruct the cosmic scenario."[300] This is because most sources dealing with the catastrophe have been shifted backward. Yet the few Western chronicles that we have for the 11th century do inform us. Such is the case of the chronicle of the monk

Rodulfus Glaber, writing between 1026 and 1040, which I quoted in the introduction (p. 10).

The birth of AD chronology

The confused perspective of eleventh-century men on earlier ages, that Patrick Geary analyses in *Phantoms of Remembrance* (see the introduction p. 9), can account for the chronological distortions that later made it into history books. Within a few generations, what Rodulfus Glaber still calls "the Roman world," destroyed by cataclysms, plague and famine only decades before his time, was idealized and pushed back in almost mythical times.

This coincides with the rise of Christianity, heavily dominated by apocalypticism in its infancy. In Matthew 24:6-8, when Jesus' disciples asked him: "Tell us, when is this going to happen, and what sign will there be of your coming (*parousia*) and of the end of the world?" he answered: "There will be famines and earthquakes in various places. All this is only the beginning of the birthpangs."[301] "In the minds of survivors," Heinsohn writes, "the ancient gods had failed, but the apocalyptic books of the Bible had been proven right. Spontaneous conversions to the various Judaism-derived sects quickly increased throughout the empire."[302] The Book of Revelation sounded like a summary of the conflagrations just passed:

> "A mighty earthquake took place, and the sun became black like animal hair sack-cloth, and the full moon became like blood, and the stars of heaven fell to the earth ... And the kings of the earth, and the great people and the generals and the rich and the powerful, and everyone, slave and free, hid themselves in the caves, and among the rocks of the mountains. ... There came hail and fire mixed with blood, and it was rained on the earth. And one third of the earth was burned up, and one third of the trees were burned up, and all the green grass was burned up. Something like a huge mountain burning with fire was hurled into the sea. ... A huge star fell from heaven, burning like a lamp, and it

fell on a third of the rivers, and on the sources of the waters." (from *Revelation of John*, chapters 6 and 8)

Heinsohn suggests that the Book of Revelation directly influenced the chronological shift, because its chapter 20 postulates a thousand period between Jesus and the catastrophe: "Then I saw an angel coming down from heaven. / He took hold of the dragon, / Satan, and chained him for 1,000 years. / He could not fool the nations anymore until the 1,000 years were completed." Church father Cyprianus (200-258 AD, i.e. 900-958 in revised chronology), a survivor of the catastrophe in his heavily hit city of Carthage, wrote: "Our Lord has foretold all this. War and famine, earth quakes and pestilence will occur everywhere" (*On Mortality*).[303] Rodulfus Glaber also wrote at the end of book 2: "All this accords with the prophecy of St John [Revelation 20:7], who said that the Devil would be freed after a thousand years." Heinsohn suggests Michael Psellos (c. 1018-1078 AD), author of the *Chronographia,* as the main engineer of the chronological shift.[304]

To understand more precisely the role played by Christianity in the chronological reset, we would need a clear vision of the history of early Christianity, which we don't have. What is almost certain is that, contrary to what Church historians have written, the Roman world was not dominated by Christianity until the eleventh-century Gregorian Reform. Excavations of Carolingian tombs cast doubt on the Christian religion of that age: "excavators recently analyzing the contents of 96 Carolingian burials from 86 different locations (dated 751-911, but mostly from the time of Charlemagne and Louis the Pious), were shocked by an extremely widespread practice resembling Charon's obol. That payment was used as a means of bribing the legendary ferryman for passage across the Styx, the river that divided the world of the living from the world of the dead."[305] Even more puzzling — but logical within the Heinsohnian paradigm —, some of those coins are Roman coins.

One likely factor in the chronological confusion of the eleventh century, leading to the stretch of 300 years into a millennium, came from the traditional Roman computation. Roman historians counted years *ab urbe condita* ("since the foundation of the city"), abbreviated AUC. A monk named Dionysius Exiguus determined that Jesus' birth took place in 753 AUC. That means that 1000 AUC falls on 246 AD, during the Third Century Crisis. People living soon after the cataclysm (like Dionysius)[306] believed they were living around 1000 AUC. They could easily be led to believe that they really lived 1000 years after Christ. It has actually been suggested that the "Dominus" in *Anno Domini* originally meant Romulus, the founder of Rome. Changing Romulus into Christ would have been easy since both legendary figures have similar mythical attributes. Like Christ, Romulus suffered a sacrificial death, and then the Romans "began to cheer Romulus, like a god born of a god, the king and the father of the city, imploring his protection, so that he should always protect his children with his benevolent favor" (Titus Livy, *History of Rome* I.16). (Whether we take the resemblance between Romulus and Christ as another clue that Livy is a medieval or Renaissance fabrication makes little difference.) At some stage, people were led by the Church to change their notion of living one millennium after Romulus into the notion of living one millennium after Christ. This shift was part and parcel of the Christianization process: just like the Church Christianized many Pagan gods, holy places and holy days, it Christianized AUD into AD. The confusion was facilitated by the fact that AUC was still used in the eleventh century (some chroniclers such as Ademar of Chabannes also counted years in *annus mundi*, based on biblical chronology).

Since, according to Dionysius, Jesus was born in 753 AUC, the confusion of AUC with AD added 753 years, which is approximately the length of phantom time added into the first millennium according to Heinsohn. The Church was then too happy to fill in the vacuum and make itself look older than it was, with forgeries such as *Liver Pontificalis,* the *Donation of Constantine,* and the *pseudo-Isidorian decretals.* Papal clerics imposed their millennium-long Christian history, when in reality, their Christ had been crucified (under Augustus) only 300 years before Gregory VII (1073-1085).

Conclusion

Heinsohn's theory still leaves many unanswered questions, but it solves a few crucial problems. I have introduced some of these problems in the first two chapters of this book.

In chapter 1, I agreed with Polydor Hochart's objection to the possibility that books from Imperial Rome were preserved until the 14th-15th century, when Florentine humanists later discovered them in the attics of European monasteries, because monks had copied them in the 9th, 10th or 11th century. Christian monks copying pagan works on expensive parchments is just too unlikely. Rather, we have every reason to believe that, whenever they got their hands on such books, monks either destroyed them or scrapped them to reuse the parchment. From the incongruity of the common assumption, Hochart concluded that most of this Roman literature was late medieval or Renaissance forgeries. But Heinsohn's revised chronology now points to an alternative solution: the original composition of these works (1st century) and their medieval copies (9th century at the earliest) are not separated by seven centuries or more, but by one or two centuries at the most. The 9th century still belonged to Roman times, and Christianity was then in its infancy. The seven centuries that our Benedictine monks are supposed to have spent copying them again and again, in defiance to their sacred duty to burn them, never existed. That doesn't eliminate suspicion of Medieval or Renaissance fraud, but that reduces it. We can now read Roman sources with a different perspective.

In chapter 2, I focused on Church history and agreed with Jean Hardouin (1646-1729), the Jesuit librarian who came to the frightening conclusion that all the works ascribed to Augustine (AD 354-430), Jerome of Stridon (AD 347-420), Ambrose of Milan (c. AD 340-397), and many others, could not have been written before the 11th or 12th century, and were therefore forgeries. We can now consider that Hardouin was both right and wrong. He was right in estimating these works much younger than officially claimed (though perhaps wih some exaggeration), but he was not necessarily right in concluding that they were forgeries; if Augustine, Jerome and Ambrose really belong, in stratigraphic time, to the end of the Early Middle Ages at the earliest, it is no wonder they are attacking the same heresies as the medieval Church who promoted them.

CHAPTER 5
Islamic chronology and geography

"Despite the best efforts of generations of distinguished Arabists, the history of the Arabs before Islam remains exasperatingly obscure," wrote Harvard scholar Barry Hoberman, managing editor of *Biblical Archaeology*.[307] Arabs themselves, when trying to tell their pre-Islamic history, "could offer no dating system of their own, and only very partial historiographical content focused on the background to Muhammad," notes Garth Fowden in *Before and After Muhammad*. Pre-Islamic history is, for Muslims, only the world of *jahiliya*, that is, "ignorance", "barbarism" or "lawlessness". "Muslims still cannot narrate with any precision what happened before the *hijra* except by using BC/AD dates."[308] The early history of Islam is in no better state: a "revisionist school of Islamic Studies" is now shattering the canonical chronology.[309] Yet new difficulties appear in the process. This chapter will document some of the problems of Arabian history, and examine Heinsohn's solutions based on his "stratigraphically corrected" (SC) chronology of the first millennium.

The Heinsohnian hypothesis

Let's recap. According to Heinsohn, the standard view of the first millennium C.E. is an arbitrary construct that doesn't stand up to modern scientific archaeological evidence. It is too long by some 700 phantom years. In reality, the period from the first Roman Emperor Augustus to the traditional *Anno Domini* 1000 lasted only about 300 years. The Crisis of the Third Century, beginning at the end of the Severan Dynasty in the 230s, coincides with the Tenth-Century Collapse starting in the 930s.

The distortion resulted from an accumulation of errors and forgeries from the post-collapse centuries, when the reckoning in *Anno Domini* became commonly used in manuscripts. It was normalized in the 16th and 17th centuries by scholars such as Joseph Scaliger (1540-1609) or Denys Pétau (1583-1652), and then internationalized by Jesuits missionaries, starting with their takeover of Chinese scholarship.[310]

As a result of stretching 230 years into 930 years, simultaneous events happening in different parts of the world were artificially sequenced, leading ultimately to the modern division of the first millennium in three major time-blocks that need to be resynchronized: Imperial Antiquity (c. 1-230s), Late Antiquity (c. 300-640) and Early Middle Ages (c. 700-930). This explains why textbook history is distributed unevenly, most of the known events attributed to each time-block being localized in one of three geographical zones: for Imperial Antiquity, we know a lot about the Roman South-West, but little about the rest of Europe; for Late Antiquity, we know a lot about the Byzantine South-East, but little about Rome and Western Europe; and for the Early Middle Ages, we know a lot about the Germanic-Slavic North, but little about Rome or Constantinople.

Because they are captive to an erroneous chronology, archaeologists digging for first-millennium artifacts date their finds differently depending on the locations, even when these finds are at the same stratigraphic depth and exhibit the same technological advancement. To explain the resemblances of excavated materials supposedly separated by 300 or 700 years, they resort to theories of "revival", "imitation", *spolia* (recycled material), or — in utter desperation — "art collections". Typically, for example, Charlemagne is said to have built in 2nd-century Roman style with materials recycled from the 2nd century. He is also supposed to have revived the classical Latin of Imperial Antiquity (1st-3rd century), down to calligraphic style.[311]

The contemporaneity of Imperial Antiquity and Late Antiquity means that the start of Imperial Rome and the foundation of Constantinople are roughly contemporary; "a geographical sequence from west to east was turned into a chronological sequence from earlier to later."[312] However, Byzantine Late Antiquity cannot be simply superimposed on Roman Imperial Antiquity, because it is itself some 120 years too long, according to Heinsohn. The Byzantine segment from the rise of Justinian (527) to the death of Heraclius (641) was in reality shorter and overlaps with the period of Anastasius (491-518). "We know that stratigraphies dated to Late Antiquity (Dyrrachium, Alexandria etc.) lack about 120 years of archaeological substance. Thus, the conventional Late Antiquity period from the 290s to 640s AD has not 350, but only some 230 years with residential strata."[313]

The contemporaneity of Imperial Antiquity and the Early Middle Ages means that the peoples living North of the Danube and East of the Rhine did not suddenly emerge from their forest-dwelling primitivism 700 years after the expansion of the Roman Empire. The Saxons competed with the Romans for the conquest of Great Britain from the early Imperial era. Thus the semi-legendary Arthur of Camelot, first mentioned as *dux bellorum* in the *Historia Brittonum* (dated 829) can be reunited with his alter-ego, Aththe of Camulodunum, the Celtic military leader in the period of Augustus.[314] However, here again, the correspondence is not a straight one, because the Carolingian Empire, traditionally placed in 800-841, must be shifted to the 890s-930s (corresponding to the 190s-230s in Imperial Antiquity). "Charlemagne and Louis [the Pious] do not belong to the 8th/9th century, but to the 9th/10th century."[315] This is consistent with the appearance of Charlemagne in the *Chansons de Geste* in the late 11th century. One source of confusion is the multiplication of one Charles into many: Carolus Magnus is in fact identical to Carolus Simplex (898-929) and with other Charles in between.[316] "Stratigraphically

... these Frankish rulers belonged to the 890s to 930s CE. Their phase of the Early Middle Ages ran parallel with the Severan period (190s-230s) of Imperial Antiquity as well as with the decades of the Justinian Dynasty in Late Antiquity."[317]

In the second chapter, I argued that the standard history of the Roman Catholic Church amounts to a counterfeit autobiography, partly motivated by Rome's rivalry with Constantinople. It is impossible to reconstruct the real history of the Church before the 11th century from the literary sources that were fabricated or adulterated in ecclesiastical scriptoriums. J.M. Wallace-Hadrill wrote about St Benedict's life: "with no supporting evidence, narrative of this kind could contain almost no historical truth. We can take it on trust or not, as we feel inclined. Scholars have been generally disposed to accept it."[318] The same can be said of more central figures like Constantine the Great, whose life and religious policies are known almost exclusively from Eusebius, whose authorship is extremely controversial. The reason why scholars tend to take Eusebius' account at face value is that, without it, they simply could hardly write anything about Constantine.

Arguably Church history is biased to the point of inversion. For instance, a strong argument was made a long time ago by Walter Bauer that, contrary to the story propagated by the victorious Church, orthodoxy was preceded, not followed, by the great heresies.[319] As a result of the Catholic Church's falsification of its own history, its emergence as the ghost of the Roman Empire, with the pope taking over most of the prerogatives of the emperor — not just the title of *pontifex maximus,* but also imperial properties, public treasury, and even military affairs — remains largely obscure to historians.[320]

In Heinsohn's stratigraphically corrected chronology, the transition happened in the 11th century, during the Gregorian Reform, the "First European Revolution" as Robert I. Moore calls it.[321] This is only one century, not eight centuries, after the end of the Severan dynasty. This explains many strange anachronisms in ecclesiastical history, such as the formal adoption of the Nicene Creed in 1014, seven centuries after the Council that produced it (325), or the standardization in the 13th century of the Latin *versio vulgate* of the Bible commissioned to saint Jerome by Pope Damasus I (366-384). This also explains why Christian architecture and decorative styles of the 11th and 12th century are hard to distinguish from those of the 4th century, prompting scholars to speak of "a Paleo-Christian revival in Rome at the beginning of the 12th century."[322]

To understand the conversion of Rome to the cult of a Galilean Messiah, the background of the Severan emperors is an important clue. The founder of the dynasty, Septimius Severus, had married in Syria the daughter of a priest of the god Elagabal worshipped in Emesa (today's Homs in Syria). His wife Julia Domna played an active role in the empire, especially when their son, Caracalla, became emperor in 211 at 13 years of age. After her death, her younger sister Julia Maesa was sent back to Phoenicia, from where she plotted to place upon the throne her grandson Elagabalus, who had served since his early youth as head priest of Elagabal. The Syrian domination was continued by the thirteen-year reign of Alexander Severus, with whom the dynasty came to an end in 235. This period is covered by the historian Herodian of Syria, probably a member of Julia Domna's Eastern-oriented literary coterie — like Philostratus who wrote for her the *Life of Apollonius of Tyana*. Herodian's information on the god Elagabal (Latinization of the Arabic *Ilah Al-Gabal*, "God of the Mountain") is quite interesting:

> "A huge temple was erected to this god, lavishly decorated with gold, silver, and costly gems. Not only is this god worshipped by the natives, but all the neighboring rulers and kings send generous and expensive gifts to him each year. No statue made by man in the likeness of the god stands in this temple, as in Greek and Roman temples. The temple does, however, contain a huge black stone with a pointed end and round base in the shape of a cone. The

Phoenicians solemnly maintain that this stone came down from Zeus." (Book 5, chapter 3)

A black stone worshipped in Syria in the 3rd century provides an appropriate transition for the main subject of this chapter: Gunnar Heinsohn's solution to the problems facing historians of Arabia and Islam.

Heinsohn on Arabia and Islam

In Heinsohn's SC chronology, the rise of Christianity in the first three centuries AD and the rise of Islam from the 7th to the 10th century are roughly contemporary. Their six-century chasm is a fiction resulting from the fact that the rise of Christianity is dated in Imperial Antiquity while the rise of Islam is dated in the Early Middle Ages, two time-blocks that are in reality contemporary. The resynchronizing of Imperial Antiquity and Early Middle Ages provides a solution to some troublesome archaeological anomalies. One of them concerns the Nabataeans.

During Imperial Antiquity, the Nabataean Arabs dominated long distance trade. Their city of Petra was a major center of trade for silk, spice and other goods on the caravan routes that linked China, India and southern Arabia with Egypt, Syria, Greece and Rome. In 106 AD, the Nabataean Kingdom was officially annexed to the Roman Empire by Trajan (whose father had been governor of Syria) and became the province of *Arabia Petraea*. Hadrian visited Petra around 130 AD and gave it the name of *Hadriane Petra Metropolis*, imprinted on his coins. Petra reached its urban flowering in the Severan period (190s-230s AD).[323]

After that, Arabia recedes into darkness. We don't find Arab coins until the Islamic period, and hardly any written record. These Arab long-distance merchants, Heinsohn writes, "are supposed to have forgotten the issuing of coins and the art of writing (Aramaic) after the 1st century AD and only learned it again in the 7th/8th century AD (Umayyad Muslims)."[324] It is assumed that Arabs fell out of civilization after Hadrian, and only emerged back into it under Islam, with an incomprehensible scientific advancement. The extreme primitivism in which pre-Islamic Arabs are supposed to have wallowed, with no writing and no money of they own, "stands in stark contrast to the Islamic Arabs who thrive from the 8th century, [whose] coins are not only found in Poland but from Norway all the way to India and beyond at a time when the rest of the known world was trying to crawl out of the darkness of the Early Middle Ages."[325] Moreover, Arab coins dated to the 8th and 9th centuries are found in the same layers as imperial Roman coins. "The coin finds of Raqqa, for example, which stratigraphically belong to the Early Middle Ages (8th-10th century), also contain imperial Roman coins from Imperial Antiquity (1st-3rd century) and Late Antiquity (4th-7th century)."[326] "Thus, we have an impressive trove of post-7th c. Arab coins lumped together with pre-7th c. Roman coins of pre-7th c. Roman times. But we have no pre-7th c. Arab coins from the centuries of their close alliance with Rome in the pre-7th c. periods."[327]

The first Islamic Umayyad coins, issued in Jerusalem, "continue supposedly 700 years earlier Nabataean coins."[328] Often displaying Jewish menorahs with Arabic lettering, they differ very little from Jewish coins dated seven centuries earlier; we are dealing here with an evolution "requiring only years or decades, but not seven centuries."[329] Below are a Jewish Hasmonean coin dated 40-37 BC (left), and a Jerusalem Umayyad coin dated 8th century AD (right).

Architecture raises similar problems. Archaeologists have no way of distinguishing Roman and Byzantine buildings from Umayyad buildings, because "8th-10th Cent. Umayyads built in 2nd Cent. technology" and followed Roman models.[330] "How could the Umayyads in the 8th c. AD perfectly imitate late Hellenistic styles," Heinsohn asks, "when there were no specialists left to teach them such sophisticated skills?"[331]

Moreover, "Umayyad structures were built right on top of Late-Hellenistic structures of the 1st c. BCE/CE."[332] One example is "the second most famous Umayyad building, their mosque in Damascus. The octagonal structure of the so-called Dome of the Treasury stands on perfect Roman columns of the 1st/2nd century. They are supposed to be *spolia*, but ... there are no known razed buildings from which they could have been taken. Even more puzzling are the enormous monolithic columns inside the building from the 8th/9th c. AD, which also belong to the 1st/2nd century. No one knows the massive structure that would have had to be demolished to obtain them."[333]

Far from rejecting the Umayyads' servile "imitation" of Roman Antiquity, their Abbasid enemies resumed it: "8th-10th c. Abbasids bewilder historians for copying, right down to the chemical fingerprint, Roman glass." Heinsohn quotes from *The David Collection: Islamic Art / Glass*, 2014:

> "The millefiori technique, which takes its name from the Italian word meaning "thousand flowers", reached a culmination in the Roman period. ... The technique seems to have been rediscovered by Islamic glassmakers in the 9th century, since examples of millefiori glass, including tiles, have been excavated in the Abbasid capital of Samarra."[334]

Heinsohn's articles contain an abundance of quotes from archaeologists puzzled by the contradictions between their hard evidence and their received chronology, yet betraying their craft by yielding to the latter. Here is, for example, Heinsohn's illustrations of identical millefiori glass bowls

ascribed respectively to the 1st-2nd century Romans (left)
and to the 8th-9th century Abbasids (right).

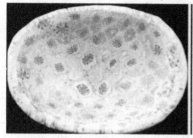 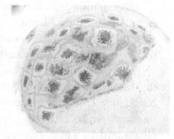

Heinsohn concludes that, "the culture of the Umayyads is
as Roman as the culture of early medieval Franks. Their
9th/10th century architecture is a direct continuation of the
2nd c. AD. The 700 years in between do not exist in
reality."[335] "The Arabs did not walk in ignorance without
coinage and writing for some 700 years. Those 700 years
represent phantom centuries. Thus, it is not true that Arabs
were backward in comparison with their immediate Roman
and Greek neighbours who, interestingly enough, are not on
record for having ever claimed any Arab backwardness. In
the stratigraphy of ancient sites, Arab coins are found at the
same stratigraphic depth as imperial Roman coins from the
1st to the early 3rd c. CE. Thus, the caliphs now dated from
the 690s to the 930s are actually the caliphs of the period
from Augustus to the 230s. The Romans from Augustus to
the 230s knew them as rulers of *Arabia Felix*."[336]

This would explain why archaeologists often find
themselves puzzled by the stratigraphy. For example, the
Israeli newspaper *Haaretz* reported (August 8, 2003) that
during a dig in Tiberias, archaeologist Moshe Hartal
"noticed a mysterious phenomenon: Alongside a layer of
earth from the time of the Umayyad era (638-750), and at
the same depth, the archeologists found a layer of earth from
the Ancient Roman era (37 B.C.E.-132). 'I encountered a
situation for which I had no explanation — two layers of

earth from hundreds of years apart lying side by side,' says
Hartal. 'I was simply dumbfounded.'"[337]

Heinsohn argues that the Umayyads of the Early Middle
Ages are not only identical with the Nabataeans of Imperial
Antiquity, but are also documented in the intermediate time-
block of Late Antiquity under the name of the Ghassanids.
"Nabataeans and Umayyads not only shared the same art,
the same metropolis Damascus, and the same stratigraphy,
but also a common territory that was home to yet another
famous Arab ethnicity that also held Damascus: the
Ghassanids. They served as Christian allies of the
Byzantines during Late Antiquity (3rd/4th to 6th c. AD).
Yet, they were already active during Imperial Antiquity (1st
to 3rd c. AD). Diodorus Siculus (90-30 BC) knew them as
Gasandoi, Pliny the Elder (23-79 AD) as *Casani*, and
Claudius Ptolemy (100-170 AD) as *Kassanitai*."[338] In the
Byzantine period, the Ghassanid caliphs had "the same
reputation for anti-trinitarian monotheism as the Abbasid
Caliphs now dated to 8th/9th centuries."[339] They also, like
the Islamic Arabs, preserved some Bedouin customs such as
polygamy.[340]

The triplication of the Western, Eastern and Northern
Roman empires, resulting from the desynchronization of
Antiquity, Late Antiquity, and Early Middle Ages, is
therefore reproduced in the Arab world, with the arbitrary
distinction of the Nabataeans (1st century), the Ghassanids
(3rd/4th-6th century), and the Umayyads (7th/8th century),
all of them having similar architecture and art.

All three are supposed to have moved toward
monotheism. An obscure connection is often recognized
between the Ghassanids' monophysitism and the Umayyads'
religion which may be called proto-Islam since Islam as we
know it was standardized by their conquerors, the Abbasids.

The Revisionist School in Islamic Studies

It is today admitted by many Western scholars that
Islamic scriptures, including the Quran, are of a later date

than claimed by the canonical account. It was under the Abbasid Caliphate (750-1258) that practically all traditional texts about Islam's beginnings were written, mostly after the 9th century and mostly outside Arabia, notably in Iraq. As the victorious party in the conflict with the Umayyads, the Abbasids had great interest in legitimizing their rule, and took sweeping measures to destroy sources that contradicted their narrative. It was under the Abbasids that the Quran reached its final stage, and that copies reflecting earlier stages were forever lost.

Another well-known aspect of early Islam is its Jewish background, best illustrated by the central place of Abraham (Ibrahim) in the Quran, and the 135 mentions of Moses (Musa), followed by Joseph, David, Jonah and Solomon. Entire surahs (Quranic chapters) are devoted to biblical legends. "Islam developed against the background of an Arabia strongly under the influence of Judaism," states Gordon Newby in his respected *History of the Jews of Arabia* (1988).[341]

Christian influence on the formation of Islam is also obvious. Besides the many Quranic references to Jesus, Muhammad's canonical biography mentions Jewish Christians known as "Nazarenes" or "Nazoreans", believers in Christ who remained faithful to Moses' Torah. Living mainly in Syria and speaking Aramean dialects, they were opposed to Trinitarian Christology and regarded the deification of Christ as a pagan deviance. Günter Lüling has argued that "considerable parts of the Koran text itself were pre-Islamic Christian strophic hymns," and that the Meccan adversaries of Muhammad, the "*mushrikun*" ("associators"), were not polytheist pagans, as previously assumed, but Trinitarian Christians.[342]

John Wansbrough's research into the early Islamic manuscripts, including analysis of the repeated use of Judeo-Christian monotheistic imagery in the Quran, led him to the conclusion that Islam was born out of a mutation in what was originally a Judeo-Christian sect that spread to Arab territories but looked back toward Jerusalem. In 1977, Wansbrough's student Patricia Crone wrote with Michael Cook a book titled *Hagarism: The Making of the Islamic World*, which traces the origin of Islam in an attempt by Jewish exiles to recover Jerusalem from which they had been expelled in the 70s, and assigning to the Ishmaelites a share in God's promise to Abraham.[343]

From this perspective, the seven-century hiatus between the two episodes is quite extraordinary. Heinsohn's shortened chronology restores the continuity. According to him, messianic Jews who were ousted by Titus from Jerusalem did not wait for 30 generations in a state of coma, before suddenly waking up with renewed fervor and plans for the reconquest of their lost city.

Linguistic and philology concur. In 2000, a Syriac scholar using the pseudonym Christoph Luxenberg published *The Syro-Aramaic Reading of the Koran,* showing that the Quran emerged in a region linguistically Syro-Aramaic rather than Arabic. And according to Gerd-Rüdiger Puin, about twenty percent of the 6000 Quranic verses are originally written in Aramaic from the 1st/2nd century AD.[344] So on the one hand, recent scholarship has pushed the final redaction of the Quran forward into the 9th century, while on the other hand, the Quran is shown to be rooted in Syriac literature and liturgy of the 1st and 2nd century. That conundrum finds a solution in Heinsohn's SC chronology, which shifts forward the 2nd century of standard chronology immediately before the 9th century. What later turned into the new religion of Islam appears to have been originally a messianic movement for reclaiming Jerusalem, not seven centuries after the expulsion of the Jews by the Romans, but merely decades after.

Dan Gibson's geographical revisionism

As mentioned above, linguistic considerations point to a Syriac (Aramaic) rather than Arabic origin of the Quran. This in itself poses a challenge to the traditional geography

of Islam. But there are other reasons for questioning the
origin of Islam in the Hejaz. The identification of "Bakkah",
the home of Muhammad's Quraych tribe according to the
Quran, with the site of "Mecca" in Saudi Arabia (the two
names are extremely close in Arabic writing) doesn't really
add up. In *Meccan Trade and the Rise of Islam* (1987),
Patricia Crone showed that what is known today as Mecca
was neither an important trading center nor a pilgrimage
destination at the time of Muhammad, and that its barren
condition does not match at all the Quranic description of
Bakkah as a fertile city with fields, grass and even gardens.
Moreover, Mecca never had city walls, while Bakkah is
described as a fortified city.

In 2011, a book by Dan Gibson titled *Qur'ānic
Geography* expounded the groundbreaking theory that the
powerful Nabataean capital of Petra fits the Quranic
description of Bakkah, as well as many stories in early
Islamic history, while Mecca doesn't.[345] In 2017, Gibson
added to his argument with *Early Islamic Qiblas,* where he
shows, with unmistakable evidence on the ground, that the
Qibla (direction of prayer) in Umayyad mosques was Petra,
not Mecca. The Qibla was changed during the second
Islamic civil war by Abd Allah Ibn al-Zubayr, leader of a
dissident caliphate that took refuge in Mecca in 683. It was
Al-Zubayr who moved the Black Stone from Petra and built
for it a new Kaaba in Mecca. For a century after that, Islam
was split between Umayyad traditionalists who continued to
build their mosques facing Petra, and the Abbasid reformers
who built their mosques facing Mecca. However, after the
earthquake that devastated Petra's water systems in 713,
Petra was abandoned and slowly faded from memory. When
the Abbasids supplanted the Umayyads in the East in 750,
Petra and Mecca were merged in canonical historiography,
and an Arabian location was determined for other Quranic
locations such as Yathrib (Medina) and Khaybar, where
Muhammad dealt with Jewish communities. Gibson's
arguments are presented in the documentary film directed by

David Taylor, "The Sacred City: Discovering the Real Birthplace of Islam" (2016).[346]

Gibson's theory is fully compatible with the Jewish root of Islam highlighted by the revisionist school of Islamic Studies, because Jews are easier to find in the region of Petra than in the Hejaz. The Nabataeans had been allies of the Maccabees during their struggle against the Seleucid monarchs. Nevertheless, there were internal divisions among them, just like among the Judeans. And the Nabataean kings' later rivalry with the Hasmonean dynasty became a factor in the disorders that prompted Pompey's intervention. A Roman army besieged Petra, after which the Nabataean king Aretas III paid tribute, receiving in exchange formal recognition by the Roman Republic. Although Petra became a Hellenized Roman city, it certainly also harbored anti-Roman Arabs and a Jewish community simmering with messianic expectations.

Gibson's geographical revisionism also dovetails with Heinsohn's chronological revisionism, since both identify the Arabs who took over Jerusalem in the 8th-9th centuries with the rulers of Petra and Damascus. According to Heinsohn, the Roman conquest of Jerusalem in Imperial Antiquity and the Judeo-Arab conquest of Jerusalem in the Early Middle Ages belong to the same broad period. Let us take a closer look at the evidence in Jerusalem.

Archaeology in Jerusalem

One source of embarrassment for Jerusalem archaeologists is their inability to locate the Roman fort hosting the Tenth Legion after the city was destroyed by Titus in 70 CE. In *Aelia Capitolina–Jerusalem in the Roman Period, in Light of Archaeological Research* (Brill, 2020), Shlomit Weksler-Bdolah insists on this problem:

> "Surprisingly, despite the long duration of military presence in Jerusalem ... no archaeological remains have been attributed with certainty to the military camp and its site has not yet been identified." "One cannot

underestimate the difficulty caused by the absence of irrefutable evidence of the Roman army camp in Jerusalem. ... At this stage, there is no acceptable solution to the problem of the 'lack of remains'."[347]

On the other hand, archaeologists and the whole world know where once stood the Herodian temple that Titus' troops burnt down, for the walls of the "Temple Mount" are still standing. Oddly, this "Temple Mount" overlooking the city has the standard dimensions of a Roman fort. The solution is obvious: the esplanade that Muslims call the Al-Aqsa Compound was originally Fort Antonia, first built by Herod in honor of Antony, then used by the Tenth Legion. It was arbitrarily determined to be the location of the Temple by the first crusaders in the 11th century, and this mistaken attribution became so entrenched that no one dared question it. When the question was finally raised a few decades ago, it was hushed by the Israeli academic establishment, and would have remained a well-kept secret if not for Ernest L. Martin, who after working for five years with archaeologist Benjamin Mazar, published his unorthodox view in 1994 (see his drawing below).[348]

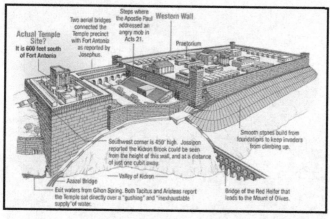

As Gregory Wesley Buchanan wrote in the *Washington Report on Middle East Affairs* in 2011, "While it has not been widely published, it assuredly has been known for more than 40 years that the 45-acre, well-fortified place that has been mistakenly called the 'Temple Mount' was really the Roman fortress — the Antonia — that Herod built."[349] The argument, based on literary sources and archaeological evidence, is presented by Bob Cornuke in a 30-minute film, "The Temple".[350]

This controversy has no direct bearing on chronology, other than to illustrate the state of confusion of archaeology in Jerusalem. What is directly supportive of Heinsohn's theory, however, is the accepted dating of the Western Wall, consisting of 45 stone courses, 28 of them above ground and 17 underground. The first seven visible layers, comprising very large stone blocks, are from the Herodian period. The four courses of medium-sized stones above them were added during the Umayyad period, while the small stones of the uppermost courses are of more recent date, especially from the Ottoman period. Do 700 years really separate the Herodian courses from the Umayyad courses?

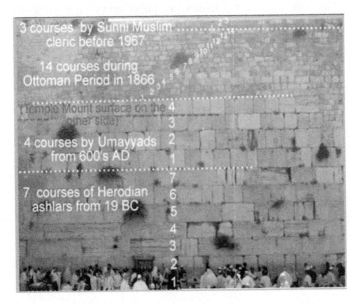

Heinsohn questions this assumption defended by archaeological architect Leen Ritmeyer: "Although Ritmeyer knows that the Umayyads have built directly on Jerusalem ruins of 70 AD, he believes that they have been waiting for over 600 years to do so. That is why the Temple Mount is said to have remained empty ('abandoned') until the 7th century."[351]

The Western Wall is not the only piece of evidence of a direct continuity between Romano-Herodian architecture and Umayyad architecture in Jerusalem. Archaeologist Orit Peleg-Barkat notes that, "the Umayyad builders used the fragments of Herodian architectural decoration as construction materials."[352] According to Heinsohn, "there are no series of settlement layers anywhere in Jerusalem which would be required to substantiate the centuries between Imperial Antiquity and the Early Middle Ages of the Umayyads. So, from a purely stratigraphic point of view, the Umayyads lived, at least since 70 AD, side by side with what is called the Jerusalem of Imperial Antiquity (1st-3rd c. AD)."[353]

This explains why the Umayyads actually called Jerusalem *Iliya*, as attested by their coins, seals and milestones. This is an Arabic form of the name that Hadrian had given the city in the 130s (*Aelia Capitolina*). Since that name is supposed to have been abandoned in between, scholars wonder why the Umayyads "revived" it; in reality, the Roman *Aelia* of Imperial Antiquity and the Muslim *Iliya* of the Early Middle Ages are one and the same.[354]

Our knowledge of the events of this period is too fragmentary and distorted by religious propaganda to reconstruct them with any precision. What seems quite certain, however, is that Jerusalem, like the rest of Syria, was inhabited by many Arabs. It is said that the Roman legions who fought for Rome in the 60s, were settled in the area, but according to Flavius Josephus these soldiers were mainly recruited in Syria, "from the kings in that neighborhood" (*Jewish Wars,* book III, chapter 1). Therefore, writes Heinsohn, "Arab Nabataean soldiers, not

men from Italy, conquered Jerusalem for Titus in 70 AD."
The construction of Hadrian's new city *Aelia Capitolina* in
the 130s was also the work of Arabs, who were master
builders (with renowned architects such as Apollodorus of
Damascus).[355]

Does that mean that the Roman subjugation of Jerusalem
with Arab mercenaries in the late 60s is identical with the
Muslim conquest of Jerusalem 700 years later? No. The
Arab mercenaries who fought for Rome against nationalist
Jews, then built *Aelia Capitolina* in honor of Hadrian,
cannot be identical with the Arabs who appropriated a
Jewish messianic movement and conquered the Levant for
themselves after defeating the Byzantine Romans at the
Battle of Yarmuk (in 636). Rather, the Arab conquest was a
reaction to the Roman conquest, as revisionist scholars
suggests — albeit failing to explain the 600 years delay.
Nevertheless, it is important to keep in mind that Arabs
lived in Jerusalem before they came to rule it under the
banner of Islam. And there is no reason to assume that Arab
alliances were uniform and stable. Depending on the
circumstances, they could fight either for or against the
Romans, and either with or against the Jews.

Moreover, there was no clear boundary between Jews
and their Arab neighbors before Islam. As Steve Mason
reminds us, "the *Ioudaioi* were understood until late
antiquity as an ethnic group comparable to other ethnic
groups, with their distinctive laws, traditions, customs, and
god. They were indeed Judaeans."[356] The Hebrew Bible
insists on their kinship with Arab tribes and nations such as
the Moabites, the Edomites, the Midianites, the Amalekites,
and the Ishmaelites — all descendants of Abraham.[357]
According to David Samuel Margoliouth, ancient Hebrew is
an Arabic dialect, and even Yahweh's name is Arabic
(*Relations Between Arabs and Israelites Prior to the Rise of
Islam,* 1921).[358]

Besides, Exodus 2-3 makes the Hebrews' conquest of
Canaan originate from the land of Midian, which roughly

corresponds to the Nabataeans' homeland. Moses was the son-in-law of a Midianite priest (*kohen*) and met Yahweh in Midian.[359] Of course, Moses is traditionally dated two millenniums before Muhammad. But the Exodus story, as we have it, may in fact date from the Hasmonean period, as "minimalist" biblical scholars now believe.[360] The Islamic conquest really seems like a remake of the Mosaic conquest from the same region, and both may be separated by just a couple of centuries; it is always about Arab nomads coveting the Fertile Crescent.

At any rate, during the formative years of Islam, Arabs and Jews were ethnically homogeneous. Only when asserting its autonomy did Islam self-consciously widen the gap between Jews and Arabs: this is illustrated by the shift in the direction of prayer from Jerusalem during Muhammad and the Rashidun caliphs, to Petra under the Umayyads, to Mecca under the Abbasids.

Islam and Christianity

If we look at the historical horizon of the Middle East from a Heinsohnian standpoint, we see the birth of Islam roughly contemporary with the birth of Christianity, and not separated by six or seven centuries. There is clear evidence that Islam arose in the context of the early doctrinal controversies surrounding the nature of Christ and the Trinity. Compressing the first millennium into roughly 300 years is not only compatible with the basic facts of religious history; it makes more sense of them.

Heinsohn identifies the monophysitism of the Ghassanids with the early Islam of the Umayyads.[361] Islam has also been tied to Arianism by Christian heresiologists. John of Damascus (c. 675-749) assumed that Muhammad devised "the heresy of the Ishmaelites" "after having conversed with an Arian monk." In the twelfth century, the Abbot of Cluny Peter the Venerable thought the same after studying the Latin translation of the Quran that he had commissioned.[362]

Strangely, Arianism left virtually no known material trace, even in Spain where it is supposed to have been the religion of the ruling Visigoths for three centuries. This is a great puzzlement for scholars like Ralf Bockmann ("The Non-Archaeology of Arianism," 2014), or Alexandra Chavarria Arnau ("Finding invisible Arians," 2017).[363] On the other hand, there is no contemporary written record of the Islamic conquest of Spain, leading some Spanish authors to claim that it never happened — as a military campaign.[364]

Arianism is the umbrella name given to the resistance against the full deification of the man Jesus. The opposite current that focuses on Christ as a divine entity falls under the broad denomination of Gnosticism. And here again, strange things are observed. Ewa Weiling-Feldthusen notes that there is in the long history of Gnosticism a "missing link", causing "the ever-ending discussions and controversies among scholars" about "the problem of how to fill the temporal gap between the occurrence of Manichaeism (app. third-sixth century) and Paulicianism (app. ninth century) in the European part of Byzantium."[365] Gnosticism was the most serious competitor to Catholicism during the first three centuries AD, but survived another seven centuries despite the fact that the Catholic Church had become all-powerful in the fourth century. Gnostic movements, covering a millennium in standard chronology — from Marcion's first compilation of Paul's epistles, to the crushing of the Bogomils' heirs in the south of France — appear as different waves of the same movement. Heinsohn has noted that the Paulicians, whose original stronghold was close to Paul's birthplace Tarsus, had as their spiritual leader a man who called himself Silvanus, a name also born by Paul's travelling companion (2Cor 1:19 ad 1Pet 5:12).[366]

Among the Eastern manifestations of Gnosticism, the "Sabeans" deserve special attention because they are mentioned in the Quran as one of the "peoples of the book," along the Jews and the Nazarenes. Their Arab name, "Subbas," means "Bathers" or "Baptists." They may be

affiliated to the Elkhasaites, the heterodox Jewish-Christian
movement where Mani grew up, according to the *Cologne
Mani Codex* (Manichaeism was still very influential in
Bagdad during the first four centuries of Islam).[367]

Here a digression about Mani, Manichaeism and
Gnosticism is in order. The standard view is that the first
Christian Gnostic was Marcion, whom Justin Martyr (100-
165) says was still living during his time. Then came Mani.
But Islamic sources, and particularly the biographer and
bibliographer Ibn al-Nadīm, who died in Baghdad in 995 or
998, places Mani before Marcion.[368] So does the sixth-
century Byzantine chronicler Malalas, placing Mani during
the reign of Nerva Augustus after Domitian ("During his
reign Manea appeared, preaching, teaching and attracting a
mob," X.54), and smearing Marcion as "a Manichaean"
(XI,19). Scholars assume that "his [Malalas'] account of
Mani himself is misplaced (X §54, Bo268)."[369] But that may
not be the case. Manichaeism may have preceded Christianity
in the Roman Empire. It may even have been the original
matrix of Christianity. Mani deemed himself "the apostle of
Jesus Christ." If you consider, in addition, that he was from a
Jewish Baptist sect (the Elchasites), and that a possible
etymology of *mani* is the Persian for "stone", then it becomes
tempting to speculate that Peter may be a duplicate of Mani.
That Mani had a mother named Maryam, twelve disciples, and
a death depicted as a crucifixion by his followers and comme-
morated by a sacred meal, allows for further speculations.[370]

Let us now go back to the Sabeans of the Quran. Besides
their identification to the Elkhasaites, from which came
Mani, they are also generally recognized as identical to the
Mandaeans (from *manda,* the Aramaic equivalent of the
Greek *gnosis*), who were until 2003 confined to a
community of thirteen thousand people in the South of Iraq.
Their sacred books are written in an Aramaic dialect bearing
much resemblance with the Aramaic once used in Palestine,
and their script is close to the Nabataean. Though they live
in Iraq and baptize themselves in the Euphrates, their

scriptures refer to Jerusalem and the Jordan River, attesting that they came from there, perhaps during the Judeo-Roman Wars. Because they refer to themselves as *Nazoraia* and honor John the Baptist, the travelling missionaries who first met them in 1652 called them "Christians of Saint John". But, as B.R.S. Mead explains in her authoritative study, their holy scriptures show John cursing Jesus, calling him a devilish false prophet. It is now assumed that the Mandaeans descend from the disciples of John the Baptist, whom the Gospels portray as competitors to the disciples of Jesus.[371] The survival of John the Baptist's sect for so many centuries is one of the most intriguing riddle in the history of religions, and makes more sense within the framework of Heinsohn's short chronology.

The history of the different offshoots of heterodox Judaism is still rife with enigmas, and arguably some of them can find a solution within the Heinsohnian paradigm that puts the births of Christianity in Imperial Antiquity, of Manichaeism in Late Antiquity, and of Islam in the Early Middle Ages, in the same time period.

The context of their appearance is that of the traumatic Collapse of the Tenth Century, which coincides with the Crisis of the Third Century. In this context, the overwhelming success of Christianity was greatly assisted by its apocalyptic message. In Matthew 24:6-8, when asked, "what will be the sign of your coming (*parousia*) and of the end of the world," Jesus announces "famines and earthquakes."[372] The Book of Revelation looked like a summary of the cosmic cataclysm that had just shaken the earth:

> "There was a great earthquake; and the sun became black as sackcloth, the full moon became like blood, and the stars of the sky fell to the earth as the fig tree sheds its winter fruit when shaken by a gale; the sky vanished like a scroll that is rolled up, and every mountain, ad island was removed from its place. Then the kings of the earth ad the great men and the generals and the rich and the strong, and every one, slave and free, hid in the caves and among the

rocks of the mountains. ... and there followed hail and fire, mixed with blood, which fell on the earth; and a third of the earth was burnt up, and a third of the trees were burnt up, and all green grass was burnt up. ... and something like a great mountain, burning with fire, was thrown into the sea; and a third of the sea became blood, a third of the living creatures in the sea died, and a third of the ships were destroyed. ... and a great star fell from heaven, blazing like a torch, and it fell on a third of the rivers and on the fountains of water, because it was made bitter." (Book of Revelation, chapters 6 ad 8)

It has been suggested by Heinsohn and others that Revelation directly influenced the chronological reset, by the reference to the dragon (comet?) and the thousand years following its appearance: "He seized the dragon, that ancient serpent, who is the devil, or Satan, and bound him for a thousand years ... until the thousand years were ended. After that, he must be set free for a short time" (Revelation 20:1-3). We know how much chronological speculations these "thousand years" enthused. Church Father Cyprianus of Carthage, a survivor of the catastrophe in his badly affected city (he died in 258, that is, around 958 in Heinsohnian chronology), wrote: "Our Lord has foretold all this. / War and famine, earth quakes and pestilence will occur everywhere" (*De mortalitate*).[373]

APPENDIX
Short chronology of the Old World

You cannot travel time as you can travel space. That makes a huge difference between geography and chronography. Anatoly Fomenko, a mathematician, once said that historians don't know what history is, because their never question the basic timeline of world history that they have been taught in primary school. Without giving it any thought, they simply assume that it is as securely established as the maps on their classroom wall.

As we saw, the main architect of our sophisticated clockwork mechanism that tells us precisely when everything happened everywhere in the world, was a French scholar named Joseph Scaliger (1540-1609), who set out to harmonize all available chronicles and calendars (Hebrew, Greek, Roman, Persian, Babylonian, Egyptian). His main works on chronology are *De Emendatione Temporum* (1583) and *Thesaurus Temporum* (1606).

Isaac Newton (1642-1727) thought Scaliger's chronology was too long by three centuries, and wrote so in *The Chronology of Ancient Kingdoms Amended*, published one year after his death. This part of his work was ignored, and we are now told to trust Scaliger as if he had a time-travel machine equipped with a digital clock. But why should we trust Scaliger rather than Newton?

As a matter of fact, many historians and archaeologists are now joining Newton in claiming that the first millennium BC is about three centuries younger than has been taught. Egyptologist David Rohl has been leading the way with his New Chronology.[374] Peter James has supported this revisionist trend in *Centuries of Darkness: a challenge to the conventional chronology of Old World archaeology*. He has a nice metaphor for the chronological conundrum:

"Imagine, then trying to complete a jigsaw where the sides are far too long; frustratingly, many pieces will appear to fit into two places in the puzzle, while many 'ghost pieces' will be needed to fill the space that is unaccounted for. / This is precisely the dilemma into which so many archaeologists have been forced."[375]

Here is Peter James's short list of "as yet unresolved, historical puzzles" for the Dark Age between 1200 and 700 BC, after the fall of he Bronze Age civilization:

"Why, for instance, would the 8th-century Greeks have borrowed an alphabet from Phoenicia that was 300 years out of date? How could the Cypriots and the Babylonians have left virtually no evidence of writing for 300 years, after which they continued to use basically the same scripts?

Why do bronzes made in Cyrpus during the 12th century BC frequently occur elsewhere in 9th-century or later deposits? How is it that the objects of Egyptian pharaohs from the 10th to 9th centuries are always found abroad in contexts 100-200 years later? What causes the gap in the apparently continuous tradition of Eastern Mediterranean ivory-working between 1175 and 850 BC? Why indeed have the Iron Age levels of Israel produced nothing reflecting the 'Golden Age' of King Solomon?

The questions do not end there. Did the Phoenician colonization of the West occur in the 12th or the 8th century BC? How is it that archaeologists cannot agree on a date for the earliest remains at Rome, traditionally founded around 750 BC? Where are the archaeological remains of the native Sicilians who were expelled by Greek colonists in the 8th century BC? Even more intractable puzzles surround how the Hittite kings and civilization of Syria could have sprung from ancestors who vanished without a trace nearly three centuries earlier. And what really happened to the people of Nubia, who supposedly vanished only to return with the same material culture 250 years later? Did the Trojans and Elamites also disappear and reappear in their homelands over the same period. Where is the archaeological evidence for the arrival of the Israelites in Palestine?

Within the presently accepted scheme these problems appear to be insoluble. So many interlocking anomalies occur at this point in history that one begins to wonder whether, as in the case of the origins of copper-working, the root cause may really be a faulty chronology." [376]

A more radical challenge for the age of the Old World had come earlier from from Russian-born scientist Immanuel Velikovsky (1895-1979), already mentioned in chapter 4 (read the full story in P. John Crowe's 1999 great article titled "The Revision of Ancient History – A Perspective" on the website of the Society for Interdisciplinary Studies (SIS).[377] Gunnar Heinsohn himself came from the Velikovskian school, but he rejected Velikovsky's reliance on the biblical framework to built a method of research compatible with academic standards, relying exclusively on stratigraphy.

Long before he started deconstructing the standard chronology of the first millennium in 2013, Heinsohn had questioned the dates of ancient pre-Roman civilizations. His first book was *Die Sumerer gab es nicht* ("The Sumerians did not exist"), published in 1988, followed in 1990 by a book co-written with Heribert Illig titled *Wann lebten die Pharaonen?* ("When did the Pharaohs live?").

Heinsohn's first synthetic paper on ancient civilizations was "The Restoration of Ancient History," delivered in 1994 at a symposium in Portland, Oregon.[378] A detailed discussion of it in 26 parts can be read on Brendan Ward's blog harlotscurse. I will quote mostly from these two sources, although I recommend, for a more thorough and updated version, two papers published by Heinsohn in 2006 for the Circle of Ancient Iranian Studies (CAIS): "Empires Lost and Found: Stratigraphy and Today's Search for the Great Powers of the Past", and "Cyaxares: Media's Great King in Egypt, Assyria & Iran." Also of interest is his paper presented at some International Congress of Egyptology in 1993, "Who Were the Hyksos?"

The main problem outlined by Heinsohn is that the timeline of ancient Mesopotamian history which is taught in universities today is more or less identical to the timeline which biblical fundamentalists deduced from the Bible in the 17th century. The keystone of this construction is Babylonian king Hammurabi, identified with King Amraphel of Genesis 14, a contemporary of Abraham, whom the Bible places in the third millennium BCE. Thus in 1857, biblical archaeologist William Kennett Loftus uses Abraham's birth in 2130 BC as an anchor point in his *Travels and Researches in Chaldaea and Susiana.*

CHRONOLOGICAL TABLE.*

FIRST CHALDÆAN EMPIRE.

B. C. about.	Names of Kings.	Cuneiform Records, where Discovered.	Dates of Corresponding Events in the Bible.
2234	Urukh.	Buwáríyya at Warka; Great Mound, Niffar; Do. Sinkara; Mûgeyer.	
	Ilgi.	Niffar; Warka; Sinkara; Mûge-yer.	B. C. Birth of Abraham, 2130
	Shinti-Shil-Khak.		
1950	Kudur-Mapula. (perhaps Chedorlaomer.)	Mûgeyer.	
1860	Ismi-Dagan.	Mûgeyer.	
	Ibil-Anu-Duma.	Mûgeyer.	
	Gurguna.	Mûgeyer.	
	Naramsin.		
1700	Purna-Puriyas.	Sinkara.	The Exodus, 1625
	Durri-Galzu.	Akker-Kûf; Mûgeyer.	
	Khammu-rabi.	Red Mound at Sinkara; Mûgeyer; Gherára near Bághdád; on Ta-blets from Tel Sifr.	
1600	Shamsu-Iluna.	On Tablets from Tel Sifr.	Death of Moses, 1585
	Sin-shada.	Upper terrace of the Búwáríyya, and Wuswas gateway, at War-ka.	First Servitude, 1558

This chronology is twice as long as the chronology recorded by the Greek Classical historians such as Hecataeus of Miletus, Herodotus, or Diodorus Siculus. But Christian historians favorably prejudiced toward the Old Testament have given preference to the Jewish computation. This, according to Heinsohn, was the original sin of our ancient historiography.

"It began with the comparative history of Greeks and Jews. This comparison focused on the question if Moses was more ancient than Homer. ... Since dates used in the Bible simply were earlier than the Greek dates, the latter lost the competition for the earlier periods of civilization. ... the Greek dates cut the biblical ones down to about one-third. When their dates were replaced by the biblical ones, the following picture emerged. Suddenly, the historians were confronted with a gap of 1,500 years. It was created by equating biblical Nimrod of Abraham's -3rd millennium with Herodotus' Ninos of the -8th century. ... Biblical dates ... openly dominated comparative world chronology up to about 1870 and — in a disguised manner — are used up to the present."

To fill the gap, ancient empires have been discovered by archaeologists that Classical historians knew nothing about. Meanwhile, those empires they knew well were said to have left hardly any archaeological trace, so that their existence was questioned. Heinsohn noticed that these two types of discrepancies came in matching pairs. It starts with Chaldaea, the first civilization according to Herodotus, founded by Ninos around -750.

"Students of Chaldaea are stunned by the archaeological absence of the most learned nation of antiquity which the Greeks considered as the cradle of knowledge. ... Yet, the same researchers take great pride in the discovery of the Sumerians (1867) in the very heartland of Chaldaea. These Sumerians became teachers of mankind. Yet, they were so ancient that even the best historians of antiquity had never heard of them."

For Heinsohn, the Sumerians are none other than the Chaldaeans wrongly dated. He drew another parallel between the Gutians discovered by modern archaeologists and the Scythians of Classical history.

"In the last 150 years the learned world was time and again struck by the discovery of lost nations and forgotten empires which were so ancient that even the best historians of antiquity had never heard of them. This caused great surprise because these superancient civilizations were found in territories which were otherwise well known to the historians of Classical and Hellenistic Greece. Yet, the surprise did not end there. The nations and empires which were described by the classical authors in great detail could hardly be verified by the spade. One and a half centuries of excavations, thus, brought as much desperation as it did provide success stories for European scholars. Modern archaeologists... dug in vain for the scientific splendor of the Chaldaeans on the Persian Gulf but hit the scientific splendor of much older and mysterious Sumerians. They dug in vain for marauding Scythians in Mesopotamia but hit the much older and mysterious Quthean/Gutaean marauders."[379]

A third example is the Medes. Since the 1980s, historians question the existence of their empire mentioned by all Classical historians and described by Diodorus Siculus as "the mighty empire of the Medes." For lack of archaeological evidence, this empire is now declared "elusive". Meanwhile, the ancient state of the Mitanni has been discovered in Upper Mesopotamia and dated between 1500 BCE and 1260 BCE. The Classical historians knew nothing of these Mitanni. Heinsohn's solution is, of course, that the Mitanni are the Medes wrongly dated, just like the Sumerians are the Chaldaeans, and the Gutaeans are the Scythians; "none of the newly discovered nations is new at all but merely provide the archaeology of the nations known since antiquity. Because they applied erroneous dating schemes, modern scholars failed to recognize their findings as the remains of the nations they only apparently looked for in vain."

According to Heinsohn, Herodotus was basically right. Upper Mesopotomia, the region centered on the River Tigris and known to Classical historians as Assyria, was the nucleus of three successive empires prior to the conquest of Alexander the Great: the Assyrians, the Medes, and the Persians, with possibly a period of Scythian domination interrupting the Empire of the Medes. Heinsohn's stratigraphy-based chronology erases 1500 ghost years created by Bible-based chronology. Brendan Ward explains in more detail:

"One of Gunnar Heinsohn's most remarkable achievements is his discovery that modern archaeologists have unwittingly triplicated some of the empires of the Ancient World, placing three copies of each of them in three different timeframes. One copy might correspond to the actual historical empire, while the other two copies are ghost empires that never really existed. For example, the so-called Akkadian Empire of Sargon the Great in Lower Mesopotamia, the Hyksos Empire in Egypt, and the Old Assyrian Empire in Upper Mesopotamia all refer in Heinsohn's opinion to the Assyrian Empire of the Classical historians. Typically, the real history belongs in the first millennium BCE, with duplicates and triplicates placed in the second and third millennia respectively."[380]

Florin Diacu illustrates the relevance of Heinsohn's stratigraphic approach in his remarkable book *The Lost Millennium*:

"Heinsohn referred to the archaeological findings at Hazor, an ancient Canaanite city in northern Israel. In1996, excavations made in the upper strata of the site uncovered four cuneiform tablets, two written in Old-Babylonian Akkadian and two in the Akkadian of the Amarna era. The problem is that traditional chronology places them in the early second millennium BC, even though they belong to a layer corresponding to the peak of the Persian Empire (550-330 BC). / To eliminate the contradiction, historians considered the tablets to be heirlooms, a claim Heinsohn found silly. How, Heinsohn asked, can they explain that the later Hazoreans kept those tablets for more than a thousand years but were incapable of producing some of their own?"[381]

Because it lies outside the biblical world, China has never been forced into the false chronological frame tied to the biblical birthdate of Abraham the Patriarch. Scholarship therefore assumes that China has been a backward civilization until it entered history, about 1500 later than Assyria.[382] According to standard chronology, Heinsohn writes:

"When the Eurasian land mass entered the Iron Age around -1600/-1400, China slowly moved into the Bronze Age. The Chinese waited an additional millennium-around 600/-400- before they could bring themselves to work iron. The Chinese did not seem to care about falling millennia behind. ... Modern students of Ancient China have no way of comprehending the behavior of such a gifted nation."

In reality, China is dated correctly, like India and pre-Columbian Central America. "It, therefore, can be used as an interesting measuring rod for the true age of the beginning of the Bronze Age." When brought in line with China's chronology, it turns out that "the emergence of post-Neolithic high civilization does not come about before the turn to the 1st millennium BCE. This reduction brings China, the Ganges Valley as well as Mesoamerica (Olmecs) etc., into line with the rest of the world." Heinsohn's shortened chronology can be summarized by the following chart (reproduced from Brendan Ward):[383]

	Years BCE						
	1150	770-750.	620	540	475	330	221
Assyria	Early Assyrians		Assyrian Empire	Medes	Persian Empire		Hellenistic period
Babylonia	Early Chaldaeans		Assyrians & Scythians	Late Chaldeans	Persian Empire		Hellenistic period
Egypt	Early Dynastic Egypt		Hyksos	18th-19th Dynasties	Persian Egypt		Ptolemaic Egypt
Indus Valley	Early Harappan		Mature Harappan	Late Harappan	Persian Satrapy		
China	Shang Dynasty		Zhou Dynasty		Warring States		Qin Dynasty

Eusebius of Caesarea

The flawed biblical chronology was passed on to the Christian world by Eusebius of Caesarea, who supposedly wrote in the decades after 300 CE in the Palestinian city of Caesarea. With his two-volume *Chronicon,* Eusebius is credited with the first systematic chronology of world events synchronizing the varied pasts of ancient Assyria, Egypt, Israel, Persia, Greece and Rome into a single work. Every entry in the *Chronicon* begins wih "the year of Abraham," and the calculations involve the life spans of biblical characters: Adam lived 930 years, Noah 950, Abraham 175, and Moses 120.[384] As Anthony Grafton explains in *Christianity and the transformation of the Book: Origen, Eusebius, and the Library of Caesarea* (2009), Eusebius used key synchronisms between Greek, Roman, and Jewish history "as the grounds for arguing that Moses was older than any Greek writer. Both the Jewish religion and its Christian offspring emerged from this argument as older than, and accordingly superior to, the traditions of the pagans."[385] The *Chronicon* remained unchallenged for thirteen centuries:

> "Once edited, translated into Latin, and brought up to date
> by Jerome, Eusebius's tables provided the model for Latin
> world chronicles for centuries to come. ... Even in the
> early seventeenth century, when Scaliger wanted to create a
> new structure for universal history, he set out to do so by
> reconstructing Eusebius's work."[386]

Interestingly, Grafton portrays Eusebius as living, working and writing pretty much like a Renaissance scholar. He compares him to Johannes Trithemius (1462-1516), a Benedictine abbot, scholar and forger, who assembled vast libraries and compiled histories of the Church. Grafton insists on "the close parallels between the activities of Eusebius and Trithemius." and claims that the similarities indicate "a deep structure of Christian scholarship, forged in late antiquity, then reproduced again and again in the Middle Ages and the early modern period." "Eusebius," writes Grafton, "specialized in producing works that required massive help from collaborators." "By 320 or so, ... Eusebius's workplace must have become a substantial research institution, at once an archive, a library, and a scriptorium."[387]

Eusebius was building on the foundation of his predecessor Origen, who is said to have authored more than 800 works, with the support of his wealthy disciple Ambrose, who "provided his teacher with an enviable support staff, including more than seven shorthand secretaries to take Origen's dictation as he composed, scribes to work up the secretaries' notes, and even [according to Eusebius] 'girls trained in beautiful writing,' whose task was presumably to prepare copies to be presented to Origen's dedicatees and other privileged readers," not to mention "Jewish informants" and "assistants literate in Hebrew as well as Greek."[388]

Origen and Eusebius, according to Grafton, "were themselves impresarios of the scriptorium and the library, and developed new forms of scholarship that depended on their abilities to collect and produce new kinds of books."[389] They were the founders of Christian scholarship: "the model of ecclesiastical learning that took shape in the library at Caesarea shaped the whole, millennial tradition of Christian scholarship, in subtle but vital ways. In many respects, we are still the heirs of Origen and Eusebius."[390]

From this description, the skeptic will suspect that neither Origen's nor Eusebius' works can possibly date from a time when Christians were still persecuted by imperial power. They reflect a situation of State-sponsored erudition. Eusebius' *Chronicon* may very well belong to the early days of the papal state in the Carolingian era, for although it was supposedly written in Greek, no Greek version appeared before the thirteenth century. Until then, it was know only in the version "edited, translated into Latin, and brought up to date by Jerome" (Grafton's words), which, just like Jerome's *Vulgate* translation of the Bible, did not surface until the eleventh century.

A deception of Biblical proportion

Although European scholarship has stopped relying explicitly on the biblical narrative, the chronology built upon biblical dates has remained the basis of our textbook historiography. In other words, the Western world sees — and has taught the rest of the world to see — the history of mankind through the lens of the Hebrew Bible.

The problem is that the Hebrew Bible was a work of historical deception, partly designed to give the Chosen People precedence over all other nations.

To start with, the biblical scribes lied about the age of their own writing. They were almost candid about it when they wrote, in chapter 22 of the Second Book of Kings, that under the reign of King Josiah (639-609 BC) the authentic "scroll of the Torah" written by Moses himself was "discovered" by the high priest Hilkiah during renovation work in the Temple. No historians today interprets this narrative as anything but a legend fabricated by priests to pass their newly crafted law code (Deuteronomy) as the reenactment of an old law. Therefore, according to the most conservative biblical scholarship, Deuteronomy dates back to the age of Josiah around 625 BC, and so do the six historical books following Deuteronomy.

Less conservative biblical historians such as Philip Davies go one step further, and consider that the "reform of Josiah" is itself "a pious legend." Deuteronomy, they say, cannot possibly have been written in a monarchy, because it is a law code adapted to a theocracy, the regime that proto-Zionists Ezra and Nehemiah sought to impose when they directed the Babylonian exiles "back" to Palestine.[391] This is not news: the apocryphal Fourth Book of Ezra, chapter 14, tells how Yahweh dictated a new edition of the Scriptures to Ezra, and Spinoza suggested as early as 1670 that Ezra was the head of the scribal school that had compiled and edited most of the Tanakh.[392]

The biblical narrative, designed to establish Ezra's legitimacy on the models of Moses and Josiah, is built on a double *mise en abyme* (a lie within a lie within a lie): first, Moses receives from Yahweh the Law (of Deuteronomy) and urges the Hebrew people to "faithfully obey the voice of Yahweh your God, by keeping and observing all his commandments" (Deuteronomy 28:1-20). Then, Josiah receives from the high priest that same "Law of Moses" (that had once fallen from the sky but now emerges from the rubble), and summons "the whole populace, high and low" to hear it being read (2 Kings 23:2). Finally, Ezra brings back from Babylon this very "Book of the Law of Moses" and summons the families of the settlers to read it to them "from dawn till noon" (Nehemiah 8:1-3). In reality, that Torah supposedly written by Moses, abandoned and then revived two centuries later by Josiah, then becoming obsolete again as the country was ravaged, and finally returned by Ezra to a people who, it seems, no longer remembered it — that Torah was written by Ezra and his band of priestly scribes, as the instrument of their new power over the Palestinian population.

Abraham is an invention of Ezra's time, or at least was fitted then into the official narrative. His journey from Mesopotamia to Palestine, prompted by Yahweh's commitment "to give you this country as your possession" (Genesis 15:7), was written as a model for the (re)conquest of Palestine by the exiles in Babylon. Abraham was unknown among pre-exilic prophets.[393]

Much of the Tanakh as we have it is, of course, much younger than Ezra. For example, the books of Ezra and Nehemiah themselves (originally a single book) cannot possibly date from the time of their eponymous heroes, because the Persian edicts that they include, supposedly issued by Cyrus, Darius and Artaxerxes, allowing the priests and Levites to rule over "the whole people of Trans-Euphrates [territories west to the Euphrates]," are fake, and it is unlikely that Jews writing under Persian rule would have taken the risk of producing false royal edicts, even in Hebrew. This brings us to the Hellenistic period. It was under the authority of the Hasmonean kings that the biblical canon was defined. It now included the Books of Chronicles, an updated version of the Books of Kings, as well as the books of Jonah, Daniel, Tobit, Judith, Esther and Sirach. Daniel and Esther are legendary stories or smart Israelites who, having reached the rank of courtier, use their influence to benefit their community — a form of tribal nepotism.

The story of Joseph that now occupies the last chapters of Genesis (37-50) follows the same pattern; for that reason, this story is dated from the same period. A secondary argument in favor of a Hellenistic dating of what exegetes call "the romance of Joseph" is its resemblance to the story of another Joseph that the historian Flavius Josephus situates at the time of the Ptolemies (*Jewish Antiquities* XII.4). This Joseph, a man "of great reputation among the people of Jerusalem, for gravity, prudence, and justice," was appointed as Judea's tax collector by Ptolemy after promising to bring back double the tax revenues of his competitors. "The king was pleased to hear that offer; and, because it augmented his revenues, said he would confirm the sale of the taxes to him." Joseph fulfilled his contract by murdering several prominent citizens and confiscating their property. He became extremely rich and was thus able to help his coreligionists. Therefore, concludes the historian, Joseph "was a good man, and of great magnanimity; and brought the Jews out of a state of poverty and meanness, to one that was more splendid." The proximity of the two Joseph narratives suggests that they derive from the same matrix, of Hellenistic date.

It was during the same Hasmonean period that a state ideology of world empire first became explicit, notably in the *Book of Jubilees*. It reaffirms that Yahweh, the god of Israel, is the Creator of the Universe, who has destined his Chosen People to rule the world:

"I am Yahweh who created the heaven and the earth, and I will increase you and multiply you exceedingly, and kings shall come forth from you, and they shall judge everywhere wherever the foot of the sons of men has trodden. And I will give to your seed all the earth which is under heaven, and they shall judge all the nations according to their desires, and after that they shall get possession of the whole earth and inherit it forever" (32:18-19).

It is also stated in the *Book of Jubilees* that any Israelite who wishes to give his daughter or his sister to a Gentile must be stoned to death, "for he has wrought shame in Israel; and they shall burn the woman with fire, because she has dishonored the name of the house of her father, and she shall be rooted out of Israel" (30:7). A strong case can be made that such extreme endogamic legislation, which is found repeated again and again in the Torah, originates from the early days of the Hasmonean kingdom established by the fundamentalist Maccabees.

Moses and the Gnostic Serpent

Here I will develop a new argument for dating the Garden of Eden story from the Book of Genesis in the last century BC. In that story, the serpent offers to the first humans the means of acquiring knowledge and immortality, attributes that would allow them to "be like gods" (Genesis 3:5). It has long been understood that this story is a polemical attack against mystery-type religious cults promising knowledge and immortality.

It is also understood that the polemic is directed against a religious practice *within* the Judean-Israeli world, rather than against Gentile religions. We learn from Numbers 21:9 that, on Yahweh's instruction, Moses fashioned a brass serpent which, placed on a standard, healed snakebites. We then read in 2 Kings 18:4 that the king of Judea, Hezekiah, a great slayer of idols, "broke in pieces the bronze serpent that Moses had made, for until those days, the people of Israel had made offerings to it; it was called Nehushtan." To delegitimize the cult of Moses' serpent which was practiced in Israel — that is, in the northern kingdom of Samaria —, the author of the Genesis story portrays the serpent as a deceiver.

We also know of Gnostic movements from the first century AD that saw the serpent of Genesis 3 as a good god or eon who comes to give men knowledge (*gnosis*) and immortality (a happy afterlife), whereas Yahweh is denounced as an evil demiurge who imprionned humans in material bodies. In the Gnostic text known as *The Testimony of Truth,* the Serpent convinces Adam and Eve to partake of knowledge (*gnosis*), while the Demiurge tries to keep them away from it by threatening them with death.

The Ophites (from the Greek *ophis* "serpent") also called Naassenes (from the Hebrew *naas*, "serpent"), were a Gnostic sect that appeared in Syria and Egypt around the year 100 AD. They had a positive interpretation of the serpent of Genesis 3. According to Irenaeus of Lyon, the Ophites taught that "the Divine Mother used the serpent to lead Adam and Eve to disobey the orders of Yaltabaoth and acquire knowledge, thus inciting the anger of the latter, who cast the serpent into the lower world, along with Adam and Eve."[394]

The latest research into this early Gnostic trend has established that it was a Jewish heresy before it became a Christian heresy. Even the oldest Christian Gnostic texts are heavily Jewish and only superficially Christian; they never refer to the earthly life of Christ, but present him as an angelic principle, a higher aeon. The *Apocryphon of John*, dated from the 2nd century, is the most representative of this current. Evidence suggests that Gnosticism originated in Palestine, more precisely in Samaria, and that it spread to Anatolia and North Africa during and after the Judeo-Roman Wars (68-135).[395]

As long as it was believed that Gnosticism was a Christian phenomenon, it was assumed that the Ophites' positive interpretation of the Genesis serpent was an anti-Jewish polemic. But since it it understood that Gnosticism stemmed from within Israel, and since the Genesis story is itself polemical in nature, that assumption makes no more sense. Rather, we are compelled to hypothesize some kind of filiation between the Samaritan cult of Moses' serpent and the Gnostic movement. And we find confirmation of this in the fact that the serpent in Genesis 3 expresses itself as a Gnostic. In other words, both the Book of Genesis and the Book of Numbers make reference to a Samaritan Gnostic or proto-Gnostic religious movement, of which the Gnostics of the first and second century AD, Ophites and Naassenes included, are the spiritual heirs.

That is only conceivable if Genesis and Numbers were written in the first century BC at the earliest, for there is no trace of Jewish Gnosticism before the first century AD. Irenaeus of Lyon, and Christian tradition in general, attribute the paternity of the Gnostic heresy to the Samaritan Simon Magus who comes into conflict with Peter in Acts 8; this means that Gnosticism was considered a recent Samaritan movement, contemporaneous or just slightly older than Christianity.

Note that I have not, here, concerned myself with the date of Moses, but only with the date of writing of the Pentateuch, the so-called "Books of Moses". But if one wants to consider that the story of Moses' serpent has any historical background, then that background too must be moved close to the first century AD.

Finally, if we choose to see the cult of Moses' healing serpent as being derived from the Greek cult of Asklepios,[396] then we are also compelled to give the story a late Hellenistic date, for the spread of the cult of Asklepios in Palestine is a Hellenistic phenomenon. An influence from the cult of Asklepios is perfectly compatible with a Gnostic origin, in the context of the syncretism of the Hellenistic period.

NOTES

1. Laurent Guyénot, *La Mort féerique. Anthropologie du merveilleux (XIIe-XVe siècles),* Gallimard, 2011.

2. Alfred Nutt, « Presidential Address to the Folk-Lore Society », *Folk-Lore* 32 (1921), quoted in Lewis Spence, *British Fairy Origins,* Watts & Co, 1946, p. 141.

3. Jean-Christophe Cassard, « *Arthur est vivant !* Jalons pour une enquête sur le messianisme royal au Moyen Âge », *Cahiers de civilisation médiévale* 32 (1989), pp. 135-146.

4. Laurent Guyénot, *La Lance qui saigne. Métatextes et hypertextes du 'Conte du Graal' de Chrétien de Troyes,* Honoré Champion, 2010.

5. Richard Barber, *The Holy Grail: Imagination and Belief,* Harvard University Press, 2004, p. 4.

6. Silvestro Fiore, « Les origines orientales de la légende du Graal : évolution du thème dans le cadre des cultures et des cultes », *Cahiers de civilisation médiévale* 10 (1967), pp. 207-219.

7. Sigfried J. De Laet, « La composition de l'ordre équestre sous Auguste et Tibère », *Revue belge de philologie et d'histoire,* tome 20, fasc. 3-4, 1941. pp. 509-531, on www.persee.fr/doc/

8. Guy Blois, *The Transformation of the Year One Thousand: The Village of Lournand from antiquity to feudalism,* Manchester UP, 1992, pp. 161, 167, 1.

9. Raoul Glaber, *Histoires,* ed. and trans. Mathieu Arnoux, Brépols, 1996, book II, § 13-17, pp. 116-125.

10. Patrick J. Geary, *Phantoms of Remembrance: Memory and Oblivion at the End of the First Millennium,* Princeton UP, 1994, p. 9.

11. *Ibid.,* p. 7.

12. www.unz.com/comments/all/?commenterfilter=eknibbs

13. www.e-codices.unifr.ch/de/list/one/csg/0272 on p. 245.

14. gallica.bnf.fr/ark:/12148/btv1b85409594

15. daten.digitale-sammlungen.de/~db/0001/bsb00012957/images/

16. Raoul Glaber, *Histoires,* ed. and trans. Mathieu Arnoux, Brépols, 1996, pp. 106-107 and 78-79.

17. Richard Landes, "The Fear of an Apocalyptic Year 1000: Augustinian Historiography, Medieval and Modern," *Speculum,* Vol. 75, No. 1 (Jan. 2000), pp. 97-145, on www.bu.edu/history/files/2011/10/11.Fear-of-an-Apocalyptic-Year-1000-Speculum.pdf

18. Mireille Chazan, *L'Empire et l'histoire universelle de Sigebert de Gembloux à Jean de Saint-Victor (XIIe -XIVe siècle),* Champion, 1999, pp. 24-25.

19. Which doesn't mean that auhors defending such theories do not have interesting things to say. See for example jefdemolder.blogspot.com.

20. Serge Gruzinski, *La Machine à remonter le temps. Quand l'Europe s'est mise à écrire l'histoire du monde,* Fayard, 2017, pp. 16-17.

21. Nicolas Standaert, "Jesuit Accounts of Chinese History and Chronology and Their Chinese Sources," *East Asian Science, Technology, and Medicine*, no. 35, 2012, pp. 11–87, on www.jstor.org/stable/i40123097

22 . Quoted in Florin Diacu, *The Lost Millennium: History's Timetables under Siege*, second edition, John Hopkins University Press, 2011, p. 202.

23. Veteran NASA astronaut Donald Roy Pettit: "The problem is we don't have the technology to do that anymore. We used to but we destroyed that technology and it's a painful process to build it back again."
https://www.youtube.com/watch?v=DpPMoIv1lxI

24. Robert Folz, *L'Idée médiévale de l'Empire en Occident*, Aubier, 1953, p. 107.

25. Heinrich Fichtenau, *Living in the Tenth Century: Mentalities and Social Orders* (German edition 1984), trans. Patrick Geary, University of Chicago Press, 1991, p. 9.

26. Eric Knibbs, *Ansgar, Rimbert and the Forged Foundations of Hamburg-Bremen*, Routledge, 2016.

27. Marcel Pacaut, *La Théocratie. L'Église et le pouvoir au Moyen Âge*, Aubier, 1957, p. 117.

28. Ferdinand Lot, *La Fin du monde antique* (1927), Albin Michel, 1989, pp. 49-50.

29. Gunnar Heinsohn, "Constantine the Great in 1st Century AD Stratigraphy", February 2223, www.academia.edu/96112108/CONSTANTINE_THE_GREAT_IN_1_st_C_AD_STRATIGRAPHY_02_2023_strongly_expanded_

30. "Aqueducts and the Water Supply System of Constantinople," on www.thebyzantinelegacy.com/aqueducts

31. Gunnar Heinsohn, "Ravenna and chronology," 2020, www.q-mag.org/gunnar-heinsohn-ravenna-and-chronology.html - 4CWXi2hA

32. Paul Stephenson, *The Byzantine World*, Routledge, 2012, p. xxi.

33. Jonathan Harris, *Byzantium and the Crusades*, 2nd ed, Bloomsbury, 2014, kindle l. 465-94.

34. Sylvain Gouguenheim, *Aristote au Mont Saint-Michel. Les racines grecques de l'Europe chrétienne*, Seuil, 2008.

35. Oswald Spengler, *The Decline of the West*, vol. 1, George Allen & Unwin Ltd, 1926, p. 17.

36. Polydor Hochart, *De l'authenticité des Annales et des Histoires de Tacite*, 1890, pp. viii-ix, on archive.org/details/delauthenticitde00hoch

37. Clarence Mendell, *Tacitus: The Man and his Work*, Yale UP/Oxford UP, 1957, as explained on www.tertullian.org/rpearse/tacitus/

38. P. W. G. Gordan, *Two Renaissance Book Hunters: The letters of Poggius Bracciolini to Nicolaus de Niccolis*, New York, 1974.

39. David Schaps, "The Found and Lost Manuscripts of Tacitus' *De Agricola*," *Classical Philology*, Vol. 74, No. 1 (Jan., 1979), pp. 28-42, on www.jstor.org.

40. Wilhelm Kammeier, *Die Fälschung der Geschichte des Urchristentums* (1942, 1956), French trans.: *La Falsification de l'histoire allemande*, Didi18, 2022.

41. Gaetano Mosca, *The Ruling Class*, McGraw-Hill Book Company, 1939, p. 118: "In describing the manners and customs of the Germans of his day Machiavelli evidently wrote under the influence of Tacitus."

42. Leo Wiener (1920) *Contributions towards a History of Arabico-Gothic Culture; vol. III: Tacitus' Germania and other Forgeries* (Philadelphia, 1920), p. 299, quoted by Uwe Topper in "Leo Wiener, a pioneer halfway through," 2020, http://www.ilya.it/chrono/en/index.html

43. Georges Minois, *Histoire de l'athéisme*, Fayard, 1998, p. 94.

44. ehne.fr/en/encyclopedia/themes/european-humanism/cultural-heritage/recovery-manuscripts

45. Jan Willem Drijvers and David Hunt, *The Late Roman World and Its Historian: Interpreting Ammianus Marcellinus*, Routledge, 2003.

46. www.tertullian.org/fathers/ammianus_14_book14.htm

47. groups.google.com/g/sci.classics/c/5fD_26bk5k0

48. Giles Constable, "Forgery and Plagiarism in the Middle Ages," in *Culture and Spirituality in Medieval Europe*, Variorum, 1996, pp. 1-41, and on www.degruyter.com/abstract/j/afd.1983.29.issue-jg/afd.1983.29.jg.1/afd.1983.29.jg.1.xml

49. Lynn Catterson, "Michelangelo's 'Laocoön?'," *Artibus Et Historiae*, vol. 26, n° 52, 2005, pp. 29–56, on www.academia.edu/1568656/_Michelangelos_Laoco%C3%B6n_Artibus_et_H istoriae_52_2005_pp_29_56. Read also here: www.nytimes.com/2005/04/20/arts/is-laocoon-a-michelangelo-forgery.html

50. Henri Pirenne, *Mahomet et Charlemagne*, 1937, Texto Tallandier, 2021, p. 23.

51. *Ibid.*, p. 34.

52. David Carrette, *L'Invention du Moyen Âge. La plus grande falsification de l'histoire*, Magazine *Top-Secret*, Hors-série n°9, 2014.

53. Gaetano Mosca, *The Ruling Class*, McGraw-Hill Book Company, 1939, p. 94.

54. hoaxes.org/archive/permalink/renaissance_forgeries

55. Jerry Brotton, *The Renaissance Bazaar: From the Silk Road to Michelangelo*, Oxford UP, 2010, pp. 66-67.

56. Louis de Beaufort, *Dissertation sur l'incertitude des cinq premiers siècles de l'histoire romaine* (1738), on www.mediterranee-antique.fr/Fichiers_PdF/ABC/Beaufort/Dissertation.pdf

57. Brotton, *The Renaissance Bazaar, op. cit.,* pp. 66-67.

58. Jacques Heers, *Le Moyen Âge, une imposture*, Perrin, 1992, pp. 55-58.

59. It is never raised, for example, by Royston Lambert in his *Beloved and God: The Story of Hadrian and Antinous*, Phoenix Giant, 1984.

60. Petronius, *The Satyricon*, trans. P. D. Walsh, Oxford UP, 1997, "Introduction," p. xxxv.

61. Gédéon Huet, "Le Roman d'Apulée était-il connu au Moyen Âge ?", *Le Moyen Âge*, 22 (1909), pp. 23-28.

62. Jacques Heurgon, "Fra Giocondo et l'édition du Xe livre de la correspondace de Pline le Jeune," *Bulletin de la Société national des Antiquaires de France*, 1958, pp. 57-63, on www.persee.fr/doc/bsnaf_0081-1181_1958_num_1956_1_5488

63. Jean-Louis Brunaux, *The Celtic Gauls: Gods, Rites, and Santuaries*, Routledge, 1987; David Henige, "He came, he saw, we counted: the

historiography and demography of Caesar's gallic numbers," *Annales de démographie historique*, 1998-1, pp. 215-242, on www.persee.fr/doc/adh_0066-2062_1998_num_1998_1_2162

64 Georges Dumézil, *Heur et malheur du guerrier. Aspects mythiques de la fonction guerrière chez les Indo-Européens* (1969), Flammarion, 1985, pp. 66 and 16.

65. Georges Dumézil, *Archaic Roman Religion,* vol. 1, John Hopkins UP, 1996 (French ed. 1966), pp. 48, 55, 58.

66. Eusebius's *Life of Constantine,* translated with introduction and commentary by Averil Cameron and Stuart G. Hall, Clarendon, 1999, on p. 1.

67. en.wikipedia.org/wiki/Diocletian - Early_life

68. *Dux Francorum* and *rex Francorum* were used interchangibly for Peppin II, for example. See en.wikipedia.org/wiki/Duke_of_the_Franks

69. Ferdinand Lot, *La Fin du monde antique* (1927), Albin Michel, 1989, p. 29.

70. Anthony Kaldellis, *Streams of Gold, Rivers of Blood: The Rise and Fall of Byzantium, 955 A.D. to the First Crusade,* Oxford UP, 2019, p. xxvii.

71. Harold J. Berman, *Law and Revolution, the Formation of the Western Legal Tradition,* Harvard UP, 1983; Aldo Schiavone, *The Invention of Law in the West,* Harvard UP, 2012.

72. Sander M. Goldberg, *Epic in Republican Rome,* Oxford UP, 1995, pp. 50-51.

73. Han Lamers, "Janus Lascaris' Florentine Oration and the 'Reception' of Ancient Aeolism," www.academia.edu/41405002/Janus_Lascaris_Florentine_Oration_and_the_Re ception_of_Ancient_Aeolism

74. Anthony Kaldellis, *Hellenism in Byzantium: The Transformation of Greek Identity and the Reception of the Classical Tradition,* Cambridge UP, 2007, p. 65.

75. Anatoly T. Fomenko, *History: Fiction or Science?* vol. 1, Delamere Publishing, 2003, p. 357.

76. Yves Cortez, *Le Français ne vient pas du latin,* L'Harmattan, 2007, pp. 11-14.

77. M. J. Harper, *The History of Britain Revealed,* Icon Books, 2006, p. 116.

78. Carme Jimenez Huertas, *Romance Did Not Begin in Rome: A Critic of the Latin Origin of Romance languages,* CreateSpace, 2018. Listen to the author's interview on Youtube: "No venimos del Latin," www.youtube.com/watch?v=SPI_Y4hdIaU

79. Clara Miller-Broomfield, "Romanian: The forgotten Romance language", 2015, on unravellingmag.com/articles/romanian-the-forgotten-romance-language/

80. en.wikipedia.org/wiki/Dacian_language

81. en.wikipedia.org/wiki/Thracian_language

82. Joseph Solodow, *Latin Alive: The Survival of Latin in English and the Romance Languages ,* Cambridge UP, 2010, p. 53.

83. "Dacians: Unsettling Truths" on Youtube, www.youtube.com/watch?v=8R99LhTukfY&t=2s

84. "Dacians: Unsettling Truths" on Youtube, www.youtube.com/watch?v=8R99LhTukfY&t=2s

85. We need to take into account that Southeastern Romania is located in the Pontic Steppe which, according to the widely held "Kurgan hypothesis", is the original home of the earliest proto-Indo-European speech community.

86. Harper, *The History of Britain Revealed, op. cit.,* pp. 130-131.

87. Steven Runciman, *The Eastern Schism: A Study of the Papacy and the Eastern Churches During the XIth and XIIth Centuries,* Clarendon Press, 1955, p. 8.

88. Angelo Mazzocco, *Linguistic Theories in Dante and the Humanists: Studies of Language and Intellectual History in Late Medieval and Early Renaissance Italy,* E.J. Brill, 1993, p. 175 (read on books.google.com).

89. Stefano Corno, « Langue originelle et langue vulgaire entre *De vulgari eloquentia* et *Divine Comédie* », *La Clé des Langues,* ENS de Lyon/DGESCO, septembre 2010, https://cle.ens-lyon.fr/italien/langue/les-origines/langue-originelle-et-langue-vulgaire-entre-de-vulgari-eloquentia-et-divine-comedie-

90. Viscount James Bryce, *The Holy Roman Empire* (1864), on www.gutenberg.org/ebooks/44101

91. François de Sarre, *Mais où est donc passé le Moyen Âge ? Le récentisme,* Hadès, 2013, on notionsdhistoire.files.wordpress.com/2017/03/ou_est_donc_passe_le_moyen-age.pdf

92. Linda M. Seymour, Janille Maragh, Paolo Sabatini, Michel Di Tommaso, James C. Weaver, and Admir Masic, "Hot Mixing: Mechanistic insights into the durability of Roman concrete," *Science Advances,* 6 Jan 2023, vol. 9, issue 1, www.science.org/doi/10.1126/sciadv.add1602

93. Uwe Topper, "The literary architect Vitruvius: Who wrote his famous book on architecture," www.ilya.it/chrono/en/index.html

94. In the words of Jerry Brotton, *The Renaissance Bazaar: From the Silk Road to Michelangelo,* Oxford UP, 2010, p. 66.

95. Jacques Heers, *Le Moyen Âge, une imposture,* Perrin, 1992, pp. 55-58.

96. Robert Folz, *L'Idée médiévale de l'Empire en Occident,* Aubier, 1953, p. 107.

97. Antonio Pucci [1362], *Libro di varie storie* (a cura di Alberto Varvaro, AAPalermo, s. IV, vol. XVI, parte II, fasc. II, 1957) [anno accademico 1955-56], pp. 136-137, mentioned in it.wikipedia.org/wiki/SPQR, brought to our attention by Chronology 2.0 in their film "La Fake Rome antique", on Youtube, www.youtube.com/watch?v=xLHknfC_OCY&t=1s

98. it.wikipedia.org/wiki/SPQR

99. Folz, *L'Idée médiévale de l'Empire en Occident, op. cit.,* p. 107.

100. Claire Levasseur et Christophe Badel, *Atlas de l'Empire romain : Construction et apogée: 300 av. J.-C. – 200 apr. J.-C.,* Édiions Autrement, 2020, p. 76.

101. Angelo Mazzocco, *Linguistic Theories in Dante and the Humanists: Studies of Language and Intellectual History in Late Medieval and Early Renaissance Italy,* E.J. Brill, 1993, p. 175.

102. Israel Finkelstein and Neil Adher Silberman, *David and Solomon: In Search of the Bible's Sacred Kings and the Roots of the Western Tradition,* S&S International, 2007.

103. Bart D. Ehrman, *Forgery and Counterforgery: The Use of Literary Deceit in Early Christian Polemics,* Oxford University Press, 2013, pp. 1, 27.

104. Quoted in Wilhelm Kammeier, *Verfälsehung der Deutschen une Europäischen Geschichte*, 1940, trans. *La Falsification de l'histoire allemande*, Didi18, 2022.

105. Heribert Illig, "Anomalous Eras - Best Evidence: Best Theory," June 2005, on fr.scribd.com/document/79623295/Anomalous-Eras-H-Illig-Toronto-2005#

106. A notice relating the promise made by Pepin the Short to Pope Stephen II to restore to him the lands taken from the Roman Church (known as the *Fragmentum Fantuzzanum*, from the name of Fantuzzi who published it in his Monumenti Ravennati), is preserved only in a manuscript of the end of the 15th or the beginning of the 16th century.

107. Herbert Edward John Cowdrey, *The Cluniacs and the Gregorian Reform*, Clarendon, 1970.

108. Marc Bloch, *Feudal Society*, vol. 1: *The Growth of Ties of Dependance*, University of Chicago Press, 1964, p. 107.

109. Robert I. Moore, *The First European Revolution, c. 970-1215*, Basil Blackwell, pp. 11, 174.

110. Harold Berman, *Law and Revolution, the Formation of the Western Legal Tradition*, Harvard UP, 1983, pp. 15, 108.

111. Laurent Morelle, "Des faux par milliers" *L'Histoire*, n° 372, February 2012.

112. Reproduced from F. Henderson, (Ed.), *Select Historical Documents of the Middle Ages*, George Bell and Sons, 1910, pp. 329-333, on archive.org/details/selecthistorical00hendiala

113. John Romanides, *Franks, Romans, Feudalism, and Doctrine: An Interplay Between Theology and Society*, Patriarch Athenagoras Memorial Lectures, Holy Cross Orthodox Press, 1981, on www.romanity.org/htm/rom.03. en.franks_romans_feudalism_and_doctrine.01.htm

114. John Meyendorff and Aristeides Papadakis, The Christian East and the Rise of the Papacy, St Vladimir's Seminary Press, 1994, pp. 55, 167, 27.

115. Aviad Kleinberg, *Histoires de saints. Leur rôle dans la formation de l'Occident*, Gallimard, 2005, p. 72.

116. Andrew J. Ekonomou, *Byzantine Rome and the Greek Popes: Eastern Influences on Rome and the Papacy from Gregory the Great to Zacharias, A.D. 590-752*, Lexington Books, 2009, p. 43.

117. Heinrich Fichtenau, *Living in the Tenth Century: Mentalities and Social Orders*, trans. Patrick Geary, University of Chicago Press, 1991 (German edition 1984), p. 13.

118. Christopher Dawson, *Religion and the Rise of Western Culture*, Doubleday, 1950, pp. 29-30, on archive.org/details/DawsonReligionAndTheRiseOfWesternCulture

119. Michel Kaplan, *Pourquoi Byzance ?: Un empire de onze siècles*, Folio/Gallimard, 2016, p. 55.

120. Eusebius, *Life of Constantine*, translated with introduction and commentary by Averil Cameron and Stuart G. Hall, Clarendon Press, 1999, p. 81.

121. *Ibid.*

122. Whether this mosaic portrays Christ or Constantine is debated. If it portrayed Christ, it would be the earliest representation of Christ known, and it would be completely unlike any other.

123. Patricia Stirnemann, *"Saint Augustin, Contre Faustus"*, on www.bibliotheque-virtuelle-clairvaux.com, quoted in fr.wikipedia.org/wiki/Contre_Faustus

124 . Hermann Detering, *O du lieber Augustin: Falsche Bekenntnisse?* Alibri Verlag, 2015.

125. Edwin Johnson, *The Rise of Christendom* (1890), p. 360, on archive.org/details/riseofchristendo008657mbp

126. *Ibid.,* p. 50.

127. *Ibid.,* pp. 7, 80.

128. James Watson, *Interpolations in Bede's Ecclesiastical history and other ancient annals affecting the early history of Scotland and Ireland,* Peebles, 1883, p. 9.

129. Leo Wiener (1920) *Contributions towards a History of Arabico-Gothic Culture; vol. III: Tacitus' Germania and other Forgeries* (Philadelphia, 1920), quoted by Uwe Topper in "Leo Wiener, a pioneer halfway through," 2020, http://www.ilya.it/chrono/en/index.html

130. Grégroire de Tours, *Histoire des rois francs,* Gallimard, 1990, ch IV, p. 103.

131. Raoul Glaber, *Histoires,* éd. et trad. Mathieu Arnoux, Turnhout, Brépols, 1996, book III, §13, pp. 163-165.

132. Thomas Creissen, "La christianisation des lieux de culte païens : 'assassinat', simple récupération ou mythe historiographique ?", *Gallia - Archéologie de la France antique,* CNRS Éditions, 2014, 71 (1), pp. 279-287, on hal.science/hal-01932515

133. Polydor Hochart, *De l'authenticité des Annales et des Histoires de Tacite,* 1890, pp. 3-5, on archive.org/details/delauthenticitde00hoch

134. Klaus Oehler, *Atike Philosophie une byzantinisches Mittelalter,* 1969, p. 16, quoted in Sylvain Gouguenheim, *La Gloire des Grecs,* Éditions du Cerf, 2017, p. 12.

135. Anthony Kaldellis, *Hellenism in Byzantium: The Transformation of Greek Identity and the Reception of the Classical Tradition,* Cambridge UP, 2007, p. 4.

136. Sylvain Gouguenheim, *Aristote au Mont Saint-Michel. Les racines grecques de l'Europe chrétienne,* Seuil, 2008.

137. Einar Joranson, "The Problem of the Spurious Letter of Emperor Alexis to the count of Flanders," *The American Historical Review,* vol. 55 n°4 (July 1950), pp. 811-832, on www.jstor.org.

138. Jonathan Harris, *Byzantium and the Crusades*, Hambledon Continuum, 2003, p. 56.

139. Robert de Clari, *La Conquête de Constantinople,* Champion Classiques, 2004, p. 171.

140. Steven Runciman, *A History of the Crusades, vol. 3: The Kingdom of Acre and the Later Crusades (1954),* Penguin Classics, 2016, p. 123.

141. Harris, *Byzantium and the Crusades, op. cit.,* p. 50.

142. Runciman, *A History of the Crusades,* vol. 3, *op. cit,* p. 130.

143. Andrew Louth, *Greek East and Latin West: The Church AD 681-1071,* St Vladimir's Seminary Press, 2007, p. 20.

144. Anthony Kaldellis, *Romanland: Ethnicity and Empire in Byzantium,* Belknap Press, 2019, kindle l. 629-641.

145. *Ibid.,* l. 1489.

146. *Ibid.,* l. 217-229.

147. *Ibid.,* l. 288.

148. *Ibid.,* l. 883.

149. Anthony Kaldellis, *Hellenism in Byzantium: The Transformation of Greek Identity and the Reception of the Classical Tradition,* Cambridge UP, 2007, p. 107.

150. en.wikipedia.org/wiki/Name_of_Greece

151. Kaldellis, *Romanland, op. cit.,* l. 2136-2226. Kaldellis, in l. 2088, adopts the dubious claim, made by Carolina Cupane, that when Byzantines mention "the language of the Romans", they sometimes meant Latin rather than Greek, but then he only provides evidence to the contrary.

152. Anthony Kaldellis, *The Byzantine Republic: People and Power in New Rome,* Harvard UP, 2015, pp. 146, 199.

153. Anthony Kaldellis, "Introduction", in Prokopios, *The Secret History with related texts,* edited and translated by Anthony Kaldellis, Hatchett Publishing, 2010.

154. *Ibid.*

155. John Bagnel Bury, *History of the Later Roman Empire, from the Death of Theodosius I. to the Death of Justinian (A.D. 395 to A.D. 565),* vol. 1, MacMillan, 1923, p. 422.

156. *Ibid.,* p. 424.

157. Kaldellis, "Introduction", *in* Prokopios, *The Secret History, op. cit.*

158. Edwin Hunt, *The Medieval Super-Companies: A Study of the Peruzzi Company of Florence,* Cambridge UP, 1994.

159. Jerry Brotton, *The Renaissance Bazaar: From the Silk Road to Michelangelo,* Oxford UP, 2010, p. 103.

160. In *Re-Dating Ancient Greece* (2008), Sylvain Tristan points to intriguing parallels between Plato's and Pletho's lives, and makes the hypothesis that Plato is in reality a fictional *personae* of Pletho.

161. John Meyendorff, *Byzantium and the Rise of Russia,* Cambridge UP, 1981, p. 2.

162. Steven Runciman, *The Fall of Constantinople 1453,* Cambridge UP, 1965, p. 190.

163. Michel Kaplan, *Pourquoi Byzance? Un empire de onze siècles,* Folio/Gallimard, 2016, p. 39.

164. Roderick Saxey II, "The Greek language through time," 1998-99, linguistics.byu.edu/classes/ling450ch/reports/greek.html

165. Margaret Alexiou, "Diglossia in Greece," in William Haas, *Standard Languages: Spoken and Written,* Manchester UP, 1982.

166. Anthony Kaldellis, *The Christian Parthenon : Classicism and Pilgrimage in Byzantine Athens,* Cambridge UP, 2009, pp. 40, 44.

167. *Ibid.,* p. 104.

168. William Miller, *The Latins in the Levant: A History of Frankish Greece (1204-1566)*, P. Dutton & Co., 1908 (on archive.org), pp. 315, 327.

169. Garth Fowden, *Before and After Muhammad*, Princeton UP, 2014, p. 10.

170. en.wikipedia.org/wiki/Theories_about_Alexander_the_Great_in_the_Quran

171. Sylvain Tristan, *Re-Dating Ancient Greece: 500 BC = 1300 AD?*, independently published, 2008.

172. Bernard Guenée, *Histoire et culture historique dans l'occident medieval*, Aubier, 2011, p. 9.

173. David Carrette, *L'Invention du Moyen Âge. La plus grande falsification de l'histoire*, Magazine *Top-Secret*, Hors-série n°9, 2014, pp. 43, 53.

174. eclipse.gsfc.nasa.gov/eclipse.html

175. Richard Stephenson, *Historical Eclipses and Earth's Rotation*, Cambridge UP, 1997, quoted in Petra Ossowski Larsson and Lars-Åke Larsson, "Astronomical dating of Roman time," February 2016, www.researchgate.net/publication/296060902_Astronomical_dating_of_Roma n_time

176. Florin Diacu, *The Lost Millennium: History's Timetables under Siege*, second edition, John Hopkins University Press, 2011, p. 85. Chapter 2 of this book, pp. 33-52, is a good exposé of the use of astronomy in chronology.

177. *Ibid.*, p. 39.

178. Robert R. Newton, *The Crime of Claudius Ptolemy*, The John Hopkins UP, 1997, p. 374.

179. Vedveer Arya, "Ptolemy's Almagest: A Great Treatise or A Successful Fraud," www.academia.edu/51299571/Ptolemys_Almagest_A_Great_Treatise_ or_A_Successful_Fraud

180. cometography.com/lcomets/1106c1.html

181. Cornell University, "Inaccuracies in radiocarbon dating," June 5, 2018, www.sciencedaily.com/releases/2018/06/180605112057.htm

182. Don Lincoln, "Carbon 14 Dating: Complications and Mitigations," September 13, 2020, www.wondriumdaily.com/carbon-14-dating-complications-and-mitigations - :~:text=The ratio of carbon 14 to carbon 12 is about,assigned a number of 100%25

183. Petra Ossowski Larsson and Lars-Åke Larsson, "Radiocarbon dates of dendro-dated timbers from Roman London show large offset," June 2019, www.researchgate.net/publication/334094183_Radiocarbon_dates_of_dendro-dated_timbers_from_Roman_London_show_large_offset

184. A. Bayliss, "Rolling Out Revolution: Using Radiocarbon Dating in Archaeology," *Radiocarbon* 51(1), 2009, pp. 123-147, www.cambridge.org/core/journals/radiocarbon/article/rolling-out-revolution-using-radiocarbon- dating-in-archaeology/0CCCCE4FB7B0BEF52F552C1039C7855Aquoted in Petra Ossowski Larsson and Lars-Åke Larsson, "Radiocarbon dates of dendro-dated timbers from Roman London show large offset," *op. cit.*

185. Peter James, *Centuries of Darkness: a challenge to the conventional chronology of Old World archaeology*, Rutgers UP, 1993, p. xix.

186. G. Lambert, "Dendrochronologie et archéologie : problèmes méthodologiques et théoriques (Exposé de synthèse)," *ArchéoSciences, revue*

d'Archéométrie, année 1980, 4, pp. 9-20, on www.persee.fr/doc/arsci_0399-1237_1980_num_4_1_1105

187. Quoted in Hans-Ulrich Niemitz, "Did the Early Middle Ages Really Exist?" 1995, revised 2000, citeseerx.ist.psu.edu/viewdoc/download;jsessionid=68593502395E97A609231B4DAF9CC4F3?doi=10.1.1.494.4845&rep=rep1&type=pdf

188. Diacu, *The Lost Millennium, op. cit.*, p. 176.

189. Petra Ossowski Larsson and Lars-Åke Larsson, "Merging Hollstein curves – an interpretation. Rebuilding the periods AD 814-1974, AD 401-1974 and 340 BC - AD 336," September 2010, https://www.cybis.se/forfun/dendro/hollstein/merging/index.htm

190. Petra Ossowski Larsson and Lars-Åke Larsson, "Redating West-Roman history," August 2016, www.researchgate.net/publication/306268333_Redating_West-Roman_history_-about_specious_twin_events_and_anachronisms_in_Late_Antiquity

191. Petra Ossowski Larsson and Lars-Åke Larsson, "Astronomical dating of Roman time," February 2016, www.researchgate.net/publication/296060902_Astronomical_dating_of_Roman_time

192. Lars-Åke Larsson and Petra Ossowski Larsson, "The validity of the European chronology. The case of the stem of the Trier Amphitheater", January 1, 2010, updated February 17, 2010, www.cybis.se/forfun/dendro/hollstein/arenakeller2/

193. Lars-Åke Larsson and Petra Ossowski Larsson, "The ambiguous match in the Hollstein chronology. Confirming the dating of the Middle collection to AD 401-716," 21 September 2010, www.cybis.se/forfun/dendro/hollstein/ambiguous/index.htm

194. Petra Ossowski Larsson and Lars-Åke Larsson, "How continuous is the European Oak Chronology?" February 2015, media.cdendro.se/2015/02/16117-19224-1-SM.pdf

195. Lars-Åke Larsson and Petra Ossowski Larsson, "Dendrochronological Dating of Roman Time" April 2015, www.researchgate.net/publication/275083761_Dendrochronological_Dating_of_Roman_Time

196. Ossowski Larsson and Larsson, "Astronomical dating of Roman time," *op. cit.*

197. Ossowski Larsson and Larsson, "Redating West-Roman history," *op. cit.* Until indicated otherwise, quotes are from this article.

198. Eivind Heldaas Seland, "The Liber Pontificalis and Red Sea Trade of the Early to Mid 4th Century AD," in D. A. Agius, J. P. Cooper, A. Trakadas & C. Zazzaro (Eds.), *Navigated Spaces, Connected Places: Proceedings of Red Sea Project V*, Archaeopress, pp. 117-126, www.academia.edu/26383437/The_Liber_Pontificalis_and_Red_Sea_Trade_of_the_Early_to_Mid_4th_Century_AD

199. Ossowski Larsson and Larsson, "Astronomical dating of Roman time," *op. cit.*

200. en.wikipedia.org/wiki/Late_antiquity - Terminology

201. Ossowski Larsson and Larsson, "Redating West-Roman history," *op. cit.*
202. Petra Ossowski Larsson and Lars-Åke Larsson, "About the obsession with Roman heirlooms in Late Antiquity," August 2019, www.researchgate.net/publication/335517926_About_the_obsession_with_Ro man_heirlooms_in_Late_Antiquity
203. www.unz.com/article/byzantine-revisionism-unlocks-world-history/?showcomments#comment-6075898
204. https://www.soulask.com/researchers-hypothesis-a-civilization-reset-happens-every-676-years-the-next-would-come-in-2024/
205. Edward Gibbon was the first to call into question the authenticity of traditional accounts of the Christian martyrs in his *History of the Decline and Fall of the Roman Empire* (1776).
206. Petra Ossowski Larsson and Lars-Åke Larsson, "Response to Rzepecki et al., 'Missing link in Late Antiquity? A critical examination of Hollstein's Central European Oak Chronology," 2019, www.researchgate.net/publication/330857300_Response_to_Rzepecki_et_al_ Missing_link_in_ Late_Antiquity_A_critical_examination_of_Hollstein%27s_Central_European _Oak_Chronology
207. Heribert Illig, "Anomalous Eras – Best Evidence: Best Theory," Toronto Conference, 2005, fr.scribd.com/document/79623295/Anomalous-Eras-H-Illig-Toronto-2005#; Hans-Ulrich Niemitz, "Did the Early Middle Ages Really Exist?" 1995, revised 2000, citeseerx.ist.psu.edu/viewdoc/download;jsessionid=68593502395E97A609231 B4DAF9CC4F3?doi=10.1.1.494.4845&rep=rep1&type=pdf
208. Quoted in Heribert Illig, "Anomalous Eras – Best Evidence: Best Theory," Toronto Conference, 2005, https://fr.scribd.com/document/79623295/Anomalous-Eras-H-Illig-Toronto-2005
209. Ossowski Larsson and Larsson, "Redating West-Roman history," *op. cit.*
210. Larsson and Ossowski Larsson, "Merging Hollstein curves," *op; cit.*
211. Ernst Hollstein, "Dendrochronologische Untersuchungen an Hölzern des frühen Mittelalters," in *Acta Praehistorica* 1(1970), p. 147-156 [p. 148], quoted in Hans-Ulrich Niemitz, "Did the Early Middle Ages Really Exist?" *op. cit.*
212. Petra Ossowski Larsson, Lars-Åke Larsson, "An Irish tree ring chronology. An interpretation of some raw dendrochronology data published by the Queen's University Belfast", September 9, 2012, www.cdendro.se/forfun/dendro/hollstein/belfast/index.htm#NewEnglishData
213. A good presentation in this Youtube video, "New Chronology by Fomenko", www.youtube.com/watch?v=HN3S8ncDehY&list =PLCOZWPrcz4SKwqQ1I0Gm6krti4yTzuDlA&index=2&t=0s
214. Anatoly Fomenko, *History, Fiction or Science,* Chronology 1, archive.org/details/bub_gb_YcjFAV4WZ9MC
215. Anatoly Fomenko and Gleb Nosovsky, *History: Fiction or Science,* volume 1: *Introducing the problem. A criticism of the Scaligerian chronology. Dating methods as offered by mathematical statistics. Eclipses and zodiacs,*

chapter 6, p. 356, on ia601300.us.archive.org/1/items/AnatolyFomenko Books/History-FictionOrScienceByAnatolyFomenkoVol.1.pdf

216. Anatoly Fomenko and Gleb Nosovsky, *History: Fiction or Science,* vol. 2: *The dynastic parallelism method. Rome. Troy. Greece. The Bible. Chronological shifts*, pp. 19-42, on archive.org/details/history-fiction-or-science-vol.-2

217. Fomenko and Nosovsky, *History: Fiction or Science,* vol. 1, ch. 6, pp. 356-358, on chronologia.org/en/seven/1N06-EN-326-372.pdf

218. Florin Diacu, *The Lost Millennium: History's Timetables under Siege,* second edition, John Hopkins University Press, 2011, p. 196.

219. www.q-mag.org/gunnar-heinsohns-latest.html Many of Heinsohn's articles are now downloadable on https://independent.academia.edu/Gheinsohn. His original German articles are on www.xn--zeitensprnge-llb.de/

220. "Gunnar Heinsohn - Toronto Conference2016," Youtube, www.youtube.com/watch?v=c876lPZ-UZU

221. Heinsohn, "Creation of the First Millennium CE," 2013.

222. Heinsohn, "Justinian's correct date in 1st Millennium chronology," 2019.

223. Heinsohn, "The Stratigraphy of Rome," 2018.

224. Heinsohn, "Heinsohn in a nutshell"

225. Heinsohn, "Letter to Heribert Illig," 2017.

226. Heinsohn, "Goths of the 4th century and Getae of the 1st century," 2014.

227. Heinsohn, "Justinian's correct date in 1st Millennium chronology," 2019.

228. Heinsohn, "Charlemagne's Correct Place in History," 2014.

229. *Ibid.*

230. Heinsohn, "Letter to Heribert Illig," 2017.

231. From Heinsohn's letter to Eric Knibbs, 2020, communicated to the author.

232. Heinsohn, "Creation of the First Millennium CE" 2013.

233. Heinsohn, "London in the first millennium AD: finding Bede's missing metropolis" 2018.

234. *Ibid.*

235. Heinsohn, "Justinian's correct date in 1st Millennium chronology," 2019.

236. Heinsohn, "Ravenna and chronology," 2020. Also "Justinian's correct date in 1st Millennium chronology," 2019.

237. Heinsohn, "Siegfried found: decoding the Nibelungen period," 2018.

238. Heinsohn, "Charlemagne's Correct Place in History" 2014.

239. Heinsohn, "The Stratigraphy of Rome," 2018.

240 Heinsohn, "Polish origins," 2018.

241 Theodor Mommsen, A History of Rome Under the Emperors. Routledge, 2005, p. 281.

242. Heinsohn, "4th century and Getae of the 1st century: are they one and the same?" 2014.

243. *Ibid.*

244. Arne Sby Christensen, *Cassiodorus Jordanes and the History of the Gothic: Studies in a Migration Myth,* Museum Tusculanum, 2002.

245. Walter Goffart, "Jordanes's 'Getica' and the Disputed Authenticity of Gothic Origins from Scandinavia," *Speculum*, Vol. 80, No. 2 (Apr. 2005), pp. 379-398, www.jstor.org/stable/20463271

246. Heinsohn, "Polish origins" 2018.
247. Heinsohn, "Did Europe and Civilization Collapse Three Times Within the 1st Millennium CE?" 2014.
248. Michael J. Decker, *The Byzantine Dark Ages,* Bloomsbury Academic, 2016; Eleonora Kountoura-Galake, ed., *The Dark Centuries of Byzantium (7th-9th C.),* National Hellenic Research Foundation, 2001.
249. John J. O'Neill, *Holy Warriors: Islam and the Demise of Classical Civilization,* Felibri.com, Ingram Books, 2009, p. 231, quoted in Heinsohn, "Were there really no people in Poland between 300 and 600 AD?" 2020.
250. Heinsohn, "Justinian's correct date in 1st Millennium chronology," 2019.
251. Heinsohn, "Creation of the First Millennium CE", 2013.
252. Heinsohn, "Augustus and Diocletian: contemporaries or 300 years apart?" 2019.
253. Quoted in Heinsohn, "Ravenna and chronology," 2020.
254. *Ibid.*
255. Heinsohn, "Charlemagne's Correct Place in History" 2014, quoting *Fortifications* (2009), "Kaiserpfalz Ingelheim: Fortifications", http://www.kaiserpfalz-ingelheim.de/en/historical_tour_10.php
256. Heinsohn, "Charlemagne's Correct Place in History" 2014 quoting https://www.kaiserpfalz-ingelheim.de/en/about_us.php
257. Heinsohn, "Ravenna and chronology," 2020; with references to internal quotations.
258. Heinsohn, "Charlemagne's Correct Place in History," 2014.
259. Heinsohn, "Ravenna and chronology," 2020.
260. Heinsohn, "London in the first millennium AD," 2018. Also Paola Supino Martini, "Société et culture écrite," dans André Vauchez, dir., *Rome au Moyen Âge,* Éditions du Cerf, 2021, pp. 351-384 [358]).
261. From Heinsohn's letter to Eric Knibbs, 2020, communicated to the author.
262. Eginhard, *Vie de Charlemagne,* Louis Halphen éd., Les Belles Lettres, 1938, 1967, quoted in Jean Meyers, « Éginhard et Suétone. À propos des chapitres 18 à 27 de la *Vita Karoli* », in *Les Historiens et le latin médiéval,* Monique Goullet et Michel Parisse (dir.), Édition de la Sorbonne, 2001, pp. 129-150, on books.openedition.org/psorbonne/21094?lang=fr
263. Robert A. Kaster, "The Transmission of Suetonius's *Caesars* in the Middle Ages," Transactions of the American Philological Association, Volume 144, Number 1, Spring 2014, pp. 133-186, on scholar.princeton.edu/ Kaster dates that archetype "late in the 8th century or very early in the 9th" but it sounds unlikely.
264. Heinsohn, "Charlemagne's Correct Place in History," 2014.
265. *Ibid.*
266. Heinsohn, "Ravenna and chronology," 2020.
267. Richard Krautheimer, *Rome: Profile of a City, 321-1308,* Princeton UP, 1980, p. 117.
268. Heinsohn, "Charlemagne's Correct Place in History," 2014.
269. *Ibid.*
270. Ferdinand Lot, *La Fin du monde antique* (1927), Albin Michel, 1989, p. 17.

271. Heinsohn, "Jerusalem in the First Millennium AD: Stratigraphy vs. the Scholarly Belief in Anno Domini Chronology," 2021, p. 109.

272. Heinsohn, "Londinium and Lundenwic were not 700 years apart," 2018, edited 22 January 2023, www.academia.edu/95458006/LONDINIUM_AND_LUNDENWIC_WERE_N OT_700_YEARS_APART_Heinsohn_January_2023. Quotation from Reinhold Kaiser, "Vom Frühzum Hochmittelalter," in Flueler-Grauwiler, M. et al., eds., *Geschichte des Kantons Zürich. Band 1: Frühzeit bis Spätmittelalter*, Zürich: Werd, 1995, pp. 130-171 [152].

273. Heinsohn, "Charlemagne's Correct Place in History," 2014.

274. Heinsohn, "London in the first millennium AD," 2018.

275. Heinsohn, "Londinium and Lundenwic were not 700 years apart," *op. cit.* The quote is from Robin Fleming, *Vanishing Plants, Animals, and Places: Britain's Transformation from Roman to Medieval,"* lecture at Fordham's Center for Medieval Studies and the New York Botanical Garden, Humanities Institute, Mertz Library, New York Botanical Garden, 30 September 2016, and reported by Clark Whelton, "A Canterbury Tale by Saucy Chaucer," 2016, malagabay.wordpress.com/2016/10/06/a-canterbury-tale-by-saucy-chaucer/

276. Heinsohn, "The Winchester of Alfred the Great and the Haithabu of his voyager, Wulfstan: Are they separated by 700 years?" 2014.

277. Heinsohn, "Vikings for 700 years without sails, ports and towns? An essay," 2014.

278. Heinsohn, "Anno Domini and the Disstortion of Scientific Dating," 2021.

279. Heinsohn, "Londinium and Lundenwic were not 700 years apart," *op. cit.*

280. *Ibid.*

281. Heinsohn, "Arthur of Camelot and the-Domaros of Camulodunum," 2017.

282. Heinsohn, "Vikings for 700 years without sails, ports and towns? An essay," 2014.

283. *Ibid.*

284. Heinsohn, "Bulgaria's early medieval capitals of Pliska and Preslav: were they really built to resemble 700 year older Roman cities?" 2015.

285. Heinsohn, "Papermaking," 2017.

286. "When a planet behaves like a comet," www.esa.int/Science_Exploration/Space_Science/When_a_planet_behaves_lik e_a_comet

287. Jeff Hecht, "Planet's tail of the unexpected," 31 May 1997, www.newscientist.com/article/mg15420842-900-science-planets-tail-of-the-unexpected/

288. James McCanney, *Planet-X, Comets & Earth Changes: A Scientific Treatise on the Effects of a New Large Planet or Comet Arriving in our Solar System and Expected Earth Weather and Earth Changes,* jmccanneyscience.com press, 2007, www.bibliotecapleyades.net/ciencia/ciencia_maccanney07.htm

289. Heinsohn, "Did Europe and Civilization Collapse Three Times Within the 1st Millennium CE?" (2014).

290. *Ibid.*

291. Wolf Liebeschuetz, "The End of the Ancient City", in J. Rich, ed., *The City in Late Antiquity*, Routledge, 1992, quoted in Heinsohn, "Justinian's correct date in 1st Millennium chronology," 2019.
292. "The Mystery of 536 AD: The Worst Climate Disaster in History" on Youtube, www.youtube.com/watch?v=cKUz5Vjq9-s Read also Ann Gibbons, "Why was 536 'the worst year to be alive'", 15 Nov. 2018, on www.science.org/content/article/why-536-was-worst-year-be-alive
293. Emma Rigby, "A comet impact in AD 536 ?" February 2004, on academic.oup.com/astrogeo/article/45/1/1.23/229520
294. John Loeffler, "How Comets Changed the Course of Human History," November 30th, 2008, on interestingengineering.com/how-comets-changed-the-course-of-human-history
295. "The Comet's Tale – BBC" on Youtube, www.youtube.com/watch?v=oiFjeYrWlL0
296. Useful article: Declan M Mills, "The Tenth-Century Collapse in West Francia and the Birth of Christian Holy War," Newcastle University Postgraduate Forum E-Journal, Edition 12, 2015, on www.societies.ncl.ac.uk/pgfnewcastle/files/2015/12/Mills-Tenth-century-collapse.pdf
297. Heinsohn, "Tenth Century Collapse," 2017.
298. *Ibid.*
299. Mark Bloch, *Feudal Society* (1940), Routledge, 2014, pp. 43-44.
300. Heinsohn, "Tenth Century Collapse," 2017.
301. Edward Adams, *The Stars Will Fall From Heaven: 'Cosmic Catastrophe' in the New Testament and its World*, The Library of New Testament Studies, 2007.
302. Heinsohn, "Ravenna and chronology," 2020.
303. Heinsohn, "Mieszko I, destructions, and Slavic mass conversions to Christianity," 2014.
304. Heinsohn, "Creation of the First Millennium CE," 2013.
305. Heinsohn, "Charlemagne's Correct Place in History," 2014).
306. Dionysius supposedly made his computation in 532 AD, but since he was living in Bulgaria, in the Byzantine world, this date corresponds to 232 in Imperial Antiquity (and to 932 AD in Early Middle Ages).
307. Barry Hoberman, "The King of Ghassan", 1983, on archive.aramcoworld.com/issue/198302/the.king.of.ghassan.htm quoted in Heinsohn, "Justinian's correct date in 1st Millennium chronology," 2019.
308. Garth Fowden, *Before and After Muhammad,* Princeton UP, 2014, p. 78.
309. https://en.wikipedia.org/wiki/Revisionist_school_of_Islamic_studies
310. Nicolas Standaert, "Jesuit Accounts of Chinese History and Chronology and Their Chinese Sources," *East Asian Science, Technology, and Medicine*, no. 35, 2012, pp. 11–87, on www.jstor.org/stable/43150809
311. According to Paola Supino Martini, the "Caroline minuscule" was a "revival of models of the ancient minuscule", and so was the majuscule "uncial" used for luxurious manuscripts (Paola Supino Martini, "Société et culture écrite," in André Vauchez ed., *Rome au Moyen Âge,* Éditions du Cerf, 2021, pp. 351-384 [358]).
312. Heinsohn, "Creation of the First Millennium CE", 2013.

313. Heinsohn, "Jerusalem in the First Millennium AD: Stratigraphy vs. the Scholarly Belief in Anno Domini Chronology," 2021, p. 91.

314. Heinsohn, "Arthur of Camelot and the-Domaros of Camulodunum," 2017.

315. Heinsohn, "Ravenna and chronology," 2020.

316. Heinsohn, "Charlemagne's Correct Place in History," 2014.

317. Heinsohn, "Jerusalem in the First Millennium AD," 2021, p. 84.

318. J.M. Wallace-Hadrill, *The Barbarian West 400-1000*, Blackwell (1967), 2004, p. 47.

319. Walter Bauer, *Orthodoxie et hérésie au début du christianisme* (1934), Cerf, 2009, pp. 74-88. Also Robert I. Moore, *The Formation of a Persecuting Society: Authority and Deviance in Western Europe 950-1250* (1987), Wiley-Blackwell, 2007..

320. Richard Krautheimer, *Rome: Profile of a City, 321-1308*, Princeton UP, 1980, pp. 70-71. J.M. Wallace-Hadrill nottes in *The Barbarian West 400-1000*, Blackwell (1967), 2004, p. 30 "the earliest papal documents (dating from the late fourth century) derives from a chancery unmistakably modelled upon the Roman imperial chancery."

321. Robert I. Moore, *The First European Revolution, c. 970-1215*, Basil Blackwell, 2000.

322. Hélène Toubert, "Le renouveau paléochrétien à Rome au début du XIIe siècle," in *Cahiers Archéologiques*, 29, 1970, pp. 99-154.

323. Main source : en.wikipedia.org/wiki/Nabataean_Kingdom - Creation_of_the_Nabataean_Kingdom

324. Heinsohn, "Arab coinage hiatus," 2021.

325. Heinsohn, "Mieszko I, destructions, and Slavic mass conversions to Christianity," 2014.

326. Heinsohn, "Justinian's correct date in 1st Millennium chronology" (2019), p. 8.

327. Heinsohn, "Mieszko I, destructions, and Slavic mass conversions to Christianity," 2014.

328. Heinsohn, "Arab coinage hiatus," 2021.

329. Heinsohn, "Jerusalem in the First Millennium AD," 2021, pp. 51-54.

330. Heinsohn, "Vikings for 700 years without sails, ports and towns? An essay," 2014, quoting otraarquitecturaesposible.blogspot.com.tr/2011/03/typologies-in-islamic-architecture-iv.html

331. Heinsohn, "Jerusalem in the First Millennium AD," 2021, p. 56.

332. Heinsohn, "Justinian's correct date in 1st Millennium chronology," 2019, p. 41.

333. Heinsohn, "Jerusalem in the First Millennium AD," 2021, p. 82.

334. *The David Collection: Islamic Art / Glass*, 2014, on www.davidmus.dk/en/collections/islamic/materials/glass), quoted in Heinsohn, "Jerusalem in the First Millennium AD," 2021, p. 56.

335. Heinsohn, "Jerusalem in the First Millennium AD," 2021, p. 98.

336. Heinsohn, "Islam's Chronology: Were Arabs Really Ignorant of Coinage and Writing for 700 Years?" 2013.

337. Amiram Barka, "The Big One Is Coming," *Haaretz*, August 8, 2003, www.haaretz.com/1.5357523 quoted in Heinsohn, "Arabs of the 8th Century: Cultural imitators or original creators?" 2018.

338. Heinsohn, "Jerusalem in the First Millennium AD," 2021, pp. 59-60, referring to M.D. Bukharin, "Towards the Earliest History of Kinda", *Arabian Archaeology and Epigraphy*, Vol. 20, No. 1, 2009, pp. 64-80 (67).

339. Heinsohn, "Islam's Chronology: Were Arabs Really Ignorant of Coinage and Writing for 700 Years?" 2013.

340. Alfred-Louis de Prémare, *Les Fondations de l'islam,* Seuil, 2002, p. 41-56; David Samuel Margoliouth, *Mohammed and the Rise of Islam,* Putnam's Sons, 1905, p. 35-39.

341. Gordon Darnell Newby, *A History of the Jews of Arabia, From Ancient Times to Their Ecclipse under Islam,* University of South Carolina Press, 1988, pp. 17, 47, 105.

342. Günther Lüling, *A Challenge to Islam for Reformation* (1993), Motilal Banarsidass Publishers, 2003 (on books.google.fr), pp. xii-xv.

343. Patricia Crone and Michael Cook, *Hagarism: The Making of the Islamic World*, Cambridge UP, 1977 (archive.org), pp. 6-30. In 1998, Robert Hoyland refined Crone and Cook's thesis by providing other sources in *Seeing Islam as Others Saw It. A Survey and Evaluation of Christian, Jewish and Zoroastrian Writings on Early Islam*, on legrandsecretdelislam.files.wordpress.com/ 2016/03/r-hoyland-seeing_islam_as_other_saw_it.pdf.

344. Gerd-Rüdiger Puin, "Observations on Early Qur'an Manuscripts in Ṣanʿāʾ'", in Stefan Wild, ed., *The Qur'an as Text*, Brill, 1996, pp. 107 ff, quoted in Heinsohn, "Hadrian Umayyads in Jerusalem. Justice for Jewish and Arab Histories," 2020.

345. Youtube, "The Sacred City: Discovering the Real Birthplace of Islam," www.youtube.com/watch?v=jtIyeREGCYI at 51:22.

346. *Ibid.*

347. Shlomit Weksler-Bdolah, *Aelia Capitolina – Jerusalem in the Roman Period: In Light of Archaeological Research*, Brill, 2020, pp. 21-22, 42-43.

348. Read this summary in *Popular Archaeology:* Marilyn Sams, "Antonia: The Fortress Jerusalem Forgot," Dc 17, 2015, popular-archaeology.com/article/antonia-the-fortress-jerusalem-forgot/

349. Gregory Wesley Buchanan, "Misunderstandings About Jerusalem's Temple Mount," *Washington Report on Middle East Affairs,* August 2011, www.wrmea.org/011-august/misunderstandings-about-jerusalem-s-temple-mount.html

350. Youtube, "The Temple – Bob Cornuke," www.youtube.com/watch?v=zKqDx3rdCos. In complement, the film "The Coming Temple" is interesting, despite its religious overtone.

351. Heinsohn, "Jerusalem in the First Millennium AD," 2021, p. 106.

352. Orit Peleg-Barkat, "The Temple Mount excavations in Jerusalem 1968–1978 directed by Benjamin Mazar final reports volume V Herodian architectural decoration and King Herod's royal portico", in *Qedem* 57, 2017, pp. 29 ff, quoted in Heinsohn, "Jerusalem in the First Millennium AD: Stratigraphy vs. the Scholarly Belief in Anno Domini Chronology" (2021), pp. 61-63.

353. Heinsohn, "Jerusalem in the First Millennium AD," 2021, p. 19.

354. *Ibid.* Heinsohn refers to I.M. Baidoun 2015/16, "Arabic names of Jerusalem on coins and in historical sources until the early 'Abbāsid period'", Israel Numismatic Journal, 19, pp. 142-150, (145-46).

355 Heinsohn, "Jerusalem in the First Millennium AD," 2021, pp. 108, 61-63.

356. Steve Mason, "Jews, Judaeans, Judaizing, Judaism: Problems of Categorization in Ancient History," *Journal for the Study of Judaism,* 1 January, 2007, www.researchgate.net/publication/233652312_Jews_Judaeans_Judaizing_Judai sm_Problems_of_Categorization_in_Ancient_History

357. Moab is Abraham's nephew (Genesis 19:31-38), Edom or Esau is Abraham's grandson (25:25), Amaleq is Esau's grandson (36:12), and the Midianites are descendants of Abraham by his second wife Keturah (25:2-4), while the Ishmaelites are descendants of Abraham by his servant Agar.

358. David Samuel Margoliouth, *Relations Between Arabs and Israelites Prior to the Rise of Islam: The Schweich Lectures 1921,* Oxford UP, 1924.

359. The Midianite hypothesis was first formulated by Friedrich Ghillany (1863, under the pseudonym of Richard von der Alm) and Karl Budde (1899), and has now gained the support of top biblical scholars such as Thomas Römer (*The Invention of God,* Harvard UP, 2016).

360. Philip Davies, *In Search of "Ancient Israel": A Study in Biblical Origins,* Journal of the Study of the Old Testament, 1992.

361. Heinsohn, "Justinian's correct date in 1st Millennium chronology," 2019.

362. Still in the early 14th century, Dante Alighieri associated Arius and Muhammad in the eighth circle of Hell: Maria Esposito Frank, "Dante's Muhammad: Parallels between Islam and Arianism," in *Dante and Islam,* ed. Jan M. Ziolkowski, Fordham UP, 2014.

363. Ralf Bockmann, "The Non-Archaeology of Arianism - What Comparing Cases in Carthage, Haidra and Ravenna can tell us about 'Arian' Churches" in *Arianism: Roman Heresy and Barbarian Creed,* ed. Gudo M. Berndt and Roland Steinacher, Ashgate, 2014; Alexandra Chavarria Arnau, "Finding invisible Arians: An archaeological perspective on churches, baptism and religious competition in 6th century Spain", 2017, also available on the Internet.

364. Ignacio Olagüe, *Les Arabes n'ont jamais envahi l'Espagne,* Flammarion, 1969. The thesis is supported by Spanish Arabist González Ferrín, on elpais.com/diario/2006/11/17/andalucia/1163719349_850215.html

365. Ewa Weiling-Feldthusen, "In search of a missing link : the Bogomils and Zoroastrianism," 2006, www.medievalists.net/2013/01/in-search-of-a-missing-link-the-bogomils-and-zoroastrianism/

366. Heinsohn, "Saint Paul: Did he live once, thrice, or not at all?" 2020.

367. Guy Monnot, *Islam et religions,* Maisonneuve & Larose, 1986.

368. Melhem Chokr, *Zandaqa et Zindīqs en islam au second siècle de l'Hégire,* Presses de l'Ifpo, 1993, Première partie, chapitre II, on books.openedition.org/ifpo/5360?lang=fr

369. Elizabeth Jeffreys, Brian Croke, Roger Scott (eds.), *Studies in John Malalas,* Brill, 2017 p. 13.

370. Read Werner Sundermann's articles "Manicheism v. Missionary activity and technique" and "CHRISTIANITY v. Christ in Manicheism," both from *Encyclopædia Iranica* (2009) and available on www.iranicaonline.org

371. B. R. S. Mead, *The Gnostic John the Baptizer: Selections from the Mandean John-Book Together with Studies on John and Christian Origins,* John M. Watkins, 1924.

372. Edward Adams, *The Stars Will Fall From Heaven: 'Cosmic Catastrophe' in the New Testament and its World,* The Library of New Testament Studies, 2007.

373. Heinsohn, "Mieszko I, destructions, and Slavic mass conversions to Christianity" (2014), *op. cit.*

374. en-academic.com/dic.nsf/enwiki/11621109

375. Peter James, *Centuries of Darkness: a challenge to the conventional chronology of Old World archaeology,* Rutgers UP, 1993, p. xxi.

376. *Ibid.,* pp. 4-5.

377. P. John Crowe, "The Revision of Ancient History – A Perspective," 1999, www.sis-group.org.uk/papers/2007/08/09/the-revision-of-ancient-history-a-perspective/

378. Gunnar Heinsohn, "The Restauration of Ancient History," now archived on archive.ph/isBHx

379. *Ibid.*

380. Brendan War, "The Evolution of the Conventional Chronology," 2021, peakd.com/heinsohn/@harlotscurse/the-evolution-of-the-conventional-chronology

381. Florin Diacu, *The Lost Millennium: History's Timetables under Siege,* second edition, John Hopkins University Press, 2011, p. 200.

382. According to Kwang-Chih Chang (*The Archaeology of China,* 1963, p. 136), quoted by Heinsohn, "the known beginning of civilization in China is approximately a millennium and a half later than the initial phases of Near Eastern civilization."

383. Brendan War, "The Chronology of Ancient China," peakd.com/heinsohn/@harlotscurse/the-chronology-of-ancient-china; peakd.com/heinsohn/@harlotscurse/taking-leave-of-the-restoration-of-ancient-history

384. Diacu, *The Lost Millennium, op. cit.*, p. 35.

385. Anthony Grafton, *Christianity and the transformation of the Book: Origen, Eusebius, and the Library of Caesarea,* Harvard UP, 2009, p. 136.

386. *Ibid.,* p. 175.

387. *Ibid.,* pp. 18, 212, 215.

388. *Ibid.,* pp. 69 and 111.

389. *Ibid.,* p. 5.

390. *Ibid.,* p. 244.

391. Philip Davies, *In Search of "Ancient Israel": A Study in Biblical Origins,* Journal of the Study of the Old Testament, 1992, p. 41.

392. Spinoza, *Theological-political treatise,* 8.11, Cambridge UP, 2007, pp. 126-128.

393. Mario Liverani, *La Bible et l'invention de l'histoire,* Gallimard, 2012, pp. 354–355.

394. Attilio Mastrocinque, *From Jewish Magic to Gnosticism,* Mohr Siebeck, 2005, pp. 7-10.

395. Gilles Quispel, *Gnostica, Judaica, Catholica. Collected Essays of Gilles Quispel,* edited by Johannes Van Oort, Brill, 2008.

396. S. Vernon McCastland, "The Asklepios Cult in Palestine," *Journal of Biblical Literature,* vol. 58, n° 3 (sept. 1939), pp. 221-227, on www.jstor.org/stable/3259486

Made in the USA
Las Vegas, NV
10 February 2024

85567875R00118